AF477968

Gender and the Political Opportunities of Democratization in South Korea

Nicola Anne Jones

First published in 2006 by
PALGRAVE MACMILLAN™
175 Fifth Avenue, New York, N.Y. 10010 and
Houndmills, Basingstoke, Hampshire, England RG21 6XS
Companies and representatives throughout the world.

PALGRAVE MACMILLAN is the global academic imprint of the Palgrave Macmillan division of St. Martin's Press, LLC and of Palgrave Macmillan Ltd. Macmillan® is a registered trademark in the United States, United Kingdom and other countries. Palgrave is a registered trademark in the European Union and other countries.

ISBN 1–4039–7249–4

Library of Congress Cataloging-in-Publication Data

Jones, Nicola Anne.
    Gender and the political opportunities of democratization in South Korea / Nicola Anne Jones.
        p. cm.
    Includes bibliographical references and index.
    ISBN 1–4039–7249–4
    1. Women and democracy—Korea (South) 2. Feminism—Korea (South) 3. Women in politics—Korea (South) 4. Women in development—Korea (South) 5. Democratization—Korea (South) I. Title.

HQ1236.5.K6J66 2006
305.42′095195—dc22   2005051460

A catalogue record for this book is available from the British Library.

Design by Newgen Imaging Systems (P) Ltd., Chennai, India.

First edition: March 2006

10 9 8 7 6 5 4 3 2 1

Printed in the United States of America.

Contents

Gender and the Political Opportunities of Democratization in South Korea

Illustrations

Abbreviations and Acronyms

CAHF	Citizens for Abolition of Family Headship System
CCWA	Congressional Standing Committee on Women's Affairs
CEDAW	Convention on Elimination of All Forms of Discrimination Against Women
CIWR	Centers for Information on Women's Rights
DLP	Democratic Labor Party
EEA	Equal Employment Act
FKI	Federation of Korean Industries
FKTU	Federation of Korean Trade Unions
GDI	Gender Development Index
GDPRA	Gender Discrimination Prevention and Relief Act
GEM	Gender Empowement Measure
GNP	Grand National Party
HDI	Human Development Index
ILO	International Labor Organization
IMF	International Monetary Fund
IPU	Inter-Parliamentary Union
KBS	Korean Broadcast System
KCTU	Korean Confederation of Trade Unions
KEF	Korea Employers' Federation
KNCW	Korean National Council for Women
KSVRC	Korean Sexual Violence Relief Center
KWAU	Korean Women's Association United
KWDI	Korean Women's Development Institute
MDP	Millennium Democratic Party
MHSW	Ministry of Health and Social Welfare
MOGAHA	Ministry of Government and Home Affairs
MoL	Ministry of Labor
MPA2	Ministry of Political Affairs 2
NGO	nongovernmental organization

NKDP	New Korean Democratic Party
NSO	(Korean) National Statistics Office
OECD	Organization for Economic Co-Operation and Development
PCWA	Presidential Commission on Women
PFLR	Pan-Women's Group for Women's Reform
POS	political opportunity structures
PR	proportional representation
SERNAM	Servicio Nacional de la Mujer
SNU	Seoul National University
ULD	United Liberal Democrats
UN	United Nations
UNDP	United Nations Development Programme
URI	Our Open Party
WBDA	Women's Basic Development Act
WFPs	Women's Focal Points
WID	Women in Development
WPEC	Women's Policy Evaluation Committee
WPM	Women's Policy Machineries
WSIWQ	Women's Solidarity for the Introduction of a Women's Quota

Acknowledgments

Over a period of six years living in Seoul, my exploration of the relationship between democratization and gender equality was shaped by a variety of experiences in the nonprofit sector, the ROK civil service, and academia. I was privileged to talk with and work alongside an array of inspirational women (and men) who generously shared their diverse understandings of Korean gender politics.

In particular, I would like to thank the following people: First, Yoon Jung-Sook from Korean WomenLink and Lee Mikyung from the Korean Sexual Violence Relief Center, who as friends and mentors provided me with untold guidance and inspiration. Second, the staff of the International Cooperation Bureau of the Ministry of Gender Equality, who kindly provided me with a window into their exciting new endeavor. Third, Professors Chang Pilwha, Kim Eunshil, and Kim SunUk as well as Kwon Ohboon, Kim Nayoun, and Choi Myongsook from the Ewha's Asian Womans Studies Center for offering their insights into the realities of Asian women scholar-activists during my time as a coordinator of the Center's Asian Women's Studies program.

Turning to my Ph.D. dissertation committee, the thesis on which this book is based owed much to the challenging questioning of my chair Professor Jonathan Hartlyn at the University of North Carolina, as well as Professors Nancy Hewitt, Evelyne Huber, John Stephens, and James White.

Finally, on a personal level, the trials of a long research process were ameliorated by close friends in Korea, fellow Koreanists Sarah Ralston and Mila Steele, as well as Michele Shevkenek, Jennifer Nicholson, and Yuri Van Der Leest. My heartfelt thanks also goes to my parents for their enduring support, and finally my deepest gratitude is owed to my partner Paul Presler, without whom this project would never have been finished.

Abstract

Since the end of military rule in 1987, South Korea has made significant progress toward gender equality. The country's advances in women's legal rights, political representation, and the development of governmental machineries to promote gender equality are all the more impressive given a profoundly conservative Confucian culture and decidedly mixed evidence from other "Third Wave" democracies. This book explores how the political opportunities afforded by democratization—including the relative balance of power between conservative and progressive civic actors and evolving political institutions—shape power relations between men and women. The central conclusion is that the democratic consolidation process need not be dominated by political parties but can provide surprising opportunities for an organized civil society to press for a deepening of political, human and socio-economic rights.

Modeling the Gendered Political Opportunity Structures of Democratization

An engaged feminist political theory and political science would help chart the path toward change by examining the varied historical and cross-cultural experiences of feminist attempts to influence State policy . . . [while recognizing that] patriarchal practices and assumptions remain embedded in [state] structures and policies.

Alvarez, 1990: 273

Contrary to initial expectations, the impact of the "Third Wave" of democratization on women's sociopolitical status has been largely disappointing.[1] Although it was widely assumed that a democratic transition would lead to improvements in women's status based on the recognition of previously repressed citizenship rights and higher levels of civic involvement in the policy process, it soon became clear that there was no direct correlation between procedural democracy and "a democratization of power relations between men and women" (Waylen, 1994: 329). Women's movements have declined in visibility as party politics have assumed central stage, and policy changes advantageous to women have proven frustratingly slow (e.g., Waylen, 1996a; Friedman, 2000). Moreover, systemic economic crises and the introduction of structural adjustment programs have had a disproportionately negative impact on women (e.g., Craske, 1998), just as changes in traditional family composition have often spawned conservative backlashes targeting family and gender relations (e.g., Frank and Mueller, 1993; Perelli, 1994). As a result, expectations that women would be able to build upon the grassroots networks and political know-how developed during their participation in the third wave have not been fulfilled. Although women have gained greater formal political or civic rights, these advances have too rarely been translated into meaningful policy reform and have often been undermined by an erosion of social and economic rights (e.g., Caldiera, 1998).

In South Korea, however, the political opportunity structures of democratization have enabled women and their allies to not only sustain their mobilization efforts over time, but to also secure significant policy, institutional, and representational changes. Although progress in women's formal political representation has been slow, a cohesive and increasingly vocal women's movement has emerged over the last decade to become recognized as among the strongest in Asia (e.g., Chin, 2000; Lee R., 2000). Surprisingly, in a profoundly conservative Confucian society in which there was little collective mobilization of women qua women until the late stages of the transition process, democratization has provided the political space for activists and "femocrats"[2] to secure important advances in civic, socioeconomic, political, and human rights (e.g., Kim K., 1998, 2002; Lee R., 2000). Women's governmental machineries have likewise benefited from better resource allocation, and have become increasingly influential and proactive over the course of democratic consolidation. These changes, combined with the influence of transnational issue networks and norms, have in turn contributed to important shifts in broader cultural attitudes toward gender relations. In sum, although effective gender equality is still far from realized, compared to the stark legal and quotidian inequalities between men and women in 1987, changes in gender relations and gender policy constitute one of the most dramatic shifts in post-authoritarian Korea.

This breadth of change suggests that we need to rethink our understanding of the gendered dynamics of democratization. Accordingly, informed by the insights of the gender and politics, social movement theory, and democratization literatures, this book develops a model to analyze how the political opportunity structures of democratization—particularly changes in political institutions and the balance of power between constellations of state and civil society actors—influence efforts to advance gender equality. This model is then used to explore how the institutional and organizational contexts of Korean women's post-transitional activism have facilitated or constrained struggles to increase women's political representation and affect gender-specific policy changes. By analyzing the democratic consolidation process through the lens of a social group that has made significant contributions to the broader democratization of social, cultural, and political relations, the book also offers a richer understanding of Korea's democratic experience.[3]

Although women's movement organizations have perhaps constituted the single most important set of actors in advocating for policy changes, this is not a conventional story of social movement emergence and progress. Instead, I examine how struggles to advance gender equality evolve over time, incorporate new civil society–state actor constellations, and interact with a shifting political institutional matrix during the course of democratic deepening. Although recent case studies have compared women's varied responses to the political windows presented by democratic transitions in different cross-regional contexts (e.g., Jaquette and Wolchik, 1998; Lee and Clark, 2000), they have not provided a clear map of the broader actor coalitions involved in the contestation of gender politics.[4] This book addresses this lacuna by decentering women's movements and examining the wider array of civil society (progressive allies, cultural and economic conservatives) and state actors (mainstream state officials and femocrats) involved in contesting gender politics.

Similarly, as the "transition point" to democratization recedes into history, it becomes necessary to move beyond regime change as a single event and examine how actors with gendered interests interact with a dynamic institutional matrix over time. Accordingly, I analyze the specific ways in which competing "gender coalitions" capitalize on new institutional openings, shifting international networks and norms, changing socioeconomic environments, and the windows opened or closed by successive presidential administrations to translate their political claims into concrete outcomes. I pay particular attention to "feedback loops," between legal changes, gendered institutions (e.g., political quotas for women or women's governmental machineries) and cultural attitudes and practices. In other words, institutional and policy reforms that at one point in time were the end goal of organized women have subsequently become contributing variables to an ongoing process of social reform. What is significant here is not simply the expansion of the objective political space available to advocates of gender equality, but activists' increasing willingness to engage with mainstream policymaking and implementation processes.

The Korean Case

Democratic consolidation in East Asia has received comparatively little attention from scholars of gender politics.[5] However, by exploring questions of gender and democratization within the East Asian and especially

Korean contexts—where the democratization trajectory has been distinct from the more extensively researched Latin American and Eastern European experiences—we are able to step back from regionally derived arguments and seek a more theoretically nuanced understanding of the gendered underpinnings of nascent democracies.

First, given the success of South Korea's general democratic reforms, we could expect that Korean women would benefit more directly from democratization than their counterparts in other regions. Despite Korea's short history with pluralistic political institutions or cultural values, its transition to democracy from 1987 has been hailed as one of the most successful within the Third Wave (e.g., Diamond and Plattner, 1998; Shin D., 1999). Over the past 15 years, Korea has implemented a series of sweeping democratic reforms, including the imprisonment of former military leaders as well as the transferal of power to opposition leaders and former political dissidents, Kim Dae-jung (1998) and Noh Moo Hyun (2003). An important goal of this study is therefore to assess the degree to which women activists have been able to capitalize on these new opportunities. For example, whereas the democracy literature privileges the importance of developing strong institutionalized parties, the Korean case suggests that well-organized social movements can take advantage of a nonideological party system to emerge as legitimate political negotiating partners (with the state) and play a surprisingly prominent role in the policy process. Moreover, although research on advanced capitalist democracies shows that left-wing parties are most likely to advance gender-friendly policies (e.g., O'Connor et al., 1999), comparing Korea with other Third Wave polities I conclude that ideologically based party systems may be less conducive to progressive social change during the democratic consolidation process.

Second, due to Korea's distinct socioeconomic development trajectory, the case represents an important litmus test for the transformatory potential of nascent democracies. In contrast to simultaneous struggles in Latin America and Eastern Europe to institutionalize political democracy while struggling with economic crisis and neoliberal reform, the (re)emergence of Korean women's political activism occurred within a context of sustained economic development throughout the initial post-transition decade. As a result, Korea's democratic governments have had significantly greater resources to devote to noneconomic policy, including demands for progressive gender reforms. We should, however, be careful to avoid simplistic economic determinism. Although East Asian polities such as Malaysia, Hong Kong, and Singapore have combined sustained economic growth over the past generation with only modest gains for women (e.g., Brinton, 2001), the Philippines, which rarely appears on any "shortlists" of economic role models, has chalked up impressive political advances for women since the 1986 transition (Lee and Clark, 2000). Thus, although economic performance no doubt facilitated efforts to advance gender equality in post-transitional Korea, we need to consider the extent to which organizational, institutional, and international influences are also part of the puzzle.

Third, the Korean case suggests that agency, particularly the choice of alliance partners and discursive strategies, plays an important role in influencing movement organizations' abilities to realize their political goals. Whereas problems pertaining to social movement mobilization (e.g., movement fatigue and loss of a coherent movement frame) have been identified as key factors behind Latin American women's limited post-transitional gains (Alvarez, 1990; Barrig, 1994; Jaquette, 1994), Korean women's gender-specific activism emerged largely post-transition, flourishing rather than fragmenting as democratic governance was consolidated. Supported by the wider mobilization of an unusually cohesive progressive civil society community, Korea's two major umbrella women's organizations have developed considerable influence within the conventional political arena. The women's movement's adaptation of its collective action frame to suit shifting political opportunities has constituted a crucial component of this success.

Finally, adopting a broad comparative perspective encourages a reassessment of the historical and sociocultural peculiarities of civil society–state relations that constrain or facilitate efforts to improve gender equality. In particular, we need to consider the institutional expression of divergent conservative cultural traditions as well as the manner in which such values underpin significant political cleavages. Although political analysts have emphasized the importance of Korean Confucianism, for example, there have been few attempts to distinguish between Confucianism as a political ideology and Confucianists as organized political actors. In contrast to Latin America, where the contestation of gender politics is heavily influenced by a firmly institutionalized Catholic Church, Korean Confucianism is first and foremost a deeply ingrained social philosophy and lacks a well-defined institutional carrier. Likewise, although religious diversity is a prominent feature of Korean society, religious cleavages have rarely become politicized as parties focus on maximizing voter support rather than on staking out strong ideological positions on cultural and moral issues. As a result, Korean conservative groups remain largely isolated and have been unable or unwilling to replicate the formidable power bloc composed of the Catholic Church, right-wing parties, and economic elites that are found in much of Latin America and parts of Eastern Europe. An important issue that this book therefore addresses is the way in which the articulation of cultural conservatives' interests shape struggles over gender relations.[6]

Theoretical Influences

Theorizing about democratization and its impact on gender relations has drawn heavily from the Latin American experience, in part because of the region's earlier return to democracy and the relatively greater visibility of organized women in the anti-authoritarian struggles. My discussion therefore begins with insights from Latin American case studies, but also incorporates work emerging from the Eastern European and East Asian contexts. To overcome some of the weaknesses in this cross-regional literature, I also draw upon the institutional strand of the democratic "consolidology" literature, historical work on the gendered construction of the state and social movement theory, in order to develop the key conceptual tools for my analytical framework.

Gender and Third Wave Democratization

In Latin America, the unique opportunities for mobilization that women's cultural image as "apolitical mothers" allowed within an authoritarian context, as well as women's active role in the resurrection of civil society during the democratic transition, contributed to cautious optimism about the prospects for greater gender equality following the establishment of procedural democracy (e.g., Nash and Safa, 1986; Fisher, 1993; Radcliffe and Westwood, 1993; Waylen, 1996a). As the initial flexibility of the transition phase waned, however, feminist scholars sought answers for the decline in the momentum and visibility of women's organizations, and the difficulties faced in turning "brave concepts into workable legislation" in the new democratic milieu (Jacquette and Wolchik, 1998: 6). Explanations spanned internal movement dynamics, restricted openings in formal political institutions, and economic crises (Friedman, 2000; Craske and Molyneux, 2002).

At the movement level, difficulties included mobilization fatigue[7] and partisan divisions, problems with reorienting the movement frame to suit the new democratic context,[8] resource/funding scarcity, and the inability to forge lasting coalitions with allies in civil society (e.g., Macaulay, 2000). At the institutional level, observers emphasized the inflexible nature of formal political institutions, the slow and uneven pace of democratic reforms, minimal change in political elites' gender-related attitudes, especially in the context of the renewed political influence of the Catholic Church (e.g., Perelli, 1994; Franco, 1998; Valenzuela, 1998), and, in some cases, an erosion of civic and human rights (e.g., Caldiera, 1996; Jelin and Hershberg, 1996).[9] Women's post-transitional marginalization was also exacerbated by structural adjustment policies, as pressures for smaller governments significantly reduced the resources available for social policies important to women (e.g., Chant and Craske, 2003). Rhetorical commitments to improving women's rights aside, "neoliberal citizenship" lowered the number of demands the public could legitimately place upon the state, making individuals responsible for their own economic survival, and thereby freeing the state from the burden of social welfare provision (e.g., Schild, 1998). In short, as the locus of political change shifted from the community back to traditionally male-dominated political parties and policymaking processes, gains in formal political and civil rights were accompanied by an erosion of women's social and economic rights.

In the Eastern European context, democratization ushered in a rather bleak period for women (e.g., Gal and Kligman, 2000). Problems included a marked decline in women's participation in the paid labor force (e.g., Jaquette and Wolchik, 1998), reduced representation in the formal political arena due to a removal of 25–30 percent quotas for women (e.g., Drakulic, 1993), a rise in neoconservative ideologies emphasizing traditional gender roles (e.g., Nowakowska, 2001), widespread antipathy toward fledgling independent women's organizations (e.g., Waylen, 1994), and a reversal of gender rights (e.g., restrictions on once easily accessible abortion). Analysts argue that these difficulties were inextricably linked to the historical legacy of former totalitarian regimes. The gendered ideological legacy, sex-segregated labor market, and limited levels of autonomous civil society mobilization inherited from the Communist era have all served as important barriers to advances in gender politics in the post-transition era. State socialist regimes may have provided women with "emancipation from above," but they did not fundamentally alter gender hierarchies (Funk and Mueller, 1993). Whereas the region's economic development model was premised on full employment for men and women, the workforce was gender-segregated, with women concentrated overwhelmingly in low-paid positions of little authority. Moreover, even the extensive maternity and sick-leave benefits that enabled women to work in such high numbers simultaneously reinforced their traditional roles in the home and legitimized gender discrimination in employment (Siemienska, 1998).

Because struggles for democracy often entail the reconstruction of civic and national identities, including a partial rejection of the paradigms and policies of prior regimes (Jaquette and Wolchik, 1998), many Eastern European women perceived "women's rights" and their incorporation into the public sphere as burdensome (Funk and Mueller, 1993). With the complete suppression of civil society under state socialism, the family had taken on many positive attributes usually associated with the public sphere in the West (discussion of socio-political issues, socialization of cultural/moral values), and was thus widely seen as a safe haven rather than a source of repression (Goven, 1993).

By contrast, the contours of East Asian democratization provide some room for cautious optimism (e.g., Kim K., 1998; Lee R., 2000; Moon S., 2002). Not only has the visibility and political influence of civic groups, including women's organizations, grown considerably (e.g., Palley, 1994; Farris, 2000), but until the foreign exchange crisis of 1997/98, political transformation did not coincide with economic crisis and restructuring (e.g., Curtis, 1998; Mo and Moon, 1999). Accordingly, the policy choices available to political leaders were less constrained, and women were able to focus on more politically oriented collective action rather than basic survival issues.

Yet, although scholars of East Asia agree with their cross-regional counterparts that women's post-transitional political influence is likely to be shaped by the overall level of democratic reforms and specific electoral arrangements affecting women, they pay particular attention to the constraining influence of cultural norms and practices (e.g. Moon S., 2003). In the first cross-country East Asian study of its kind, Clark and Lee (2000) hypothesized that the impact of democratization would be particularly weak in the region because (a) Confucian patriarchy historically placed severe restrictions on women's political empowerment, and (b) Confucian cultural values proved relatively resilient during the process of industrialization. Although their findings show that women's groups have become more active post-transition and that legal reforms have begun to erode traditional patriarchal practices, women's representation and access to political elites has remained limited, with the exceptions of the upper house in Taiwan and Japan (Christensen, 2000; Clark and Lee, 2000). Similarly, while there has been considerable growth in the acceptance of Western notions of feminism and women's rights, especially among the younger generation, Confucian ideals persist among both political elites and in the populace more generally.

Ling (2000), for example, emphasizes that East Asia's

> hyper-masculine development represents a perverse combination of patriarchal East Asian culture with the logic of the market to justify limiting women to traditional family roles and to being a source of cheap, repressed labor. (20)

In sum, both the specific patterning of women's political mobilization post-transition and the temporal sequencing of this mobilization show significant cross-regional variation. By drawing on the divergent theoretical emphases of the Latin American, Eastern European, and East Asian literatures, a more comprehensive model of the factors that shape gender politics in recently democratized polities can be devised. The Latin American cases highlight the importance of internal movement dynamics, restricted openings in formal political institutions beyond the initial transition phase, the impact of the economic climate on elite policy choices and grassroots groups' mobilizational opportunities, and the impact of transnational issue networks and international norms and conventions. The Eastern European literature demonstrates the importance of the authoritarian period's historical legacy in shaping the trajectory of democratic gender politics. Depending on the mode of transition (by pact, collapse, or pressure from below) and how the former regime is evaluated by the populace, the economic structure, ideological underpinnings, and previous civil society–state relations all influence struggles to change power relations between men and women. Finally, in the context of continued economic growth and the absence of movement demobilization, the East Asian literature underscores the importance of political culture in constraining the political struggles of reform-oriented social movements and sympathetic politicians.

However, these literatures suffer from several important weaknesses: insufficient attention to the variety of institutional arenas where policy struggles can be played out (e.g., courts, bureaucracy); a weak theorization of the impact of institutional change as democracies consolidate; and inadequate consideration of other actors with gender-related interests. Equally importantly, the conceptualization of what constitutes "advances in gender equality" or improvements in "women's status" has remained unclear. I argue that the general democratic consolidation literature, with its emphasis on institutional variables, can provide us with insights into the first two lacunae, and that the women's history literature on the gendered construction of the state helps to conceptualize the broader array of actors involved in gender-related policy negotiations.

Democratic Consolidation

Theorists interested in explaining variation in "democratic performance" across regions agree that the presence of basic procedural democracy is far from sufficient for good governance. Institutional design plays a major role in determining the quality and stability of a new democratic polity (e.g., O'Donnell and Schmitter, 1989; Karl, 1990; Mainwaring and Scully, 1995; Diamond and Plattner, 1998). Four key post-transitional challenges discussed in this literature have particular relevance to my analysis: the importance of establishing the rule of law, developing an institutionalized party system, strengthening mechanisms to promote a balance of power between the legislature and executive, and shifts in the socioeconomic and ideological positioning of personnel who staff political institutions.

Establishing the rule of law has been identified as a minimum condition for a democratic system. However, implementation is dependent on a broader legal culture, including the development of an independent judiciary and citizens' confidence therein (e.g., Yoon, 1990); the types of rights enshrined within the constitution for specific groups of citizens (e.g., former military officials, minorities, etc.) (Linz and Stepan, 1996); the extent to which citizens internalize respect for democratic procedures as well as notions of individual civic and human rights (Shin D., 1999). How the "rule of law" is practiced within different democratic contexts can be especially important in determining whether new democracies facilitate gender reform. The degree to which individuals are conceptualized as rights-holders, as well as the mechanisms in place to protect such rights from a zealous majority (e.g., an independent judiciary), are crucial in advancing women's rights to, for example, reproductive freedom and protection from violence (Caldiera, 1998).

A second key determinant of how new democracies function relates to political parties. The extent to which the party system is institutionalized—the degree of party stability over time, the quality of parties' linkages with civil society, the degree of ideological polarization, and the level of internal party democracy—has a significant impact on the ability of new democratic governments to respond to citizens' demands (Mainwaring and Scully, 1995; Payne et al., 2002). As the main conduits for articulating and aggregating citizens' interests, stable programmatic parties with strong linkages to civic groups are more likely to facilitate democratic governance. In reality, though, relatively few new democracies boast such a system; more frequently the political arena is plagued by corruption and clientelism, with populists bypassing party organizations and appealing directly to voters on the basis of personality rather than policy choices. Ironically, however, my research suggests that ideologically based party systems may be less conducive to progressive social change in the democratic consolidation process, and instead weak nonprogrammatic parties may indirectly provide the political space for new social movements, including women's organizations, to emerge as legitimate negotiating partners in the policy process.

A third area of concern involves the often excessive power of the executive within nascent democracies. Executive dominance or what O'Donnell (1994) dubs "delegative democracy" reduces the access points open to social groups attempting to shape policy change and generally lowers citizens' ability to substantively participate in the democratic process. By the same token, however, gender scholars recognize that presidential commitment to advancing women's rights can play an important role in accelerating legislative debates on gender-related reforms, in ensuring that women's political machineries are adequately backed (in terms of institutional positioning and resources), and by lending gravity to the gender-mainstreaming process (e.g., Rai, 2003).

Finally, the degree to which the personnel composition of the main branches of government—in terms of class, ideology, gender, ethnicity—is reconfigured post-transition has an important impact on the implementation of democratic reforms. Although we can expect some change in elected elites, civil service and judicial personnel are likely to prove more stable, with the exception of possible purges of close associates of the previous regime. The significance of such continuity should not be underestimated, as the socioeconomic positioning of political incumbents is likely to influence their assumptions and policy choices (Petras et al., 1994). Newly elected leaders are involved in policy *development*, but a large percentage of those responsible for *implementing and monitoring* these policies worked under, and were often supportive of, the authoritarian regime. More specifically, in countries where the judiciary has a strong interpretive role, a lack of change in judicial personnel between authoritarian and democratic governments may have a strong conservatizing effect on the implementation of legislative reforms (Upham, 1987; Prillman, 2000). Conversely, the emergence of an activist court system can be used by civic groups as a fulcrum to prise additional rights from a more conservative polity.

Gender and the State

Building upon these insights about the importance of the social positioning and interests of state actors, women's history scholarship has drawn attention to the fact that the terrain of gender politics is rarely monopolized by mobilized women but is rather contested by a broad array of state and non-state actors (e.g., Stoner, 1991; Rosemblatt, 1997; Dore and Molyneux, 2000). State elites often endorse policies that reinforce particular gender roles in order to (re)construct national historical identities, to distinguish themselves from their predecessors, or to promote a particular model of economic accumulation. Besse (1996), for example, argues that the society-wide preoccupation in Brazil with women's roles and behavior in the early twentieth century "reflected deep and widespread anxieties among the rising urban elites over the rapidity and disorderliness of socioeconomic change" (2). Whereas urban middle-class women successfully mobilized to introduce the "woman question" into the political agenda, the issue was reframed by prominent professionals and politicians who imposed new "hygienic" or "rational" gender norms on society.

State officials are not always united in the kinds of gender power relations they seek to promote, and intra-bureaucratic struggles may result from officials' short-term political calculations. For example, Guy's (1991) work on the white slave trade in early-twentieth-century Argentina highlights how divisions among state officials (e.g., public health officials, police, politicians) affected attempts to define and control the sex trade. Whether linked to the fear of urban crime, a desire to promote public health, or the need to create new municipal revenues, control of prostitution served as the battlefield on which certain groups of men attempted to assert their authority over other men.

Finally, non-state actors such as religious or cultural conservatives, as well as economic groups with a stake in the composition and education of the workforce, often have their own gender-related interests, on the basis of which they form alliances and influence the policymaking process. As Deutsch (1991), in the Argentine context, and Haas (2000), in the Chilean case, have shown, the strength and cohesiveness of such groups can play a major role in shaping the political opportunities available to women's rights advocates.

Modeling the Political Opportunities of Democratization

Building on these divergent but complementary literatures, this book seeks to synthesize a new theoretical framework to explain post-transitional changes in gender relations (see figure 1.1). As a starting point, I borrow the concept of political opportunity structures (POS) from social

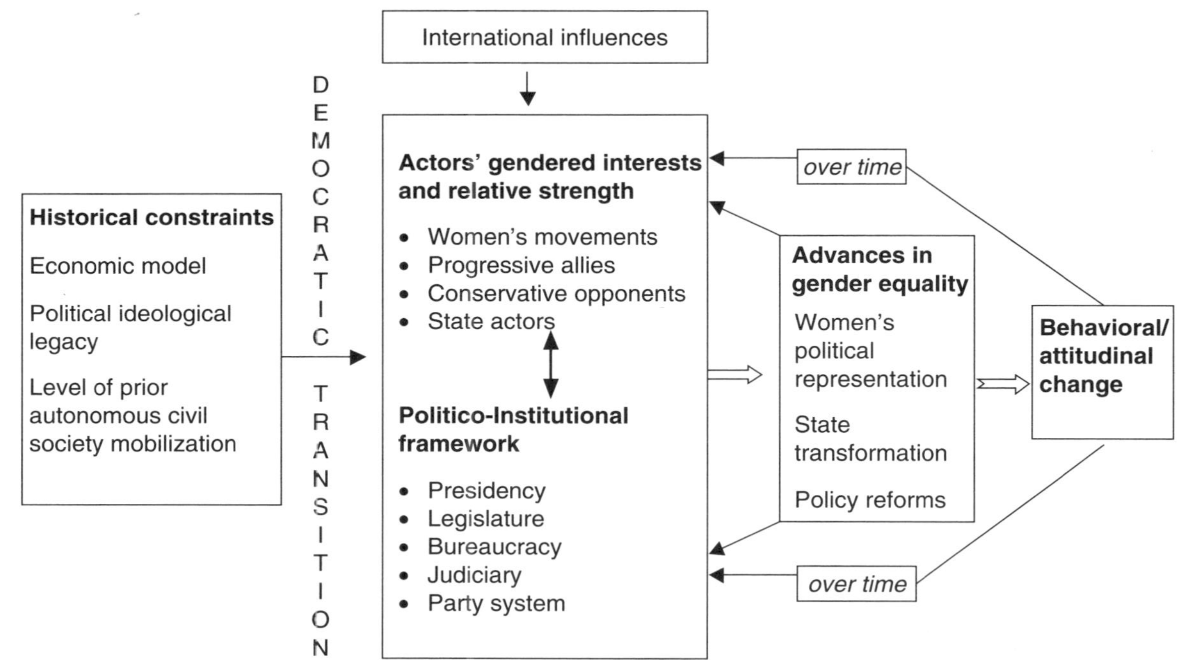

Figure 1.1   Modeling the gendered political opportunity structures of democratization.

movement theory to unpack the broader political context in which gender politics are contested. Whereas existing analyses of democracy and gender relations often treat "democratization" as the range of social, political and economic changes that have occurred since the inauguration of civilian governments, the concept of POS provides a useful tool to disaggregate changes resulting from the political transition from those that are exogenous. My primary focus is on post-transition shifts in the political institutional framework (presidency, legislature, party system, bureaucracy, judiciary) and actor constellations (both conservative and progressive coalitions with gendered interests). However, it is also necessary to consider the way in which these variables are shaped by and interact with political, ideological, and socioeconomic historical legacies, changing international norms and transnational networks, as well as an evolving macroeconomic environment.

Political Opportunities

Eisenger (1973) introduced the concept of "political opportunity structure" to underscore the pivotal role played by the political environment in conditioning social movement mobilization and influence. According to this approach, collective action is not a simple expression of grievances arising from structural change (Smelser, 1962), but encompasses an array of factors more complex than just resource availability (e.g., McCarthy and Zald, 1977) or the capacity to forge a collective identity based on shared sociocultural understandings (Melucci, 1980). POS is a dynamic concept that moves beyond micropolitics and highlights the importance of shifts in political alignments and changes in institutional access that are for the most part *external* to movement groups, but which serve to limit their political influence (e.g., Friedman, 2000). POSs encourage the formation of social movements by providing:

> external resources for people who lack internal ones, openings where there were only walls before, alliances that did not previously seem possible and realignments that appear capable of bringing new groups to power. (Tarrow, 1994: 99)

This is not to argue that movements cannot at various junctures also *create* opportunities. More audacious activists or so-called early risers may generate opportunities by confronting political authority directly when few others dare, prising open new political spaces or proactively networking among civic or political organizations to bring about shifts in actor alliances (Jenkins and Klandermans, 1995). Building on these insights, my theoretical framework incorporates four broad elements of POSs: historical constraints, the politico-institutional matrix, actor constellations, and international norms and transnational networks.[10]

Historical Constraints

The democratization process does not unfold in a vacuum. The economic and political tools available to new democratic leaders and organized citizens are shaped by (a) the country's economic development model, (b) its political ideological framework, and (c) the patterning of civil society–state relations that developed prior to the transition to democracy. Each of these "historical constraints" is in turn affected by the historically specific set of gender relations (as well as class and race relations) embodied in the state (e.g., Alvarez, 1990; Friedman, 2000).

Rather than merely providing the background or context for the consolidation period, these historical legacies mold the post-transitional paths that can be taken to deepen democracy (Linz and Stepan, 1996). They delimit the new regime's economic resources, provide parameters for emerging political discourses and influence the balance of power between the state and competing political and civic groups. In other words, they allow us to identify the baseline from which actors with gender-related interests initiate collective action and formulate their gendered political claims at the point of transition. In particular, the choice of economic development model and the degree to which it is effectively implemented profoundly shapes the subsequent evolution of political and civil society. It can therefore be considered what Collier and Collier (1991: 35) terms an "historical cause" or a causal sequence whereby a particular legacy that emerged at one period is subsequently reproduced without the recurrence of the original cause. The authoritarian ideological legacy and the patterning of civil society–state relations, although perhaps not "historical causes" in the strict sense, also have a lingering influence on public discourses and political/civil society organizational capacities.

Politico-Institutional Matrix

Historical constraints notwithstanding, post-transitional shifts in the politico-institutional matrix, which encompasses the *legislature, executive, bureaucracy, judiciary, electoral,* and *party systems,* can provide important political opportunities for advocates of gender equality. Although the gender and democracy literature has tended to focus on the problems of "institutional inertia" to explain the disappointing progress made in improving women's political representation and the passage and implementation of gender-specific policies (e.g., Craske, 1999), few studies have systematically disaggregated the country-specific contours of the political institutional matrix and their impact on gender equality initiatives.[11] In order to address this lacuna, a more fine-grained approach is required to identify the meso-level political windows that open/shut as democracy consolidates, as well as to reflect on the concrete strategies that are most conducive to change. Certainly, political institutions represent important continuities with the authoritarian past, but in addition to reforms of formal/legal arrangements, I argue that the potential for post-transitional dynamism can be considerable as a new generation of officials emerges and citizens become willing to utilize new channels of access to the state. Accordingly, whereas a macro-level snapshot may suggest relatively limited scope for change, a more detailed analysis allows us to recognize incremental yet important shifts over time.

Gender Coalitions

Shifts in elite alignments and the availability of allies constitute a second central component of the POS. Actors' interests and relative political influence are key determinants of the politicization of gender-related issues and eventual policy outcomes. In order to fully understand post-transitional politics, the gendered interests of a wider array of actor constellations, as well as their respective capacities to articulate and mobilize around such claims, need to be examined. My research suggests that the relative balance of power among progressive civil society allies (e.g., labor unions, citizens' movements) and conservative opponents (cultural, religious, or economic)—and particularly their ability to align with powerful state allies—is a major determinant of efforts to improve women's political representation and secure gender-related policy advances. In keeping with the dynamism of the concept of POS, these gender-related interests and strategies are likely to evolve over time. Civil society–state relations tend to become less antagonistic, whereas the relative influence of particular civic groups may increase or wane depending on their ability to adapt to the new democratic milieu and to capitalize on shifting domestic and international political contexts. Likewise, we can expect that the constellation of allies available to women's groups will vary depending on the type of policy changes advocated, whether labor policy, family law, or prevention of violence against women.

International Norms and Networks

In the context of globalization, international norms, action repertoires, and networks can significantly shape domestic political environments. As Diamond (1999) argues:

> The most distinctive feature of the third wave is the considerable contribution that international actors have made to democratic development by enhancing the resources, skills, techniques, ideas, linkages, and legitimacy of civil society organizations, civic education efforts, the mass media, legislatures, local governments, judicial systems and electoral commissions in the developing and post-communist worlds. (272)

United Nations (UN) conferences in the 1990s provided key networking and material resources for women's movement organizations (e.g., Sternbach et. al., 1992; Alvarez et. al., 1998; Franco, 1998), with the "Beijing process"[12] in particular providing an important opportunity to bring gender perspectives into global debates and national policymaking. Equally importantly, these forums enhanced women's understanding of the processes and actors that obstruct their empowerment (e.g., the new Right and the Vatican), while strengthening the interaction between the "triangle of empowerment," that is, women's movements, femocrats, and feminist politicians (Lycklama a Nijeholt et al., 1998: 33).

The extent to which movements draw on global norms and networks as policy leveraging and legitimating tools is likely to be shaped by a country's openness to international influences as well as the availability of domestic allies. Transnational issue networks and norms may take on relatively greater importance in polities where advocates of gender equality face a dearth of progressive domestic allies. For example, scholars have emphasized the importance of the Latin American feminist *encuentros* (regional meetings) for local women's movements over the past two decades (e.g., Meyer and Prugl, 1999). In cases where international influence is interpreted as Western imperialism, however, they are likely to play a less positive role. In the Eastern European context, for example, international feminist efforts have been perceived as unwanted interference, with little relevance to local social, political, and economic experiences (Jaquette and Wolchik, 1998: 4).

Although the significance of advances in gendered notions of citizenship and conventions has clearly increased over the last two decades, we should also bear in mind that international forums and ties do not only benefit progressive groups. Conservatives (whether they be culturo-religious, economic, or party-based) also derive strength from international linkages such as the Catholic Church and Opus Dei, global conservative/right-wing party alliances (International Democrat Union or Christian Democrats International), or international employers' federations. Stevenson (2000), for example, points out that advocacy by international pro-life groups, combined with pronouncements by the Vatican, effectively countered the efforts of feminists to legalize abortion in the Mexican case (6). Similarly, Htun (2003) analyses how conservative think-tanks and powerful U.S. legal firms provided Chilean conservatives with crucial funding and legitimacy so as to stave off reproductive rights and family law reforms.

Measuring Advances in Gender Equality

The gender and democracy literature has engaged in surprisingly few theoretical debates on what represents progress in "gender equality." Instead, most analysts have taken a social movement or bottom-up perspective, and focused on factors that facilitate or hinder women's collective mobilization *qua* women (e.g., Corcoran-Nantes, 1993; Friedman, 2000). As a result, there is often analytical slippage between the agents of change and the actual outcomes observed. In particular, autonomous women's organizations are often seen both as the initiators of gender-policy reforms and as a yardstick for assessing the impact of democracy on gender relations.[13] (e.g., Jaquette, 1994; Kim K., 1998). There have also been few attempts to provide clear indicators of different types of change. In the case of legislative reform, for instance, there is a lack of clarity as to whether evaluations should be based on the number of bills passed, the range of legislative changes, or the specific content of individual laws. As a result, meaningful intra- and cross-regional comparisons are rendered difficult.

In an effort to provide greater analytical clarity, I define "advances in gender equality" as:

(a) policy changes that seek to promote women's individual and collective rights,
(b) "state transformation" through the establishment and efficacy of women's political machineries, and
(c) improvements in the quantity and quality of women's formal political representation.

Rather than an examination of absolute outcome-oriented variables such as women's educational access, labor market positioning, health status, or their eligibility for pensions my focus is on areas under the control of both state and non-state actors following democratization.[13] Moreover, although cultural change among state and civil society actors is also essential to reduce the gap between de jure and de facto equality, culture is not included as a primary dependent variable. This is due to a dearth of longitudinal data and considerable methodological difficulties involved in attributing causality to shifts in citizens' gender-related behaviors and attitudes. Cultural transformation is likely to involve a complex interplay of post-transitional initiatives to improve gender equality as well as broader generational and modernization-related changes already in motion. Yet, aware that the practical impact of legislative reforms will be circumscribed if the populace is either uninformed or strongly opposed to initiatives that alter extant gender dynamics, I reflect upon changes in gender-related attitudes and values in the concluding chapter.

Policy Reforms

Utilizing the legislative arena to effect change is one of the key strategies employed by women's organizations in the post-transition era. I employ three broad indicators with cross-regional applicability to analyze these changes: (a) the range of policy reforms undertaken, (b) the content of the legislation passed, especially the degree of specificity and the provision of enforcement mechanisms, and (c) its implementation. Although individual policy reform cases can provide interesting insights into the constellation of actors involved in contesting a specific issue, only by considering the broader *range* of policy reforms passed will we be able to gauge the relative strength of women's organizations and their allies. For example, although Htun (2003) argues that democratization does not necessarily provide greater opportunities than authoritarianism for gender reforms, but rather provides both political openings and closures, her analysis is narrowly premised on the contestation of abortion and family law, both of which are notoriously contentious in the Southern Cone of Latin America. I would hypothesize, however, that if Htun were to extend her analytical lens to include a broader array of policy issues (e.g., employment rights, political quotas, violence against women) and hence interested actors, it is doubtful that her findings would hold up consistently.

The second indicator relates to the *content* of gender-related legislation. Does the legislation reflect the demands of women's groups or was the content watered down in order to satisfy conservative objections? To what extent does the legislation conform to international standards?

The final indicator—*implementation*—is concerned with whether the government's commitment to reform is largely symbolic or extends to active implementation. Due to space constraints and a relative dearth of data, my analysis of this dimension is brief. Where possible, however, I discuss the allocation of resources and the provision of penalties for violations, as well as related monitoring mechanisms, all of which are important to ensure effective enforcement.

Women's Formal Political Representation

Initial hopes that women's mobilization would be translated into greater formal representation following the Third Wave have been only partially met. Women's presence in national legislatures actually declined in some countries following the advent of democracy and few exceeded ten percent congressional representation for women prior to the introduction of quota laws (Craske, 1999; Htun and Jones, 2002). Moreover, greater female representation does not neatly translate into greater political access for progressive women's organizations or the development of more gender-egalitarian policies. Although the presence of feminists in the formal political arena has increased at the margins, many women representatives have conformed to rather than challenged gender stereotypes (e.g., Feijoo, 1998) or have assumed responsibility in social reproductive, or so-called soft/caring portfolios, rather than in more politically influential policy areas (Soh, 1994).

To evaluate women's formal political representation, I use three separate but related indicators: (a) the percentage change of women representatives in the main branches of government and political parties since the transition, (b) the presence of quotas for women, and (c) women officials' level of commitment toward and capacity to advance gender equality. First, both formal rules—such as multimember districts or proportional representation, which are known to facilitate women's representation (e.g., Darcy et al., 1994)—and the subjective attitudes of politicians, officials, voters, and women themselves need to be considered. Second, quota systems are an important proactive device through which to redress women's political underrepresentation (e.g., Dahlerup, 1998). Their efficacy, however, also depends on the type of electoral system in place—especially on whether there is a closed-list system, a list placement requirement, or a large district magnitude—and the political will of parties to adhere to good-faith compliance with the new rules (Htun and Jones, 2002). Third, as the number of women representatives per se is no guarantee that gender issues will be promoted, their level of commitment to advancing gender equality is important (e.g., Soh, 1994).

To what extent have female officials promoted policy or legislative reforms aimed at advancing gender equality? What is their relationship to autonomous women's organizations? And equally importantly, did they have sufficient capacity to translate these commitments into results?

Women's Policy Machineries
Besides increased representation of individual women, progress toward gender equality may also be enhanced by the establishment of women's policy machineries (WPMs) or special state and/or party bodies charged with promoting women's interests. Such machineries represent what Hochstetler (1997) terms efforts at "state transformation":

> In this role, social movements target the organization and nature of the state and its political institutions directly . . . they demand increased accountability and responsiveness from decision-makers and a devolution of power from the state to society. (198–99)

Whereas activists approached authoritarian states as agents of repression, the relative flexibility of the transition period suggested that democratic regimes were not immutably masculine and could potentially serve as an empowerment tool for women (e.g., Waylen, 1996b). This shift in attitudes led to the creation, for example, of Brazilian Women's Councils (at both state and national levels) as well as SERNAM in Chile[14] (e.g., Valenzuela, 1998; Macaulay, 2000). With the passage of time, however, analysts have observed important limitations in the efficacy of WPMs due to insufficient budget and staff resources, ambiguous briefs, and a lack of formal channels to oversee the operations of other government ministries with gender-related responsibilities.

Given these complexities, I build on Stetson and Mazur's (1995) model of comparative state feminism and their emphasis on the circumstances under which WPMs emerged and the interrelated reasons for success or failure. In the case of WPM emergence, I identify four key variables: (a) the constellation of actors either endorsing or opposing its establishment, (b) the degree of presidential political will, (c) the relative importance of international norms and conventions, and, over time, (d) pressure from WPM officials for the expansion of existing agencies or the creation of new machineries. I argue that in the initial stages of democratization, the creation of a WPM—a specific institutional space dedicated to addressing gender equality—constitutes an important measure in itself. Over time, however, as these agencies become more firmly embedded within the state apparatus, they can also function as independent actors, helping to promote the further expansion of WPMs and gender-related policy reforms. My assessment of WPM success is based on (a) a machinery's institutional positioning and available resources, (b) the political will of the executive and WPM personnel (c) its policy capacity/achievements, and (d) the level of access that the WPM affords autonomous nongovernmental (NGO) women's organizations to influence the policy agenda and process.

Methodology

The book draws on a multilayered qualitative research methodology based on field research conducted in South Korea between August 1998 and September 2003. First, in addition to secondary sources, information was gathered from (a) congressional records, political party manifestos, policy statements and articles published by relevant government ministries; (b) policy research papers and surveys conducted by the state-funded women's policy think-tank, the Korean Women's Development Institute; (c) documents and periodicals produced by major women's NGOs, religious organizations and Confucian groups, labor unions and employers' associations; and (d) newspaper archives from several major dailies spanning the ideological spectrum as well as the feminist press.[15]

Second, given limited existing research on gender and democratization in Korea, particularly when I first embarked on this project, interviews with state and civil society actors, as well as academic observers, were crucial in developing a comprehensive overview of the contours of gender politics during the first decade-and–a-half of democratization. These semi-structured interviews explored the behind-the-scenes dynamics of legislative negotiations, including the constraining role of conservative groups and political officials that often escapes the public record, the changing attitudes and relations between state and non-state actors across the four post-transitional presidential administrations, and the filtering impact of intervening factors such as political culture, economic restructuring, and international norms.

I interviewed a total of 67 key informants between September and December 2000, with 26 subsequent follow-up interviews between 2001 and 2005 (see the appendix).[16] The informants were selected on the basis of their positions within, or understanding of, formal political institutions or major civil society organizations that have gender-related interests. A balance was attempted between actors who were involved before the transition as well as across the four post-transitional administrations of Roh Tae Woo (1988–92), Kim Young-sam (1992–97), Kim Dae-jung (1998–2002), and Noh Moo Hyun (2003–).

I also gained a wealth of insights from my role as a participant observer in two national women's organizations with distinct origins and focuses: Korean WomenLink, one of the larger progressive women's groups, and the Korean Sexual Violence Relief Center, which has been active in sexual violence prevention initiatives since 1990. Similarly, my experience of working with the Korean Secretariat for the Seoul 2000 Asian European Meeting Summit NGO parallel forum, and participating in the Korean Women's Environmental Network delegation to the Johannesburg 2002 World Summit for Sustainable Development enabled me to gain a closer picture of the dynamics of the progressive Korean *shimin undong* (Citizens' Movement) and its international interactions.

Finally employment in the Korean Ministry of Gender Equality (2001–03) provided an invaluable opportunity to observe intra- and inter-ministerial negotiating patterns on gender relations, and the relationship between femocrats and long-term career bureaucrats. Likewise, my involvement with an eight-country project on Asian women's studies housed at Ewha Womans [*sic*] University Asian Center for Women's Studies afforded deeper knowledge of the evolution of Korean women's studies, particularly in the context of a wider East/South-East Asian perspective.

Chapter Organization

The book is divided into four parts. Part I (chapters 1–2) introduces key themes and questions, outlines the rationale behind my conceptual approach, and provides a brief historical overview of postindependence Korean politics during the authoritarian period.

Part II (chapters 3–5) is concerned with my key explanatory variable, the political opportunity structures of democratization. Chapter 3 focuses on the evolution of the Korean women's movement within the context of democratization, and chapter 4 explores the balance of power between the movement's progressive civic allies and their economic and cultural conservative opponents. It seeks to account for the cohesive, well-coordinated, and dynamic quality of Korea's progressive "gender coalition" on the one hand, and the fragmented, single-issue-focused, and often weakly articulated conservative camp on the other. Chapter 5 discusses the Korean political institutional matrix, and analyses how post-transitional changes have affected the contestation of gender politics.

Part III (chapters 6–8) assesses post-transitional advances in gender equality based on three main indicators: gender-policy reforms, the establishment and relative efficacy of women's policy machineries, and advances in women's political representation. After an overview of the wide range of legislative reforms that have been enacted to advance women's civic, socioeconomic welfare, human and political rights, chapter 6 presents three detailed case studies—the Equal Employment Act, the Family Law, and the Sexual Violence Prevention and Family Violence Prevention Acts—to tease out the divergent sublogics of struggles to secure different types of gender rights. Chapter 7 turns to women's policy machineries and the question of state transformation. It assesses the relative capacity of women's policy units in the bureaucracy and legislature to shape policy outcomes, as well as the level of access these units provide women's organizations to influence the policy process. Drawing on indepth interviews with women political elites and activists, Chapter 8 examines the attitudinal and institutional barriers that have contributed to the particularly tough battle that Korean women have faced in increasing their formal representation in the executive, legislature, bureaucracy, and political parties. However, it also allows for cautious optimism by tracing the evolution of women's political quotas, the constellation of actors involved, and their relative merits in promoting women's visibility at the legislative, civil service, and party levels.

Part IV (chapter 9) ties together the book's empirical and theoretical contributions. Mindful of the fact that gender-related practices and beliefs are culturally bound, the discussion first reflects on the extent to which changes at the formal politico-legal level have filtered down to affect average citizens' way of thinking about gender relations. Drawing on survey data and ethnographic studies, I examine changes in attitudes regarding family and sexuality, women's economic roles and political participation. The second part of the chapter reflects on the broader cross-regional lessons suggested by the Korean case concerning gender relations, the political opportunities of democratization, and civil society development.

CHAPTER 2

Setting the Stage: Historical Constraints and Democratization Dynamics

The central thread running through Korean history is the oppression of the laboring masses and the true national identity of Korea can be discovered in the lives, culture, and struggles of the minjung—*the locked out, the exploited, the down-trodden, the have-nots.*

Ching and Yoon, 1995: 418

Research on democratic consolidation suggests that a nation's historical legacy has "profound implications for the . . . tasks different countries face when they begin their struggles to develop consolidated democracies" (e.g., Linz and Stepan, 1996: 55). The economic resources available to the new government, the parameters for emerging political discourse, as well as the relative strength of state actors and competing civil and political society groups are all shaped by developments prior to the transition. This chapter discusses three major "historical constraints" within the Korean context: the economic development model, the ideological foundations of the authoritarian regime, and the degree of civil society mobilization and autonomy. To highlight the unique characteristics of Korea's historical legacy, the discussion is framed within a comparative perspective with Latin America, the experiences of which have informed much of the democratization literature. In each section, I consider the gendered dimensions of broader historical legacies so as to map the factors that have facilitated or constrained initiatives to advance gender-related policies and women's representation post-transition. Finally, I discuss the transition process itself, which democratization scholars argue has an important impact on the subsequent quality of democratic deepening (e.g., Kim S. H., 2000).

Korea's Economic Development Model

Patterns of economic development, particularly the degree of income inequality and the sustainability of real wages and GDP growth over time, strongly influence the democratization trajectory (e.g., Hahm and Plein, 1997). In Korea, rapid economic growth during authoritarianism (1961–87) created a very different macrostructural environment for the democratic consolidation process to unfold, relative to its Latin American peers (e.g., Gereffi and Wyman, 1990). Unlike the *class-based* development projects of the Latin American bureaucratic authoritarian regimes, Korea's capitalist developmental state contributed, by intention or coincidence, to *national* development (Moon and Rhyu, 2002). Because economic cleavages were less pronounced, conflicts over distribution rarely degenerated into a zero–sum game and thus could be resolved with a lower degree of repression than frequently found in the Southern Cone.

The Korean state's higher degree of "relative autonomy" from economic elites—foreign and domestic, agrarian and industrial (e.g., Evans, 1995) was also significant. Whereas Southern Cone military regimes were instrumental in reestablishing the dominance of business groups by forcefully demobilizing labor (e.g., Collier, 1979), Park's 1961 coup d'etat was carried out in the context of limited industrialization and without an influential bourgeoisie or landed elite. Moreover, although fledgling labor organizations affiliated with the communist movement had emerged in the 1920s and 1930s, and briefly resurfaced from 1945 to 1948, the U.S. military government forcefully destroyed autonomous unions. Indeed, whereas the process of proletarianization escalated rapidly during the 1960s, it was not until the 1970s that workers began to develop a *nodongja* (class-based) identity and to organize collective responses to the exploitative underbelly of Korea's export-oriented industrialization model (Koo, 2001).

Accordingly, without either politically salient economic elites or a "mobilized" labor movement, the rationale for the military's involvement in politics was distinct from its Latin American peers. Partially motivated by the endemic corruption of the Rhee administration (1948–60), the Park junta

> arrested the import-substituting businessmen who had fattened at Syngman Rhee's trough, and marched them through the streets Cultural Revolution-style, with dunce caps and sandwich placards displaying "I am a corrupt swine," "I ate the people." (Cumings, 1997: 312)

This humbling of business groups further solidified the relative autonomy of state policy planners and opened a two-decade window during which most key levers of economic growth and (re)distribution were state controlled. Although the relationship between the military Government and the *chaebŏl* (business conglomerates) became close-knit, the balance of power was consistently weighted in favor of the state until at least the mid-1980s thanks to rapid economic growth fueled by cheap, state-directed credit (Moon and Lim, 2001). The centerpiece of the Korean economic miracle was an export-led industrialization model that initially (1962–66) concentrated on labor-intensive light industries before turning to the promotion of heavy and chemical industries from the 1970s (e.g., Amsden, 1989). Although the 1979–81 recession, brought about by the second oil shock and a global slowdown, pushed Park's successor, Chun Du Whan (1980–87), to slowly liberalize economic policy away from state-controlled finance and industrial targeting, the Korean state remained actively involved in setting the broad parameters of economic development until at least the early 1990s (e.g., Evans, 1995).

Critics (e.g., Cumings, 1997; Koo, 2001) have rightly called attention to the negative dimensions of corporatist modes of social control and exploitative labor practices. However, in terms of unrivaled growth and comparatively egalitarian income distribution, the Korean economic model has merited global accolades (e.g., Cha et al., 1997). During its transition from an agrarian to an urban-industrial society, Korea averaged eight percent annual growth, recording a dramatic rise in GNI per capita from $249 in 1970 to $1,600 in 1980, to $5,900 in 1990 and $12,646 in 2003. Despite privileging the *chaebŏl* at the expense of smaller businesses, the state simultaneously encouraged relatively progressive income redistribution programs and succeeded in retaining a comparatively low GINI coefficient.[1] This was not simply the by-product of economic growth. Rather, from a relatively egalitarian base—facilitated by the destruction of the Korean War and subsequent agrarian reform—the government can be credited with ongoing efforts to smooth resource distribution among industrial and agricultural sectors, through, for example, the New Village Movement and rice subsidies (Leipziger, 1992: 29).

The absence of major class cleavages and unprecedented growth rates over four decades eased the democratic transition process, rendering the tasks facing Korea's new democratic leaders comparatively narrower and less complex than in other Third Wave polities. Whereas fledgling democratic governments in Latin America and East Europe had to devote considerable resources to cope with run-away inflation, surging budget deficits (and demands to cut discretionary spending), potential defaults on foreign loans, and a generalized economic crisis, the Korean government spent the first decade post-transition preparing for greater integration into the world economy, including entry into the Organization of Economic Cooperation and Development. Robust economic growth, both pre- and post-transition, allowed the Korean government greater scope to focus on issues of democratic deepening, including (limited) expansion of the welfare state, consolidation of civilian control over the military, and greater civil and human rights protections (Kil and Moon, 2001).

Gendered Limits of Korea's Development Model

Feminist scholarship has shown that the mode of women's incorporation into the economic development model—for instance, mobilization as a cheap labor-force or exclusion from the formal economy as part of de-industrialization—impacts their economic and educational standing at the time of the transition, as well as their capacity to take advantage of new opportunities to participate in the public arena (e.g., Siklova, 1993; Waylen, 1996a). In the Korean case, rapid growth and industrialization notwithstanding, the gendered dynamics of the capitalist development state proved mixed (e.g., Chang, 1995; Cho, 1996). On the one hand, the promotion of a two-child-only family policy and widely available contraception significantly reduced women's childbearing/rearing burden. Combined with rising incomes for the newly emergent middle class and the government's emphasis on education for all, middle-class women were provided with unprecedented opportunities to acquire higher education and enter the labor force. Yet, for the majority, becoming economically active did not equate with individual empowerment. The mobilization of women workers was crucial to the manufacturing industry—"the engine" of Korean development—though capitalist transformation did not significantly reduce gender inequalities (e.g., Kim H., 1996).

Family Planning and Education
The Park regime's two-child policy played a pivotal role in enabling women to control their fertility. In a remarkably short time, widespread education and publicity campaigns facilitated a decline in the average number of children per family from 6.0 in 1960 to 2.9 in 1980 and to the world's lowest rate of 1.17 in 2002 (KWDI, 2004). Although these policies were implemented in the name of broader national development

Table 2.1 University enrollment rate by sex (%)

1975		1985		1995		2000		2004	
F	*M*	*F*	*M*	*F*	*M*	*F*	*M*	*F*	*M*
4.5	11	21	47	39	70	61	99	76.5	120

Source: KWDI, 2004: 126.

rather than out of a specific concern to improve women's quality of life (Moon, 1994), the indirect consequences of this policy were largely positive, especially in terms of opening up women's life options and improvements in maternal and child health.[2]

Simultaneously, due to a cultural emphasis on education,[3] and the need to develop a skilled workforce to fulfill the regime's developmentalist goals, Park advanced a national education policy for all. Accordingly, girls' enrollment in middle school doubled to 67 percent between 1965 and 1975 and rose to 100 percent by 1985; at the senior high school level, it rose from 20 percent in 1965 to 51 percent in 1975 and had reached 90 percent by 1990 (KWDI, 2000). The high costs of higher education notwithstanding, aspiring to send one's children to college was not just a middle-class dream, but a driving force behind the arduously long hours worked by lower-class families. Moreover, although sons' education was initially prioritized in accordance with Confucian gender roles, women's tertiary education rates grew rapidly as general economic prosperity improved, as seen in table 2.1 (Lee H., 1994).

Women's Labor Market Incorporation
Despite these important changes, however, women's higher education was viewed less as a path for self-development, economic independence, or public sphere achievement than as a mechanism to attract higher status marriage partners and equip women to be "wise mothers" and supervisors of their children's education (Moon, 1994). Indeed, one striking characteristic of Korean women's employment patterns across the lifespan has been the absence of a strong correlation between educational achievement and paid workforce participation (see table 2.2) (Kim K., 1998). Not only were women subject to discrimination in the recruitment process, but whereas men typically enjoyed "rice-bowl" employment protection, they struggled to reenter the workforce except in the informal sector or in low paying/status factory positions (e.g., Bai and Cho, 1995; Cho U., 1996: 58).[4]

Table 2.2 Workforce participation by educational achievement (%)

	2002		1998		1994		1990		1986	
Education	*F*	*M*	*F*	*M*	*F*	*M*	*F*	*M*	*F*	*M*
Less than junior high	43	57	42	58	45	63	46	63	40	67
High school graduate	51	78	48	80	49	81	47	80	39	91
Junior college graduate	66	93	65	93	63	94	66	93	25	43
University graduate	59	88	57	91	57	93	53	93	42	94

Source: KWDI, 2004.

Middle-class women benefited significantly from the steadily increasing disposable incomes afforded by rapid economic growth, but advancement came at a steep price for working-class and peasant women and their families (e.g., Cho O., 1998). Record numbers of women entered the workforce during the 1960s–1980s (48 percent in 1994 up from 27 percent in 1963) as industrialization required an abundant supply of cheap "docile" labor (Kim K., 1998).[5] Indeed the culturally sanctioned subordination of women became particularly important in efforts to strategically remold the labor force and carry out repressive labor control techniques.[6] As sociologist Chang (1995) argues:

> . . . gender-differentiated class restructuring was not automatically established but purposefully produced by the state and business elites to ensure a timely supply of marginalized workers and to stabilize social mechanisms of labor exploitation. (75)

Because women's employment was generally constructed as temporary, before forced retirement upon either marriage or childbirth, women worked consistently longer average hours than men. However, they earned significantly less for all education and skill levels (e.g., Park, 1993). Although women's wages began to catch up quickly with men's from the early 1990s, up from 53.4 percent in 1990 to 61 percent in 1997, the average ratio of women's to men's wages was still 65.2 percent in 2003 (see figure 2.1). Moreover, women were concentrated in low-status positions with minimal opportunities for advancement and were routinely subjected to physical and verbal abuse by male coworkers and employers (Kim S. K., 1997).

In short, Korea's export-oriented industrial development model fundamentally reshaped the socioeconomic fabric, but modernized rather than undermined patriarchal gender relations. Whereas women's access

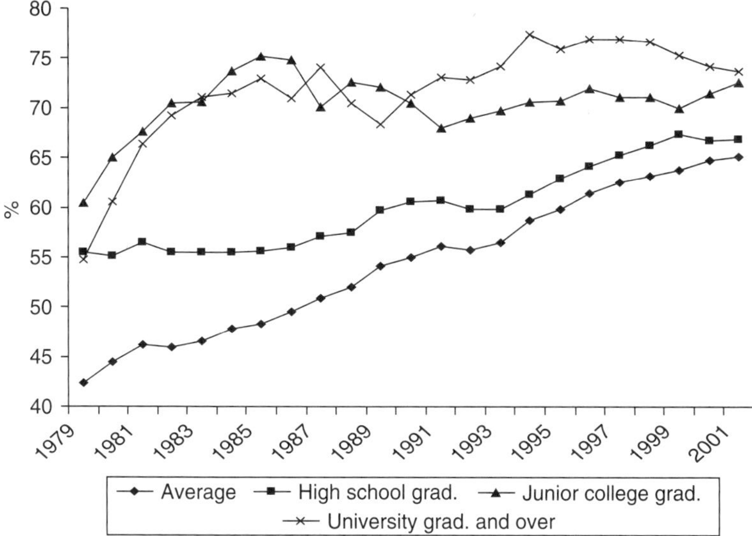

Figure 2.1 Women's wages relative to men's by educational attainment.

to fertility control and higher education was comparatively high, "South Korea was one of the most sex-biased societies in the world in terms of its wage structure" (Koo, 2001: 59), thereby limiting women's economic and social clout.

Ideological Legacies

Democratic consolidation necessitates that authoritarian values are uprooted and replaced with those of political freedom, mass participation, the rule of law, and the like. The process, however, is often nonlinear, resulting in a complicated mix of old authoritarian values/practices and new democratic principles (Helgesen, 1997). In Korea, the transition resulted less from the outright rejection of the military regime's economic and social policies than from citizens' demands for economic growth *with* political freedom. Public resentment toward the authoritarian past was thus neither as intense nor all-encompassing as in other democratizing polities. Because the authoritarian regime's economic model and anti-Communist doctrine were not discredited, Korea's new democratic government had only limited incentives to reorient the country's economic model and expand the welfare state. By contrast, given that the military's legitimacy was undermined by its human rights record and repressive measures against independent political and civil society, successive presidents have sought to improve civic rights by forging closer relations with civic groups and incorporating their voices into the policy process.

According to the Korean Democratic Barometer, only nine percent of Koreans could be categorized as "representative democrats" by the mid-1990s, that is, citizens who not only endorse democratic institutions but also fully reject authoritarian solutions (Shin D., 1999). Moreover, the ongoing division of the Peninsula and related truncation of the political Left has lent considerable continuity to the political environment. As Shin Doh-Chull (1999) argues, "democratization has been mostly a conservative movement that falls short of major policy restructuring and ideological or partisan realignment" (19). The underpinnings of this conservative democratization can be found in three strands of the political legacy of the Korean postcolonial state, that is, anti-Communism/militarism, state-led capitalism, and neo-Confucianism.

The gendered implications of this legacy have been similarly complex. A lack of fundamental questioning of the mode of accumulation and the state's associated reliance on the family for welfare provision has resulted in the coexistence of discourses about "women's human rights" and "gender equality" alongside the state's ongoing promotion of women as a flexible, supplementary workforce (Shin, 2002 interview). Similarly, although the democratic state's desire to approximate international norms has helped focus attention on gender inequalities, concern with how to best channel women's unpaid contributions to the family and community has not faded, but has instead been modernized under the banner of "harnessing women's human resources to promote national development" (Ha, 2000 interview).

Anti-Communism/Militarism

The forced partition of the Peninsula profoundly retarded Korea's democratic aspirations, as anti-Communism became the state's primary basis of legitimacy.

> The experience of the war left Koreans permanently scarred and "colorblind," unable or unwilling to distinguish between social democracy and brutal Stalinism . . . With such an image of the "Left" frozen in the minds of Koreans, the political fate of would-be Leftists was sealed. (Kim B., 1998: 124)

Ongoing tensions with the North "justified" the oppression of political dissidents and contributed to a "crude anti-communist mentality" that equated communism with other progressive models promoting economic equality and social justice (Shin D., 1999). These conservative values have been enforced by state policy, particularly the far-reaching National Security Law that stipulates prison sentences for South Korean citizens who demonstrate overt support for their Northern neighbor. With leftism branded as subversive, ideological polarization played a major role in prolonging the military dictatorship.

The anti-Communist legacy has also exacted a high price in terms of state budgets and human resources. Although civilian control over the armed forces was cemented with the military purge of 1993, South Korea's military spending, at near three percent of GDP remains among the highest in Asia and significantly higher than most of its Latin American counterparts (SIPRI, 2002).[7] Another significant cost is the compulsory unpaid 39-month military service for all able-bodied men, which entails not only a major sacrifice of time and resources, but also has important cultural spillover effects. With almost half the population subjected to, at times, physically abusive training within an authoritarian, military culture, it is not surprising that these values influence broader society (Koo, 2001). Describing Korean culture as "militarized masculinity," Moon (1994) argues that the social order is best characterized by a pattern of "militant repression and hierarchical control, rational calculation and discipline, and distance from culturally feminine activities of reproduction" (135). In order to perpetuate a conscripted military, army service has been equated in public discourse with one's civic duty, thereby reinforcing women's status as auxiliary citizens (Kwon, 2000).[8]

State-Led Capitalism

An emphasis on state-led national economic development constituted a second strand of the military regime's ideological underpinnings. To ensure the colonial era destruction would never be repeated, and to keep apace with the North's economic development, President Park (1968) urged all citizens to sacrifice for the national good:

> I want you to understand that both improvements in workers' lives and the growth of corporations depend on our national development, so I ask for your cooperation to take pride and responsibility for the establishment of the nation . . . I promise all of you, workers, will be amply rewarded for the price you have paid in "blood and sweat." (2–3)

Korea's modernization project capitalized on Confucian hierarchy and family values to discipline workers (i.e., as loyal "sons" and "daughters" of the "father" employer and nation) and to maximize growth (Kim S. K., 1997). Work was accordingly conceptualized not as a "contractual relationship but as [a] moral and ethical one between workers and employers" (Kim H., 1999: 4).

As real income soared, the broad middle class largely accepted the military regime's "growth first" mantra and came to associate democracy with political uncertainty and economic risk. Even in 1993, five years post-transition, respondents to a nationwide opinion survey ranked economic prosperity and security above political freedom, participation, and competition when asked to identify the important components of democratic political development (Shin and Shyu, 1997). Greater economic well-being subsequently provided space for the burgeoning middle class to support political reforms but their demands were for procedural democracy rather than an endorsement of the *Minjung's* (People's Movement) more radical call for progressive socioeconomic rights and to dismantle the *chaebŏl* (Shin D., 1999). Similarly, following the 1997 financial crisis, economic hardship and uncertainty contributed to a collective nostalgia for Park's strong leadership, as citizens blamed democratically elected President Kim Young-sam for the country's financial woes (Shin D., 2003).

Neo-Confucianism

Neo-Confucianism further buttressed Korea's profoundly conservative political culture (Hahm, 1997). Drawing on the nineteenth century *Tonghak* revolutionaries' philosophy of *tongdo sŏgi* (technology of the West, morality of the East), the Park regime made a concerted effort to (selectively) revive Confucian traditions. Notions of filial piety, the complementary but unequal relationship between the sexes, loyalty to the state and its leaders, and privileging of the collective over individual interests were all harnessed to foster a stronger sense of national identity and counter the influx of Western values perceived as a threat to Korea's still precarious social stability (Kim K. O., 1996). The conceptualization of Korean democracy as *minbon juŭi*, whereby politics is defined as "taking care of the ruled," was also heavily promoted to legitimize the lack of civic freedoms (Kim S. H., 2000).

In order to disseminate these nationalist values, public institutions on national history and ethics were established, and subjects such as "Anti-Communist Morality," "Right Living," and "National Ethics" were introduced into the school curriculum (Moon, 1998: 34–35). Although the state's heavy-handed approach to moral education has been tempered post-transition, neo-Confucian cultural values continue to influence democratic Korea. As Chang (1997) explains, for example, the country's "unique family-centered culture" has been used to justify government resistance to expanding social welfare programs:

> Most Koreans . . . believe that the nuclear family is something to oppose for the good of society and individuals alike . . . Various social problems that threaten stable family life usually induce society-wide moral criticism of the individuals in the troubled families instead of governmental or communitarian efforts to help relieve the troubles collectively. (58)

As a sociopolitical philosophy, Confucianism stipulates a finely tuned set of relationships between the individual and the family, community and the state (e.g., Deuchler, 1992). Many aspects of this tradition have survived, but in a "fundamentally mutated or distorted way," which is often incompatible with democratic norms (Chang, 1997: 54). Because basic social structures were destroyed during the tumultuous 1950–53 War, Koreans were forced to rely on personal connections to cope in a society in extreme flux. In contrast to other industrializing societies, the importance of the family was strengthened and reinforced resulting in "neo-familism," whereby the notion of the family functions as a conceptual device to explain all levels of sociopolitical life—the village, the state, the nation (Ha, 1995). Lacking absolute sovereignty, the individual is conceived of as a relational being performing multiple roles, each entailing a different set of rights and duties. As a result of these cross-cutting loyalties, the formation of social cleavages along class or religious lines was largely preempted:

> Instead of drawing a line of cleavage, too deep and wide for individuals to cross, Koreans drew concentric circles of the self, permanently tying it to others, and searched for the bonds that would dissolve "you" and "I" into a common "we." The concentric circles of blood, school, and regional ties joined individuals of different class backgrounds. There were always larger circles of social identity ready to reduce the sense of difference that individuals might have found among themselves at the lower levels of personal ties. (Kim B., 1998: 125)

Within Confucianism such exclusive familial ties are not limited to blood family relations, but also extend to pseudo-familial groups including clan or hometown associations, high school and university alumni, and military units. Overwhelmingly dominant in Korean social life, these groups are organized on the basis of hierarchical nepotistic ties (Ha, 1995). Rather than facilitate civic virtues, such organizations can undermine democratic cultural values by diluting class-based or ideological alliances. As suggested by social capital theorists (e.g., Putnam, 1993; Grootaert and van Bastelaer, 2002), whereas networks that foster norms of reciprocity, voluntary civic engagement, and horizontal linkages help to overcome collective action problems that thwart community development, vertical (e.g. patron–client) relations, and kinship ties, which tend to bind together only narrow segments of the population, retard the emergence of a strong civic-minded culture.

In this regard, the importance of particularistic Confucian relations—primarily kin, alumni, or regional ties—has served as a perplexing counterweight to a relatively new but vibrant social movement culture. Dual strands of social networking (i.e., *yŏnjul* [close personal relations that typically transcend institutionalized rules and ideologically oriented values] and *yongyul* [interactions based on universal rules and common philosophical or political values]) have shaped civil society in unique ways (Yee, 2000). Despite the rapid diffusion of modern values through industrialization, urbanization, and universal access to education, as well as the institutionalization of democratic institutions, there is still a strong tendency for people to rely on regional, school, and family ties as important channels of information, business networks, and decisionmaking.

Gendered Dimensions

In keeping with the feminist thesis that nation-building and economic development processes are intrinsically gendered, a fundamental pillar of the Korean authoritarian state's ideological framework was its differential incorporation of men and women into the nation. Whereas the role of men lay first and foremost in their capacities as breadwinners and patriotic soldiers, women's primary responsibility was to be loyal wives and wise mothers, who raised a limited number of highly educated children. Not considered as actors in their own right, women were cherished as bearers of sons who would defend the nation and support their parents as they aged (e.g., Kim E., 2005). This valuation of women as bodies was seen most clearly in the linking of population control and national economic development (KIHASA, 1992). Birth control was incorporated as a core element of the 1961–65 Economic Plan on the grounds that it would enable the country to earn $2 billion by 1971

(Kim, 1983). In this context, women were viewed more as statistics for IUD insertion and sterilization rather than autonomous actors (Moon, 1994).

Women's auxiliary status also extended to the workplace. In need of a cheap, flexible reserve supply of labor, the junta followed Meiji Japan's model and actively recruited young women as *sanŏp chŏnsa* (industrial soldiers) to work in factories, especially within export zones.[9] Within a broader industrial lexicon infused with Confucian familial scripts, these "daughter workers" were valued for their "docility" and "obedience," as well as their "willingness to sacrifice themselves for the good of the nation" (e.g., Ching and Yoon, 1995). As feminist anthropologist Kim Eun-Shil notes, the discursive emphasis centered on young women's contribution to national development:

> Even if at a personal level they were referred to in disparaging terms such as *kongsuni* (factory girl), at a societal level they were recognized as industrial warriors fighting for the growth and welfare of the nation and as dutiful daughters supporting their male family members.(2005)

Although less publicized, the authoritarian regime did not confine itself to the ideal of the "virtuous woman," but also fostered sex tourism as a method to generate scarce foreign exchange (Moon, 1994). Government-certified *kisaeng* (*geisha*) numbered approximately 40,000 in the 1970s, and were praised by the Ministry of Education for "their contribution to Korea's economic growth" (Lie, 1995: 213). Not until the early 1980s, in response to protests by Christian and women's groups, was the system gradually phased out. Similarly, on the national security front, the easy availability of prostitutes around military camp towns was, and still is, part and parcel of joint security agreements with the United States. As Moon (1997) argues, part of the price of maintaining the Cold War alliance was the personal insecurity and exploitation of thousands of young women, for whom the government provided protection or rehabilitation services.

The third key role assigned to women by the state was that of "mothers of the nation," which included the volunteer community labor behind a variety of developmental and political propaganda programs. Mostly under the rubric of the New Village Movement and organizations such as the Korean Federation of Housewives Clubs and the Mothers' Clubs, these programs included frugal consumption campaigns, family planning advocacy, rural development programs, and anti-Communist propaganda dissemination (Kim S. H., 2000). The government viewed women outside the paid workforce as a resource to be exploited and carried out its development policies largely on the backs of women's time and labor (Moon, 1994).

State–Civil Society Patterning

Developing an independent and robust civil society constitutes a core task in the democratization process, discouraging authoritarian reversals and facilitating democratic deepening (e.g., Oxhorn, 1995). The scope of this challenge is determined largely by historical patterning, which influences the organizational capacity of movement groups, their potential state and non-state alliance partners, as well as the ease with which they can reorient their movement frame to take advantage of the political opportunities opened by democratization. In the totalitarian societies of Eastern Europe, for example, new democratic leaders were faced with overcoming the "flattened" nature of civil society (Linz and Stepan, 1996) and widespread civic distrust of collective action initiatives. By contrast, in Latin America, where a strong civil society contributed significantly to the demise of authoritarian rule, the post-transitional challenge has centered on reorienting previously mobilized groups from anti-regime protest to political action appropriate to the rules of the new party-centered system (e.g., Alvarez et al., 1998). In Korea, I argue that the comparative strength of civil society groups post-transition, especially compared to political society, has played a key role in the gains of gender rights activists and organizations. This section therefore analyzes the roots of this political influence: a historical pattern of strong cross-sectoral organizing, relatively non-violent tactics, and the development and articulation of a comprehensive master movement frame.

Three Democratic Junctures

The evolution of an autonomous civil society did not follow a linear process, but rather unfolded over what Kim Sun-Hyuk (2000) terms three "democratic junctures": 1956–61, 1973–80, and 1984–87.[10] Whereas civil society was never completely demobilized, these junctures were notable for mass coordinated civic action that seriously challenged the existing political order. Each successive political opening gave rise to more sophisticated and robust coalition-building initiatives, as well as the development of an increasingly cohesive metapolitical narrative— the *minjung* philosophy—within which activists could situate their collective action.

In the first democratic juncture, Syngman Rhee's authoritarian regime (1948–60) was brought down by a series of nationwide student protests in April 1960. Following the suppression of a fledgling political Left by the United States Army Military Government (1945–47), the Rhee regime had relied on elections (not necessarily free and fair) and the mobilization of diverse pro-state civic organizations—anti-Communist leagues, state-sponsored unions and political parties, youth and housewives associations—to foster support for its pro-American, capitalist policies (Moon S., 2002: 483). However, while presidential elections in 1953 afforded some legitimacy, increasing reliance on anti-Communist campaigns to silence regime opponents and blatant political corruption in the late 1950s aggravated civic dissatisfaction, culminating in the student-led 1960 April Uprising.

A "Democratic Spring" led by Chang Myon ensued that year, providing Korea's most authentic democratic experience prior to 1987. The student-led opposition, however, ultimately proved unsustainable due to limited linkages between students and the broader populace, as well as growing dissatisfaction over Chang's failure to purge the bureaucracy and security forces and clearly establish himself as a champion of democracy. Park Chung-Hee and his military cohort capitalized on growing ideological polarization and social tensions to carry out a coup d'etat in May 1961, inaugurating what would become an 18-year-long military dictatorship.

The second democratic juncture involved a significantly broader spectrum of civic groups, including students, labor unions, and religious groups. Although dissidents had protested Korean–Japanese normalization in 1965, deployment of troops to the Vietnam War, as well as Park's 1969 constitutional revision to allow himself a third presidential term, these protests had failed to spill over into broader society. The main obstacles included the political legitimacy afforded by impressively high economic growth, symbolic but regular elections, mobilization of pro-state corporatist groups, and surveillance by the Korean Central Intelligence Agency. Social cohesion was further facilitated by the presence of an external enemy, North Korea, rather than the internal security threats generally identified by Latin American militaries. As a result, state repression was significantly less intense than in, for example, the Southern Cone, and highly selective, with the exception of the infamous 1980 Kwangju massacre.[11]

In the early 1970s, however, slowing economic growth encouraged a rapidly expanding urban workforce[12] to more directly challenge exploitative employment conditions, and, in turn, brought about a concomitant shift in the composition of civil society, namely the emergence of *chaeya* (national civic peak associations). Characterized by labor unions, progressive religious leaders, and dissident intellectuals/journalists, this triple alliance, in tandem with political opposition leaders, protested Park's 1972 *Yushin* (revitalization) Constitution, which dissolved the National Assembly, banned political parties, and provided for indirect presidential elections:

> Ironically, it was during the dark moments under *Yushin* that many civil society groups emerged, gained greater influence, and moved toward unity . . . The nature of *Yushin*—that is, a wholesale denial of liberal democracy in the name of "efficiency" and "national security"— manifestly recapitulated and eloquently stated to the anti-government groups in civil society the illegitimacy, illegality, immorality, and violence of the Park regime. (Kim S. H., 2000: 58)

This emphasis on the authoritarian state's illegitimacy gave rise to new theorizing about Korean history, culture, and politics from the standpoint of the *minjung* or marginalized masses (Abelmann, 1997). In response to an increasingly sophisticated, multifaceted civic challenge, Park intensified state repression, exacerbating tensions between regime hard-and soft-liners. These internal conflicts ultimately contributed to Park's assassination—the outcome of a heated post-dinner squabble with his national security chief—and the collapse of the regime in October 1979. Although the ensuing political chaos provided a window of opportunity for greater democracy, tenuous links among the triple alliance partners limited the capacity of civic opposition leaders to reign in an increasingly radicalized labor movement and facilitated the military's ability to exploit public fears and successfully execute another multistage coup (Kil and Moon, 2001).

By contrast, in the third and ultimately successful democratic juncture of 1983–87, civil society *chaeya* and political society groups forged a coalition that was both tightly coordinated and broad based, involving support from the working as well as middle classes. This alliance, which had been gradually built up over previous periods of social unrest, proved decisive in the mass protests of 1987, and was one of the key factors in the military junta's withdrawal from power the same year.

Transition Dynamics

The mode of transition from military rule plays an important role in setting the tone for a new democratic polity. The extent to which authoritarian elites are replaced and the degree to which they and their ruling ideologies are discredited have been shown to have an important impact on the subsequent quality of democratic deepening (e.g., Karl, 1990; O'Donnell and Schmitter, 1989). In the Korean case, mass civil society protest against the Chun regime constituted the singularly most important variable in shaping and ultimately accelerating the transition process. The illegitimacy of the Chun regime stemmed from the 1980 coup and brutal suppression of the Kwangju Uprising, when both professional activists and ordinary citizens briefly seized the city in protest of the military putsch. Although political repression intensified from 1980 to 1983, the Chun regime's "original sin" had undermined the military in the eyes of most Koreans, helping to reduce the viability of violence as a political option.

As the *minjung* became increasingly active, the junta was forced to accept gradual political liberalization, including the removal of the ban on opposition political parties and blacklisted activists in 1984 (Lee and Bishop, 1998). With the strong showing by the New Korea Democratic Party under the de facto leadership of Kim Young-sam and Kim Dae-jung in the February 1985 National Assembly elections, the junta quickly found itself confronted with a strong and relatively unified parliamentary opposition, as well as increasingly visible *minjung* and public protests. Chun promised constitutional revisions prior to the 1988 presidential election to quell the unrest, but these belated efforts to compromise proved too little too late (Burton and Ryu, 1997). In particular, the middle class, which had traditionally hesitated to join the democratization movement, joined the ranks of demonstrators, thereby forcing military hard-liners to cede ground. In Chun's poorly calculated effort to maintain a grip on power by postponing constitutional reforms until after the 1987 presidential elections sparked a general revolt with over one million protesters taking to the streets across the nation. International pressure, particularly in advance of the Seoul 1988 Olympics, as well as the refusal of opposition leader Kim Young-sam to resume negotiations with the government, tilted the balance from military action toward compromise. Accordingly, on June 29, 1987, Noh Tae Woo, the leader of the soft-liners and ruling party presidential candidate, announced his eight-point "June Declaration," promising direct presidential elections, a reduction in human rights restrictions, and freedom of the press (e.g., Dong, 1993).

Significantly, the Korean case avoided several key elements of a "pacted transition": the military was not institutionalized in the new political order, there were no special institutional arrangements to guarantee the continued representation of conservative parties, and few divisive issues were kept off the public agenda (Kim S. H., 2000). Within the context of continued protests and a mounting wave of strikes, constitutional negotiations between ruling and opposition forces were concluded by the end of August. The final agreement included a single-term presidency, congressional oversight of the executive, military neutrality, and basic civic freedoms (Burton and Ryu, 1997).

Disappointingly, however, the broad opposition coalition that emerged to influence constitutional reforms and the upcoming presidential elections quickly unraveled. Key opposition figures Kim Young-sam and Kim Dae-jung contracted what was dubbed "the presidential disease," and were unable to agree on a single presidential candidate. The cross-class pro-democratic alliances also proved short-lived as the middle class, having secured guarantees for civic and political freedoms, was anxious to restore social stability and unwilling to support the *minjung*'s demands for greater economic and social democratization (e.g., Dong, 1993). On account of a combination of internal competition and the fragmentation of the mass base, the opposition lost the December 1987 elections with Kim Young-sam and Kim Dae-jung splitting 45 percent of the vote, enabling the military candidate Noh Tae Woo to win a plurality with 36.6 percent. The opposition, however, organized again in time for the 1988 National Assembly elections, depriving the executive of control over the Congress. The ruling party was therefore forced to seek allies among the more conservative elements of the opposition, which resulted in a back-room merger of the parties associated with Kim Jong-pil and Kim Young-sam (see chapter 5). As a result, a fundamental shift in both the development strategy and the ideological framework of the authoritarian period was precluded, and instead Korea embarked on a protracted transition. It would be five years before a civilian president was elected and a full decade before power was handed over to the opposition.

Conclusion

Korea's historical economic development and ideological and civic organizational legacies shaped the basic contours of the democratization process. Due to the military regime's economic success, relatively less painful memories of the authoritarian past, and the persistence of a divided peninsula, citizens were unwilling to endorse dramatic socioeconomic change after the political transition and rather supported a more reformist approach. Social movements—influenced by the pro-democracy coalition's inability to sustain a lasting alliance post-transition, as well as the collapse of Communism and the resultant demise of a clear alternative to capitalism—also opted to work within the new political system and lobby for legislative and policy change. In short, despite the absence of a formal pact, these historical legacies limited the range of issues open to negotiation.

The gendered dimensions of the economic development model, its conservative Confucian ideological buttress as well as the gender-blindness of the *minjung* movement, however, were to be increasingly called into question by proponents of greater gender equity. Women's organizations in tandem with their progressive civic and state allies sought to capitalize on the new domestic and international political opportunity structures opened up by the democratization process to shape policy, as well as representational and cultural changes. The story of the post-transitional contestation of gender politics is the focus of the remainder of the book.

CHAPTER 3

The Korean Women's Movement: From *Minjung* Feminism to Gender Mainstreaming

Most women's movement activists were originally student movement activists in the 1980s. . . . We never regarded ourselves as women but rather focused on larger political issues. My enlightenment about gender issues started when we worked in factories trying to establish a women's union. We struggled to organize women laborers as they never reflected on social issues . . . and were always eager to get married to a prince . . . This experience motivated us to study about women's issues and to understand gender concepts.

Cho Y., 2000 interview

Whereas the experiences of feminists in other Third Wave regions have been fraught with disappointment, including movement fatigue, the disproportionately negative impact of neoliberal economic reforms on women's status, the renewed strength of cultural conservative groups, and divisive party politics (e.g., Jaquette and Wolchik, 1998; Siemienska, 1998; Vargas, 2002), such concerns have been largely absent in Korea. Although the reform process has been neither smooth nor linear, the Korean case suggests that democratization can afford organized women's groups significant and more varied spaces within which to effect political change. Moreover, the Korean women's movement has proven sufficiently cohesive and flexible as to provide demands for gender equality with an increasingly visible and respected sociopolitical platform. To account for this evolving influence, this chapter draws on a political process social movement framework (e.g., Tarrow, 1994) to analyze the movement's organizational structure, tactical repertoires, framing strategies, and networking capacity.

Historical Origins

A first wave of women's movement organization in the 1910s and 1920s notwithstanding,[1] there was little autonomous organizing by Korean women qua women until the 1970s. Thousands of women participated in government-sponsored groups in the 1960s and 1970s, such as the Korean National Council of Women (KNCW) and the Korean Federation of Housewives' Clubs, but these were aimed at building support for the state's development policies. As a Korea Women's Association United (KWAU) member noted:

> After the division of our nation, the women's movement meant leisurely class women's activities for social welfare, if not, government-sponsored activities for supporting the ruling regime. We can hardly find a women's movement, which aimed to fundamentally change the society. (Quoted in Cho H., 1994: 335)

Similarly, although women were actively involved in progressive social movement organizations from the 1970s, it is difficult to speak of a coherent second wave women's movement until *after* the democratic transition. Middle-class women mobilized around electoral rights (e.g., the League of Women Voters [1969–] and the Korean Family Law Reform Movement [1957–]), but were generally narrowly focused and limited in numbers (e.g., Sohn, 1999). In the early 1980s, several precursor organizations to the progressive women's movement emerged (e.g., Women for Equality and Peace, Korean Women's Hotline) but also struggled unsuccessfully to forge sustainable coalitions or impact the macropolitical field (Cho H., 1994).

The broader reentry of women into the political arena was linked to their participation in labor movements and struggles against authoritarianism. Contradictions in women's lived experiences following rapid economic development and increased access to higher education led to their involvement in mixed-sex student, labor, anti-authoritarian, and agrarian organizations. Yet, whereas Latin American women's movements explicitly linked democracy in everyday gender relations to the larger anti-authoritarian movement (e.g., Chuchryk, 1994), Korean activists generally remained within a broader social movement frame of *minjung* democracy, and only began to prioritize gender issues in significant numbers in the post-transition period (e.g., Lee and Jong, 1999).

Even in the case of the labor movement, where women workers played a decisive role in the emergence of a stronger working-class consciousness,[2] women's political activism generally did not serve as a springboard for organizing around gender issues. The primary focus remained demands for "humanitarian treatment" and "economic justice," despite the additional gender-related suffering they faced, in the form of significantly lower wages, sexual harassment, and gendered violence (Kim S. K., 1997). Whereas women in other cultural contexts were afforded some degree of immunity from state violence due to their perceived "non-political" status (e.g., Jaquette, 1994), being female in Korea offered little protection and often rendered women vulnerable to physical and sexual assault from male unionists and law enforcement groups (Koo, 2001).

Consciousness-raising efforts organized by the progressive Korean Christian Academy in the late 1970s and the 1980s, however, helped generate a more explicit focus on gender inequalities and, along with international publicity of the women's liberation movement in the West, served as an important impetus for future feminist activists (Matsui, 1999). Progressive women were divided, however, as to the relative importance of patriarchal versus class-based oppression. "Cultural feminists" emphasized the importance of establishing autonomous women's organizations to combat male-dominance (Cho H., 1994), whereas the more visible strand of progressive women's activism (developed within the *minjung* social movement frame) privileged general anti-authoritarian and pro-unification struggles at the expense of specific gender concerns.

Even so, whereas discourses of political motherhood allowed Latin American women to develop a specifically gender-focused movement during military rule, Korean women were not afforded the discursive space to forge separate organizations and movement goals until the *minjung* paradigm began to lose relevancy in the late 1980s. Only as activists gradually realized that the *minjung* framework was inadequate to account for women's specific subordination did they begin to make independent gender demands on the state. Founding members of the progressive umbrella group, the KWAU, argued that the causes of Korean women's oppression lay in *both* patriarchal culture *and* structural contradictions within the Korean polity (i.e., authoritarianism, political and economic subordination to the United States, and a divided Peninsula) (Cho, 2005).

Democratization

Although only a fledgling presence on the eve of the transition, the women's movement has adapted to the expanding political opportunities of democratization and has come to enjoy an increasingly influential public presence. In the initial post-transition period (1988–92), feminist activists, like their progressive civil society allies, maintained an oppositional stance toward the Roh Tae Woo administration due to its continuities with the authoritarian past. Changes in both the domestic and international environment in the early 1990s, however, prompted women's organizations to reexamine their stance vis-à-vis formal institutional politics. On the home front, Kim Young-sam's 1992 election as the first civilian president represented a major turning point. Although his democratic legitimacy had been eroded by his participation in a back room merger with the New Democratic Republican Party—the party of the former military junta—this marriage of convenience did not preclude far-reaching reform efforts (Lee Y., 2000). Kim Young-sam used his position within the ruling coalition to curb military power, introduce open nominations for presidential candidates, and reduce corruption by introducing "real name" financial transactions and a mandatory annual publication of bureaucrats' and politicians' assets (Kil and Moon, 2001). Not only did his administration purge the military hierarchy and revise national security laws to limit the powers of the intelligence agency, but he also oversaw the 1995 trial and imprisonment of ex-presidents Chun and Roh and related military cronies for human rights abuses.

These reform initiatives as well as efforts by political parties to court female voters provided the impetus for women's organizations to begin to engage with the state. In 1993, the KWAU registered with the government in order to improve its formal legitimacy and gain access to public funds, while the introduction of local government elections spurred women's organizations to reorient their focus toward demanding full implementation of reform policies and laws rather than simply rejecting the government's top-down, showcase policies (Kim, Y. A., 2000 interview).

Internationally, the collapse of the Communist bloc in the late 1980s profoundly altered political opportunity structures and compelled activists to rethink their socialist orientation and the *minjung* framework. As a result, activists began to turn their attention to pan-class gender issues. As former trade union organizer Cho Young-Sook noted:

> Although there was still a kind of nostalgia for class issues following the collapse of the Soviet Union . . . I felt lost and my instinct told me that we

needed greater clarity . . . I became more interested in gender issues as I started to think about myself as a woman. Until then I had ignored too much about my identity and had regarded myself just as an activist . . . So I decided to work with the KWAU. (2000 interview)

Equally important was the confluence of Korea's entry into the UN in 1990, acceptance into the Organisation for Economic Co-operation and Development (OECD) in 1996, and the Kim Young-sam administration's launch of a full-scale *segyehwa* (globalization) campaign in 1995.[3] Designed to ensure that policy measures meet international standards while facilitating global competitiveness, the sociocultural impact of the globalization drive has included a greater questioning of authority, more concern for human rights, and a growing acceptance of diversity (e.g., Samuel Kim, 2000). Similarly, increased global attention on issues of gender equality, especially in the context of major UN conferences and conventions on human rights (Vienna), population issues (Cairo), and women (Beijing) held in the mid-1990s, provided women's organizations with greater legitimacy, ideological/discursive resources, and models of best practice in their lobbying efforts. In the same vein, women's historically low status and the country's embarrassing rankings on international gender-related indicators have constituted a weak point in the government's search for greater global legitimacy (Park Y., 2000 interview).

At the NGO level, the 1995 Beijing World Conference on Women and the related East Asian preparatory conferences marked a major turning point (Nam, 2000 interview). Beijing attracted over 600 NGO participants from Korea as well as a sizeable state delegation, garnered unprecedented media attention, and, perhaps most importantly, demonstrated the willingness of Korean women to use an international forum to demand government intervention to address gender inequalities. Participants used the international spotlight to draw attention to the inadequacies of Korea's legal system in dealing with sexual harassment, for example, as well as the failure of the government to persuade Japan to compensate victims of its military sexual slavery system (Lee Y., 2000 interview). Post-Beijing, the women's movement community has continued to capitalize on international conventions to pressure public officials to enact gender-related reforms (e.g., Kim J., 2001 interview).

Movement Strands

Although there is no single ideal model of movement organization (e.g., Smith, 1991; Oxhorn, 1995), a comparative analysis of the Korean and

Latin American women's movement structures suggests that some organizational forms are more conducive to realizing state transformative and policy changes than others. Whereas women's movements have often struggled to sustain broad, overarching coalitions post-transition, the Korean case is characterized by two stable umbrella groups representing "progressive" and "conservative"/"moderate" gendered interests. These centrally coordinated umbrella organizations have served as cohesive representative and lobbying bodies, and have advanced the political influence and legitimacy of the women's movement vis-à-vis both civil society and state actors.

Establishing and sustaining an umbrella organization is, however, neither easy nor free from controversy. On a practical level, developing a coordinating body to identify common concerns and serve as a "spokesperson" for the wider community is problematized by the fact that women's "interests" span diverse practical and strategic gender arenas and are based on divergent class, partisan, ethnic, and other such positionings (Molyneux, 1985; Friedman, 2000). Moreover, because feminism as a philosophy generally critiques centralized forms of power, activists may be wary of establishing overarching organizations due to the potential dangers of bureaucratization and distancing from the grassroots (e.g., Jaquette, 1994). Although these organizational dilemmas have been much discussed in the Korean context (e.g., Kim K., 2000 interview; Yoon, 2000 interview), the presence of stable umbrella groups has provided a level of cohesion of which few other women's movements can boast.[4] Centrally coordinated movement campaigns allow groups to pool resources and build upon one another's strategies, to focus activist energies by concentrating on select issues, to present a united front when lobbying political society and conservative groups, and, through greater visibility, enhance public awareness of movement activities.

The diversity and dynamism of the movement notwithstanding, the limited size and breadth of the membership base, along with scarce funding, have hampered the post-transitional contestation of gender politics. First, although women's organizations have gradually become more representative in terms of geographic coverage,[5] membership numbers remain low, especially versus civic groups such as the environmental and political reform movements. Many of the larger women's groups are structured around practical gender interests (e.g., household management issues, hobby programs, child education concerns), whereas more explicitly feminist groups tend to be smaller, ranging anywhere from under 100 to 10,000 members. Second, funding constraints remain a recurring problem that limit public awareness efforts and the provision of programs and services, as well as activists' remuneration.[6] Korea's successful economic development model, symbolized by entry into the OECD in 1996, has led to a reduction in international funding options of most civic groups and NGOs as international agencies reduced financial support to a "newly developed" Korea. As a result, the state has become a major funding source, contributing to women's groups' decision to "engage" the formal political arena but also placing limits on the strategies to be employed (Soh, 2002 interview). Even so, economic growth has not led to a concomitant increase in public spending on civic/welfare initiatives, and the structure of governmental support (i.e., project-based funding) fails to provide much-needed financial stability to women's organizations. Equally importantly, private sector funding opportunities are limited for women's organizations, even relative to other (male-dominated) civic groups, which can often access resource-rich alumni or hometown networks (e.g., Kim P., 2002).

Korean Women's Association United

The KWAU emerged in 1987 as a national umbrella group to unite progressive women's voices and to explicitly target working-class women who had been largely ignored by the more conservative KNCW and more targeted women's political groups such as the League of Women Voters. By 2000, the KWAU had grown to include some 28 affiliated organizations with specific target groups or thematic foci including white- and blue-collar workers, farmers, housewives, violence prevention groups, peace promotion, environmental protection, women's health, and Christian and Buddhist feminism (Nam, 2000 interview). Sociocultural barriers, including women's care-work burden, cultural prescriptions against women's public sector participation, and gender-role socialization, combined with limited resources, had prevented the KWAU from attracting more than 50,000 active members by 2000 (e.g., Moon S., 2002). Core activists tend to be middle class and university educated, with lifestyles that are perceived as rather distant from the lives of ordinary women, who remain the KWAU's target audience. Political science professor Chin Mi-kyong notes:

> There is a gap between the highbrow women activists and ordinary house-wives. "Here life is much more comfortable—we want to live under the protection of our husbands". . . . Many feminist leaders are divorced . . . and so the general population got the impression that if you are exposed

to feminism, then divorce will follow . . . Feminism is like an "anti-family science." (2000, interview)

The KWAU has nevertheless emerged as the single most proactive actor struggling for greater gender equality. Having been at the forefront of most major gender-reform initiatives, it has become widely respected as a legitimate political player by civil society groups, political society, and state officials alike. In addition, it has provided valuable leadership experience for feminist activists; most famously, National Assembly representative Lee Mikyung, the former and current ministers of Gender Equality, Han Myung-Sook and Ji Uhn-Hee, and United Nations Convention on the Elimination of All Forms of Discrimination Against Women (CEDAW) Committee Vice-Chair Shin Heisoo, are all former KWAU copresidents.

The KWAU's strength stems in part from the gravity with which its leaders take the association's responsibility as a representative organization (e.g., Nam, 2000 interview).[7] Leadership is shared between three corepresentatives from member organizations and rotates biannually. More specific policy direction and campaign tactics are developed in five thematic committees (Labor, Reunification and Peace, Welfare, Human Rights, and Small Business) composed of member group leaders and supportive outside experts, while the affiliated Korean Institute for Alternative Social Policy conducts independent research on topical gender issues and prepares policy recommendation papers (Kang N., 2000 interview). Despite the more radical backgrounds of its core staff and activists, the KWAU has been generally cautious about adopting controversial issues and has been prepared to allow "indie" or "guerilla" groups to champion vanguard gender concerns such as lesbian rights or abortion on demand (e.g., Yoon, 2000 interview). Despite criticism from some movement participants and academics for its declining radicalism (e.g., Kim H., 2000 interview), the KWAU seeks to bolster its legitimacy in the eyes of broader civil movements, as well as political society, while also serving as a voice that represents the diversity of its members:

> The KWAU is an umbrella organization with members from a diverse ideological spectrum. Each year we decide on common goals and then cooperate for change. Because of this democratic structure and mutual compromise we can work together . . . We [KWAU headquarters] don't usually carry out specific programs as our role is to pressure lawmakers . . . and negotiate with government agencies about the detailed enactment. (Nam, 2000 interview)

Korean National Council of Women

The KNCW has a much longer history (established in 1959) and larger membership base (some 46 member groups and approximately one million members) than the KWAU, but has not shared the same post-transitional mantle of legitimacy that *minjung* or *shimin undong* organizations enjoy due to its origins as a government-mobilized and funded civilian organization. While some KNCW member groups were at the forefront of the 30-year struggle to reform the Family Law, others were recruited to disseminate the authoritarian regime's anti-Communist, national security, and frugality campaigns (e.g., Moon S., 2002). Moreover, on account of the diversity of its member organizations, which range from professional associations (e.g., business, medicine, law) to anti-Communist leagues and housewives' clubs, the KNCW's goals encompass professional advancement and community development–related concerns as well as gender-equality reforms (Oh, 1997).

As successive leaders have sought to distance themselves from clientelistic organizing practices and adapt to the new democratic milieu, the KNCW has grown increasingly independent and active in promoting women's rights (Lee Y., 2000 interview). In addition to involvement in campaigns to introduce women's political quotas, to demand equality in inheritance tax legislation and redress for the Japanese colonial era military sexual slaves, KNCW member groups have also tackled discrimination in educational and professional fields such as the formerly unequal high school entrance examination system and sex-biased job advertisements (Oh, 1997).

Whereas some feminist academics and activists have remained critical of the KNCW, political parties and government officials have been unable to ignore the KNCW given its numerical strength and extensive social networks. Moreover, the forging of more cooperative ties with the KWAU since the mid-1990s secured its role as an influential actor in the contestation of gender politics. Despite divergent membership bases, ideological foci, and activist strategies, the KWAU and KNCW have been able to develop effective, issue-based coalitions for the sake of key gender-policy reforms (e.g., political quotas for women, women's employment programs, the 1995 Women's Basic Development Act, and violence prevention). The KNCW's mobilization capacity and ability to appeal to more conservative community and political leaders complements the KWAU's explicit focus on gender inequality and member groups' field experience, which often informs the content of reform initiatives. As one senior KWAU activist explained:

> The dilemma is when we cooperate with the KNCW, the KWAU always provides the content, plus our perspective is different. For instance, when job training is discussed, the KNCW focuses on college-educated women but we focus on the gender division of labor and unemployment, irregular jobs etc . . . Sometimes I wonder whether we should collaborate because of these different values and attitudes . . . But [the real benefit in cooperating is] numbers and dealing with the Government—it always lends more legitimacy. Funding is easier as is media attention. (Anon., 2000 interview)

The Cultural/Academic Wing

Although this book's analytical focus on institutional rather than cultural/attitudinal changes renders these twin umbrella groups the most visible players of the Korean women's movement, it would be doing a disservice to the complexity and richness of the movement to omit any discussion of what I term the "cultural/academic wing" and the "indie" or "guerilla" groups.[8] These diverse organizations serve as important critics of the more institutionalized, lobbying strand of the movement. As generators of new ideas and alternative perspectives, they fill the role of what Fraser (1993) has termed a "subaltern counterpublic":

> [I]nsofar as these counterpublics emerge in response to exclusion within dominant publics, they help expand discursive space. In principle, assumptions that were previously exempt from contestation will now have to be publicly argued out. In general, the proliferation of subaltern counterpublics means a widening of discursive contestation, a good thing in stratified societies. (15)

Rejecting the notion that gendered political claims should be subordinated to class struggles, groups such as Alternative Culture established in the early 1980s were critical of the male-dominated anti-dictatorship movements and sought to promote an alternative, non-patriarchal culture (Cho, 2005). Since the end of authoritarianism, the number of cultural activist groups has expanded significantly. Various women's media groups have been established, for instance, including several major feminist newspapers and magazines as well as a feminist publishing house.[9] The Feminist Artist Network, which coordinates art exhibitions and demonstrations, has developed the annual "Women's Film Festival in Seoul" into the largest international women's film festival. Activists have also opposed what feminist sociologist Cho Ju-Hyun (2005) terms the "Confucian patriarchal symbolic system" by, for instance, organizing feminist performances at national Confucian monuments/shrines in order to protest the *hojuje* (family headship system), or organizing events such as the anti–Miss Korea pageant (e.g., Choy, 2001).

On the academic front, the women's studies department at Ewha Womans University, the world's largest university for women, has grown rapidly since its establishment in 1984 and now includes a Ph.D. program. Moreover, women's studies degree programs have been established at over 15 universities and M.A. programs in 10, with undergraduate classes taught at many more tertiary institutions (Chang, 2000 interview). Similarly, the Korean Association of Women's Studies, also established in 1984, boasts 700 members and holds annual conferences and monthly seminars, and publishes a journal (Shim, 2002). Moreover, whereas movement groups have looked to international examples and conventions, but remained comparatively isolated from regional and international networks, feminist scholars enjoy strong international connections. Many leading professors have returned from graduate training in Europe or North America; and since 1997, the Asian Center of Women's Studies at Ewha has played a significant role in fostering an Asia-wide network of women's studies academics.

"Indie" or "Guerilla" Groups

An additional movement strand involves more radical "indie" or "guerilla" groups that have sprung up on campuses among women's studies students, combining reading/discussion circles with more action-oriented components. Critical of a perceived "mainstreaming" of more established movement organizations, these groups organize initiatives ranging from the annual menstruation and National Young Feminist festivals to off-line/on-line interventions in controversial gender-related debates about lesbian rights and sexual harassment by male professors and students (Shin S., 2003 interview). The high rate of Internet penetration in Korea (over two-thirds of all homes) has facilitated the proliferation of such groups (e.g., Kim P., 2002), with now dozens of feminist thematic chat rooms and electronic community boards.[10] These groups serve as an important check on more established movement organizations, and encourage younger generations of women to develop practical action as well as discursive strategies that are relevant to their own lives (e.g., Shin S., 2003 interview).

Tactical Repertoires

Tactical flexibility has emerged as an important element of successful movement struggles in nascent democracies where substantive policy change depends on the development of "a flexible multidimensional feminist strategy—one that organizes gender-conscious political pressure at the base, both within and without the State" (Alvarez, 1990: 273). Depending on the goal in question, the nature and strategy of opposition groups, and the availability of allies at a particular historical juncture, Korean activists have drawn creatively on a variety of collective action forms. Tactics have ranged from small-group study and conscientization meetings to conferences and poster/leaflet and media campaigns; from street theater and festivals to signature petitions and demonstrations; and from monitoring and the evaluation of policy implementation to the provision of alternative (e.g., health- and violence-related) feminist services (Ji, 2002). As KWAU policy officer Cho Young-Sook explained: "We pursue a plural strategy: we fight, we persuade, we flatter" (2003 interview).

Unlike traditional interest groups organized around securing tangible resources, new social movements are equally concerned with cultural politics (e.g., Mainwaring and Viola, 1984). Movements calling for environmental protection, indigenous or gender rights, and the like, frequently disrupt conventional understandings, politicize new kinds of noneconomic issues, and blur the distinction between the social and political, private and public (e.g., Radcliffe and Westwood, 1993). For instance, initiatives by women's organizations to ". . . question structures of authority both public and private . . . and resignify everyday practices and people's lives" (Caldiera, 1998: 83) are often viewed as one of the women's movement's most important achievements.

To counter mainstream society's hierarchical and male-dominated culture, Korean feminist groups have tried to develop "new ways of doing politics" by reshaping not just formal structures and institutions but also daily life interactions (Yoon, 2004 interview). They have set up community-based study and consciousness-raising groups that meet regularly to discuss, for example, sexuality and reproductive health issues, environment-friendly consumption patterns, participation in local politics, and feminist psychology and spirituality. Although such efforts are small in scale, movement leaders view them as an important part of feminist praxis and as a means to maintain the vitality of the movement, particularly in the context of its increasing institutionalization (e.g., Oh, 2002 interview; Yoon, 2002 interview). Movement organizations have also engaged in culturo-political interventions at the broader public level, creatively drawing on a diverse array of both Korean and Western-inspired action strategies to attract public interest and introduce new ideas and campaign efforts. These include signature campaigns and demonstrations in front of the National Assembly, City Hall, or the symbolic Myungdong Cathedral, street/subway theater, festivals, and media-monitoring campaigns. Such activities aim to challenge conventional biases, break down taboos, and initiate debates on gender dynamics among ordinary citizens, as well as those in positions of political power.

The importance of cultural politics notwithstanding, to secure recognition as legitimate players in the mainstream political process, women's organizations have been forced to reorient their movement frame from one of protest to "critical engagement." Mindful of the feminist insight that autonomous organizational structures are essential for women in patriarchal society, activists nevertheless have come to view mainstream political institutions as an "absolutely necessary terrain of political struggle" (Kim K., 1998: 196). Accordingly, the movement has gradually shifted from its blanket critiques of the government to more targeted demands for politicians and bureaucrats to fulfill their campaign pledges and open up institutional spaces for women. The elections of presidents Kim Dae-jung in 1997 and Noh Moo Hyun in 2002 should not be underestimated as a driving force behind the more cooperative relationships between progressive civic groups more generally and the state (see chapter 5).

In order to effect legislative and policy change, social movement groups need to expand their tactical repertoire to include the provision of policy expertise and lobbying. This is often far from easy, as emphasized by Jaquette and Wolchik's (1998) study of women's movements in Latin America and Eastern Europe:

> [There is] a need for permanently organized groups that are capable of mobilizing political resources to maintain existing gains and push new agendas, but it is precisely at this level that the loss of momentum and divisions among those who remain active take their toll. (10)

In the Korean case, the KWAU and KNCW serve as the main interlocutors for women's groups' demands and often negotiate directly with political parties, legislative committees, and civil servants so as to counter the influence of more conservative groups such as employers' associations, or veteran and Confucian organizations. Over time the lobbying targets have become increasingly specific, attesting to the activist community's growing level of expertise. For example, women's health organizations campaigned in 2001/02 for a review of health insurance policies due to the excessively high national rate of Caesarian section births and associated dangers to women's health (Myung et al., 2002); while women's groups working with rural women successfully secured government support for maternity and postpartum care for farming households.

In order to foster policy competence, the umbrella groups have promoted connections between movement organizations and progressive academics and professionals, as well as founding autonomous research centers such as the KWAU's Korea Women's Research Center and the Korean Research Institute of Sexual Violence. Although formal channels of cooperation between university-based feminists and movement activists remain relatively limited, women's groups frequently work with individual scholars who conduct research on international best practices, serve as presenters at intra-movement or public forums, and participate in planning committees to assist the development of policy alternatives. These academic–activist links also play an important role in enhancing the legitimacy of movement groups in the eyes of the public and political society. As sociologist Cho Soon-Kyung explains:

> Women's studies researchers analyze issues raised by the women's movement . . . drawing attention to gender issues that weren't even seen as problematic before, such as sexual harassment . . . It's a reciprocal relationship . . . in our society, if the message is delivered through professors it tends to carry significantly more weight. We academics can also contribute our analytical skills. For example, I sometimes appear as an expert witness in court cases organized by women's NGOs . . . I also raise new concepts such as "punitive damage awards" or "class action suits" when presenting in front of politicians or legal scholars. (2002 interview)

The NGO community has also been resourceful in networking with other professionals, especially lawyers and medical professionals (Lee M., 2000 interview; e.g., Shin H., 2000 interview). Moreover, internal professionalism has been strengthened over time through attracting increasing numbers of university women's studies and social work graduates as full-time staff. Often having written M.A. theses on gender policy–related issues, these women offer research expertise and serve as spokespersons in dealing with the media and political officials (e.g., Chang, 2000 interview; Myung, 2000 interview).

Monitoring

Legislative reform is a crucial first step but only effective monitoring can ensure changes are implemented. To date the Korean movement has relied on four main methods: negotiation with bureaucrats on the content of policy enforcement ordinances, the development of NGO shadow reports on major domestic and international policies, the preparation of gender-related lawsuits to test the parameters of new legislation, and gender budget analysis.

First, because of the rapid pace of legislative passage and the still rudimentary level of policy expertise that characterizes the Korean National Assembly on the one hand, and the political dominance of the bureaucracy on the other, ministerial *shihaengnyŏng* (enforcement ordinances) have a powerful influence on the ultimate efficacy of new legislation (see chapter 5). Accordingly, to ensure that their demands are not diluted in this final stage, movement leaders devote considerable time and energy to negotiating with individual government departments as they draw up implementation guidelines. As KWAU policy officer Cho Young-Sook explains:

> Sometimes the law is good but the implementation guidelines are poor and the meaning of the law vanishes. So although we first focus on the National Assembly, we have to immediately turn and monitor whether government officials fully follow the spirit of the law or ignore its real significance . . . We know that the *shihaengnyŏng* is sometimes more important than the law itself. (2000 interview)

This process often involves the organization of public hearings, and, following the finalization of the implementation guidelines, monitoring reports. If still unsatisfied, movement organizations have not shied away from initiating fresh campaigns to push for a revision of the original law.

A second important monitoring channel involves the courts. To test the practical application of new legislation, women's organizations have been involved in filing lawsuits, for example, on the behalf of women victims of violence who retaliated against their attackers, a suit against multiple corporations with discriminatory appearance requirements, and cases concerning sexual harassment and workplace discrimination (e.g., Chong, 2000 interview). Again, in instances where results have been unsatisfactory, activists have used these experiences to prepare proposals for legislative revision (e.g., Nam, 2000 interview).

A third approach entails shadow monitoring of lawmakers' annual screening of the bureaucracy. This technique was initiated in conjunction with other progressive civic movements in 1999 to pressure lawmakers to adopt a more professional stance vis-à-vis their civil service monitoring duties (Kim S. H., 2003). Women's group representatives assessed National Assembly members based on their performance in gender-related areas, and, along with their civic partners, publicly released their evaluation results. As women's movement leader Chong Kang-Ja noted, the publicity surrounding this approach has been an effective tool to motivate lawmakers to follow through on legislative pledges (2000 interview). Similarly, at the international level, to maximize pressure on the government's gender policymaking, NGOs have drawn up shadow reports that provide international bodies that monitor Korea's progress with a more critical interpretation of women's status. Examples include shadow reports to the third and fourth CEDAW reports prepared by the Korean government (1998), the Beijing +5 and +10 Conferences (2000 and 2005), and the UN Committee for Economic, Social and Cultural Rights NGO Report (2001).

Finally, gender budget analysis, initiated by Korean WomenLink in 2001, has served to highlight the limited resources allocated to implementing the flurry of new policies seen in the last 15 years. To document their discontent and pressure state actors for change, Korean WomenLink, along with sympathetic academics, has drawn on the United Nations Development Programme's participatory budget model to assess seven local governments' gender-related budgets, and most recently those of central government ministries (Yoon, 2002b; Cha, 2004). In the case of Kangwon Provincial Government's Women's Division, for example, it was revealed that funding had been allocated to awards that lauded stereotypical gender roles, educational projects using expensive technology that would only reach an elite group of women, and efforts to mobilize women to volunteer in provincial projects with no gender-related content (Yoon, 2002a). This budget monitoring methodology has not only served to improve women's groups' financial literacy and understanding of bureaucratic processes, but also signaled to government officials that spending and policy decisions on women-related issues are now under closer scrutiny. Moreover, this NGO initiative has influenced the KWDI and Ministry of Gender Equality (MOGE) to embark on their own gendered analyses of government budgets and incorporate these methods into the Second Women's Development Plan 2003–2007 (Yoon, 2002 interview).

Service provision

Given an underdeveloped welfare state and wary of the underlining ideologies of services provided by private individuals or religious-based groups (e.g., Lee M., 2002 interview), a general consensus has emerged that women would be better served by a broader range of services from which to select (e.g., Chong, 2000 interview). Women's movement organizations are accordingly involved in providing a range of gender-related social services, which activists hope will encourage women to break social taboos, and to come forward and seek assistance. Examples range from vocational training and childcare to sexual and family violence counseling and shelters, from family law counseling to rehabilitation facilities and services for sex workers.

Although some outside analysts have worried that this hands-on approach to social policy change can compromise the independence of NGOs by increasing their reliance on government funding for their service provision endeavors (Park Y., 2000 interview), it has nevertheless enabled women's organizations to better provide government departments with policy-relevant data and recommendations. Moreover, because feminists are directly involved with the management of partially state-funded social services, they are in a stronger position to assess the government's budgetary and resource commitment. As a result, women's movement providers often team up with government research institutes to conduct evaluations of welfare service provision for women, enabling activists to influence the evaluation criteria as well as utilize the information gathered to lobby relevant agencies for greater resources and more rigorous, gender-sensitive guidelines for facility managers (Lee M., 2000 interview).

Discursive Sensitivity

Creative but culturally palatable issue-framing has been one of the hallmarks of the Korean women's movement. Because collective action does not result from a simple conversion of objective socioeconomic conditions into protest, "movements [need to] frame their collective action around cultural symbols that are selectively chosen from a cultural tool chest" (Tarrow, 1994: 119) and which resonate with broader discourses of "injustice" employed by both domestic and international social change movements. Whereas other Third Wave movements often struggled to adapt their ideological strategies and language of protest to the democratic environment, the Korean movement has flexibly adopted new ideological frames to suit an evolving political opportunity structure (e.g., Kim K., 2002).

In the 1980s, feminist activists' ideological resources were strongly influenced by the wider *minjung* master frame. Radical and liberal feminist perspectives were critiqued as Western imports with limited relevance, and instead the "woman question" was defined within a "socialist" tradition whereby women's oppression would be eradicated through their work as "revolutionary agents" and "laborers" alongside men. (Kim K. A., 1996; Ching and Yoon, 1995).[11] By the late 1980s, however, feminists had begun to question the *minjung* frame's ongoing utility in the context of the post-transitional bifurcation of the *minjung* movement and the collapse of the international Communist bloc. As part of the new *shimin undong* paradigm, which involved demands for equal citizenship rights and issue-specific institutional reforms, the women's movement reoriented their movement frame to incorporate pan-class gender issues such as access to childcare, protection from sexual and domestic violence, employment discrimination, and opposition to son preference (Kim K., 1998):

> Most women's movement activists [were] originally student movement activists in the 1980s . . . We never regarded ourselves as women but rather focused on larger political issues . . . My enlightenment about gender issues started when we worked in factories trying to establish a women's union. We struggled to organize women laborers as they never reflected on social issues . . . It was difficult to make them speak out because gentleness is the prescribed etiquette for women. This experience motivated us to study about women's issues and to understand gender concepts. (Cho Y., 2000 interview)

In framing these new rights-based claims, activists sought to avoid being branded as mere importers of Western feminism. For example, to counter claims that violence prevention initiatives "would destroy the Korean family" and that feminists were "turning the Korean male into the enemy" (Yoon, 2000 interview), advocates emphasized their concern for family health and stability. Similarly, in recognition of Korea's entrenched Confucian cultural underpinnings, body- and sexuality-related issues (except sexual assault) were largely shelved at this juncture to avoid alienating the more conservative elements of the movement's member base. As activist Myung Jin-sook reflected:

> The women's movement has been slow to address women's health issues, aside from the dramatic concerns of violence against women and female feticide. In this Confucian society, discussing bodies is still pretty much taboo, even something as central as childbirth. Women have been kept largely ignorant of their bodies and reproductive health issues, and taught to follow the prescriptions of medical authorities. (2002 interview)

Signature feminist issues in the West, such as abortion rights, women's general health and reproductive health, sexual morality, and sexual orientation, have therefore only recently become the focus of feminist campaigns (Lee M., 2000 interview). Whereas framing demands to resonate with broader civil society discourses has improved the movement's political legitimacy within a profoundly conservative cultural context and reduced public resistance to challenges of traditional gender scripts (e.g., Moon S., 2002), some observers caution that it simultaneously limits the development of women's own, more gender-focused, discourses (e.g., Yoon, 2000 interview).

Korean women's groups have also increasingly drawn upon the language of international forums, organizations, and treaties so as to capitalize on global best practices and norms to pressure the government for needed reforms. A powerful indicator of the growing convergence of movement, government, and international gendered discourses is the increasing popularity of "gender mainstreaming." First introduced on the international stage in the early 1990s, the concept was endorsed in the 1995 Beijing Platform for Action, and has since been increasingly employed by Korean feminists to refer to the incorporation of gender-sensitive policies into all social arenas—private and public, civil society, and the state (Kim K., 2002). Mainstreaming has served as a useful discursive tool to call for the recognition of gender inequality as not just a "women's issue," as well as to provide specific methodological approaches, including gender sensitivity analysis, gender budgeting, and gender disaggregated data collection. Given the Korean state's eagerness to improve its standing within the international community, ministries are highly attuned to the importance of being well versed in this new international parlance, thus providing a common language between state and non-state actors. Feminists, however, are also finding that given political society's limited gender sensitivity, the concept's transformative content has been diluted. As women's studies scholar Chang Pilwha notes:

> The concept of gender mainstreaming has not been worked out in detail. There is a wide range of understandings and little serious engagement with the term's theoretical dimensions. It has become a word rather than content—and thus there is no clear link with the implementation of government programs. (2000 interview)

Networking Capacity

Because of the diversity of women's interests and associated difficulties in sustaining long-term partnerships, an approach that involves "a variety of political action arenas, loosely coordinated by conjunctural coalitions, may prove to be the best way to advance the multiple goals of socially, politically, and ideologically heterogeneous movements" (Alvarez, 1990: 237). In the Korean case, women have forged alliances at particular political conjunctures to effect gender-policy change, but rather than the formation of coalitions across party lines as emphasized in the Latin American context (Friedman, 2000: 51), the development of intra- and inter-movement alliances have been most influential. In the context of a weak, non-ideological party system, ties with other progressive civic and labor movements have enhanced the policy influence of the women's movement by inflating their numerical strength, increasing public legitimacy, and providing opportunities to exchange tactical expertise. Moreover, these alliances have facilitated the women's movement's contribution to broader democratic reforms, which in turn has potentially positive spillover effects on women's sociopolitical status. Promoting political transparency, for example, serves not only to deepen democracy, but also helps reduce the barriers that women face when entering formal politics by reducing the influence of old boys' networks and money politics.

An excellent example is the civic Congressional Blacklist Campaign organized prior to the 2000 National Assembly elections. In the largest political mobilization since the June 1987 Uprising, some 470 organizations sparked a press sensation by publicly announcing a list of candidates deemed unfit for office (Shin E., 2003). The participation of 100 women's groups in this effort marked a turning point in their recognition as important contributors to the mainstream political reform process. Although women's organizations did not introduce gender-specific issues into the movement (e.g., blacklisting candidates who failed to support gender-related legislation in Congress), the KWAU and other groups were content to participate in the joint struggle. As feminist historian Chon Hyun-baek notes:

> The KWAU participated in the blacklist campaign not as a public relations effort for women's concerns but because it's imperative to change general political culture . . . But women's participation in civil society issues was really recognized through our involvement—Ji Eun-hee [KWAU president] appeared in every press conference . . . This publicity changed ordinary people's awareness about women's important societal roles. (2000 interview)

On the international front, however, while the Korean women's movement draws heavily on global conventions, norms, and best practices, it has remained relatively isolated from international organizations, especially other Asian women's movements. Some 30 international women's groups have branches in Korea (True and Mintrom, 2001: 39), but, with the exception of the YWCA, they have not played a major role in the women's movement to date. Likewise, although women's groups organized exchanges with international women workers' groups, several environmental cooperatives, and the East Asian Women's Forum in the lead-up to the 1995 Beijing Women's Conference, these exchanges have not played a central role in the trajectory or framing of the Korean domestic movement. In the academic realm, Ewha Womans University's Asian Center for Women's Studies was at the forefront of establishing an eight-country Women's Studies in Asia Network in 1997 with over 350 scholars from some 220 institutions, but this has yet to extend its reach to a broader cross-section of local scholars and activists. Part of the explanation lies in linguistic and historico-cultural differences. Whereas broad similarities have facilitated Latin American biannual *encuentros* (meetings) and issue networks as well as a common platform in international fora (Alvarez et al., 1998), Asia is characterized by a plethora of languages, culturo-historical traditions and development levels, rendering networking more difficult. Korea's unique geopolitics has also played a role, with the North–South division providing a strong impetus for civic groups to prioritize inter-peninsular exchanges at the expense of inter-Asian alliances.

Conclusion

Although a central thesis of this book is that the relative balance of power among progressive and conservative groups constitutes a key determinant of efforts to advance gender equality, the Korean women's movement has consistently been at the forefront of such initiatives. This chapter has drawn attention to the distinguishing characteristics of the Korean movement that have facilitated post-transitional improvements in women's political representation and gender-related policy outcomes. The first source of strength is the movement's hybrid organizational structure, comprising two relatively complementary umbrella organizations that facilitate lobbying in the formal political arena complemented by more diffuse cultural/academic and "indie/guerilla" strands. Second, the movement's multifaceted tactical repertoire, balancing institutional ("engagement with the state") and cultural politics, corroborates the thesis that double militancy lies at the heart of successful feminist reform efforts. The ability of women's organizations to frame movement demands in a way that resonates with wider movements/sentiments for social change constitutes a third key variable. Finally, the Korean case highlights the efficacy of forging strong cross-movement networks. Seeking social change as part of a broader civil society community provides crucial political legitimacy as well as a sense of identity and emotional solidarity that should not be underestimated.

Competing "Gender Coalitions": Progressive Allies, Fragmented Opponents, and Contradictory State Interests

One of the prominent aspects of the Korean shimin undong *is its continual strength—in terms of its militancy, its protest spirit . . . The movement has been very successful at revitalizing itself in the face of new challenges . . . globalization, neo-liberalism, the Asian crisis.*

Cho H., 2002 interview

Employers associations don't support any particular group, regardless of whether they are religious or educational organizations . . . Besides our interest in the economy, we don't have any broader goals per se. . . .

Choi, 2002 interview

Although women's organizations are most often at the forefront of post-transitional gender-equality reform initiatives, the political opportunities that facilitate or constrain the realization of these demands are shaped by the balance of power among a broader array of state and civil society actors. To understand the contestation of gender politics we therefore need to examine the specific gendered interests of the state, progressive civil society allies, and conservative opponents, as well as their respective capacities to address these political concerns. In keeping with the dynamic nature of political opportunity structures, such interests and strategies are likely to evolve over the democratization process. Civil society–state relations tend to become less antagonistic, whereas the relative influence of civil society groups is shaped by their ability to adapt to the new democratic environment and capitalize on the shifting domestic and international political context (Doh, 2001).

Compared to other Third Wave polities, the composition of and balance of power between progressive and conservative "gender coalitions" in Korea is distinctive, and has played a significant role in the relatively greater advances in post-transition gender policy. Progressive women's organizations have been able to take advantage of an unusually strong and vibrant *shimin undong* and position themselves "separately but together." Conversely, despite a profoundly conservative Confucian political culture, opposition to gender equality initiatives has been weaker than in many other nascent democracies. Whereas recent feminist analyses have drawn attention to the importance of conservative opposition groups, especially the Catholic Church, in the contestation of Latin American and Eastern European gender politics (e.g., Franco, 1998; Htun, 2003), culturally conservative voices in Korea lack strong institutional representation. Moreover, cultural and economic conservatives have been unable, or unwilling, to develop politically significant linkages. As such, I argue that the relative strength of organized opposition appears to be a more useful explanatory factor for advances in gender equality than general political culture.

This chapter also considers the state's role in negotiating gender politics, building on the insights of feminist historians, who have highlighted how political elites employ gendered arguments and policies to further broader state projects, including nation-building, economic development, and distinguishing a new regime from its predecessors (Scott, 1988; Dore and Molyneux, 2000). Although studies on post-transitional gender politics have focused predominantly on the social movement rather than the state side of the equation, to assume that the state only reacts to pressures from women's organizations and their allies blinkers us to the state's independent gendered interests. We therefore need to consider both explicitly gender-related policy goals (e.g., maternity leave policies that enable women to combine their productive and reproductive roles), as well as the gendered nature of ostensibly gender-neutral policy aims (e.g., restructuring of industrial sectors in which women are concentrated).

Progressive Allies

Although the creation of democratic institutions in other regions often resulted in a rather competitive relationship between social movements and political society whereby once highly visible movement groups were sidelined by the (re)emergence of political parties (e.g., Chalmers et al., 1997), a distinguishing feature of Korea's democratization experience has been the sustained political strength of civil society. Broadly speaking, the "386" generation *(sam p'al yuk shidae) minjung* activists born in the 1960s, active in the anti-authoritarian struggles in the 1980s and in their thirties in the 1990s aligned themselves post-authoritarianism with one of two main civil society groupings: the *shimin undong* or the labor movement. The following section discusses the organizational structure, political strength, and gendered interests and strategies of each movement group in turn.

Shimin Undong

The late 1980s/early 1990s Korean "NGO renaissance" was marked by a flourishing of NGOs and was symbolized by the emergence of the so-called Big Three—Citizens' Coalition for Economic Justice (CCEJ); Korean Federation of the Environmental Movement (KFEM); and People's Solidarity for Participatory Democracy (PSPD). In contrast to the *minjung* movement, which had called for a more radical social revolution, *shimin undong* groups sought issue-specific reforms within the parameters of extant political institutions, including electoral transparency, environmental protection, education reform and consumer rights. This narrower scope of day-to-day activism did not, however, preclude a broader call for participatory democracy. To coordinate this, the Korean Council of Citizens' Movements was established in 1994, and various permeations of the Council have since coordinated a wide array of campaigns relating to political and economic reforms, human rights, peace and unification, social service provision, and the like (Kim S. H., 2000). Movement ties have been further strengthened by the widely read NGO weekly the *Citizen Times* (founded in 1993) and the recently established on-line news service *OhMyNews* (http://www.ohmynews.com). In addition to offering an alternative news source to mainstream newspapers, both provide information on diverse movement activities and facilitate cross-movement debate.

The emergence of progressive civil society groups as a vibrant, comparatively cohesive, and increasingly influential political force can be partly attributed to the converse weaknesses of Korean political society (e.g., Kim S. H., 2000). In particular, although inviting its own problems (see chapter 5), the lack of a historic party system with established patterns of dominant and working-class partisan organizing has expanded the political space available to civil society. As Cho Hee-Yeon (2000) argues:

> When parliamentary democracy and the representative system are under-developed, NGOs act as a proxy for civil society's diverse demands. As the

> Government is incapable of duly reflecting the demands of civil society, through resistance from either the bureaucracy or vested interests, and as institutional political parties are unable to properly execute representative functions, these roles cannot but be played by non-institutional civil society movement organizations. (287)

A weak inchoate party system, however, is not so exceptional in fledgling democracies and constitutes only one part of the puzzle (Mainwaring and Scully, 1995). Perhaps as importantly, the political opportunity structure of the gradual transition under the Roh Tae Woo presidency (1987–92) ironically provided civic groups with room to develop a new ideological paradigm and discursive strategies, while remaining relatively autonomous from political society. Whereas transitions in Latin American and Eastern Europe often resulted in the election of leaders directly opposed to the dictatorship and entailed a more symbolic distancing from the past, the administration of popularly elected (ex-General) Roh was at best "a *dictablanda* (liberalized authoritarianism) and hence [there was a] need to continue the pro-democracy struggle" (Kim S. H., 2000: 118). In contrast to the tensions and frequent splintering of alliances that occurred in other nascent democracies as the political space became increasingly dominated by parties (e.g., Vargas, 2002), the challenge of reorienting movement frames and strategies to deal with political society proved relatively less tumultuous and divisive in the Korean context.

Identity constitutes a third key dimension of civil society strength. *Shimin undong* groups see themselves not simply as a contemporary phenomenon but rather the bearers of a longer historical legacy. Perhaps dating as far back as the *Tonghak* (Eastern Learning Movement) peasant rebels of the 1890s (Steinberg, 1997), this trajectory certainly extends from the April 1960 Student Uprising:

> The Korean *shimin undong* activists are very proud [of their] legitimate status as the sole inheritors of the social conscience or voice of the little people in this country against imperial powers, against corrupt Government, against American dominance on the Korean peninsula . . . . (Cho H., 2002 interview)

Moreover, although the *shimin undong* movement is predominantly middle class, at least among the leadership and full-time activists, it has a broader rapport with the general populace.

As Han (1997) explains:

> [A] new backbone of civil society has evolved in Korea . . . the middling grassroots . . . [They are] a rational core of the middle class which is capable of understanding repressed others and pursuing solidarity with them. (95)

Having defined themselves as "part of a national-civic community to be constructed in opposition to the injustice of the authoritarian capitalist development" (86), many former activists of this generation retained a "grassroots identity" even after moving into paid employment (Callahan, 1998: 312). Thus, although membership numbers of civic groups are relatively small, their platforms have wider resonance (Cho H. Y., 2000: 295).

Combined with the experience of pan-movement organization, this broad commitment to sociopolitical change has in turn facilitated the formation of strong cross-sectoral coalitions. Whereas *minjung* groups[1] draw on a base of peasant or blue-collar workers, and sometimes still resort to confrontational protest methods, *shimin undong* participants are largely white-collar workers, professionals, religious leaders, and intellectuals. Relying primarily on publicity campaigns, lectures, and lobbying, the latter have sought to establish a new mode of movement politics that is less class based and less confrontational. As sociologist Cho Hyo-je explains, the *shimin undong* has undergone "continual renewal in terms of its strength, militancy, and protest/resistance spirit" and maintained the same "ethos and spirit of resistance," regardless of the political problems facing the country—whether it be globalization and neoliberalism, the Asian financial crisis, or political corruption:

> This demonstrates a remarkable organizational strength—not in the sense of clear lines of authority, established forms of management etc.—but rather the power that allows the movement to be renewed and make a comeback again and again. (2002 interview)

This sustained militancy has been interpreted as both a strength and a limitation. Kim Sun-Hyuk (2000), for instance, cautions that a strategy of persistent "conflictual engagement" may hinder civil society from serving other important roles, for example, the provision of policy expertise, or from promoting an appreciation of the obligations and rights of democratic citizenship. However, while an antagonistic approach to civil society–state interactions may encourage civic distrust among more radical groups (e.g., specific student and labor organizations), there has simultaneously been a parallel process of dialogue with the state: "official or unofficial, publicly or behind the scenes between civic leaders and political leaders which defies a simplification of the process as one-dimensional" (Cho H., 2002 interview). Moreover, as civil society activists have increasingly been drawn into the state and political parties, they have helped to infuse political institutions with new blood and ideas, and facilitated more cooperative state–civil society relations (e.g., Han, 2002 interview).

Gendered Interests

Given the at best gender-blind but often gender discriminatory underpinnings of progressive political groups (e.g., Hartmann, 1981), it should come as no surprise that the Korean *shimin undong* movement has largely lacked its own gender-related agenda. Mixed-sex *shimin undong* organizations and the women's movement have, however, forged cooperative linkages around a range of issues. These include the Sexual Violence Prevention Law reform movement (1992–93): an ongoing campaign to demand justice for victims of Japanese military sexual slavery (*Ilbongun "sŏngnoye"* or *"wianbu"*); family violence prevention struggles (1997); sexual harassment awareness and reform efforts (1999); women's demands for a 30 percent quota in Congress and ministerial committees (2000); and the abolition of the veterans' affirmative action policy in the national civil service examinations (1999–2000) as well as the *hojuje* (family headship system) (1999–2005). Indeed, women's movement veteran Lee Mikyong was unable to think of a single issue for which civic groups had refused to lend their support (2002 interview).

Although some *shimin undong* organizations have gradually become more willing to take on gender issues as their own, due to a gradual deepening of intergroup linkages and greater social awareness of gender-equality issues (Lee H., 2002 interview),[2] we should not prematurely tout the emerging "feminist consciousness" of civic groups. Changes during the past decade indicate a marked increase in gender sensitivity, but the endorsement of gender-related issues has yet to become an integral part of the *shimin undong* political agenda. Women activists are also quick to point out that progressive civic group leaders have often lent their names to gender-reform campaigns without engaging in substantive discussions on gender equality or gender awareness:

> Many male members still have a poor understanding of gender issues . . .
> When we contact them to ask them to support a reform campaign they
> often claim inadequate knowledge or that they're really busy and so we
> just ask for their signatures. (Nam, 2000 interview)

Such superficial intellectual reflection is in part due to the limited time
and resources available to overtaxed activists, rather than representative
of a lack of commitment:

> Since university most activists were socialized in an environment in which
> gender issues were prominent, so they stand apart from the ordinary public.
> Although they may only pay lip-service to women's group causes, its not
> necessarily out of ignorance . . . its also an issue of capacity, a resource
> problem and a perceived lack of expertise. (Cho H., 2002 interview)

Reports and testimonies of continued widespread sexual discrimination within civic groups, however, suggest that women's organizations
have not sufficiently challenged their comfortable alliances so as to fundamentally reshape the gendered attitudes and behavior of their activist
colleagues. Indeed, there is a general tendency within activist circles for
men to subscribe to a progressive stance in the public realm, but to
degenerate into "typical Korean men" (read patriarchal, sexist) in their
interpersonal relationships with junior female colleagues or within the
family (e.g., Shim, 2002). This problem came into sharp relief, for example, in the widely publicized 2001 case of a young female activist who
filed rape charges against a respected environment movement leader.
A 2001 cyberspace exposé of top civic and labor movement leaders by
women activists, however, served as an important catalyst of change. A
network called the 100-Member Committee compiled a list of labor and
civic activists who were accused of sexual harassment/assault and published their names on the Internet, framing the issue as a human rights
violation (Lee M., 2002 interview). The Committee's "radical guerilla"
methodology, as well as its willingness to acknowledge gender injustices
among activists, sent shockwaves through civil society circles (e.g.,
Cho H., 2002 interview). Following heated debates, the response was
largely proactive: *shimin undong* groups initiated in-house sexual harassment awareness lectures and developed related literature for their members. On an individual level the "eliminating patriarchy from civil society"

campaign also bore fruit: as Korean WomenLink codirector Yoon Jung-Sook noted, "It made for big changes—it raised men's sensitivity to these problems so they now have to be much more careful" (2002 interview).

Strategies

Shimin undong groups have supported gender-reform efforts by signing petitions, attending press conferences and court hearings, participating in demonstrations and helping to raise funds, involving male lawyers when drafting new legislation, and organizing mixed-sex delegations when lobbying public officials (e.g., Park K., 1999). Such support has provided women's organizations with a much-needed source of legitimacy. Politicians and officials are more likely to accept demands for gender-related reforms if they are endorsed by a broad spectrum of civic groups, especially as major *shimin undong* organizations have considerably larger membership numbers than their women's movement counterparts (Park S., 2000 interview).

By the same token, even the women's movement's closest civic allies have rarely been proactive, lending a lopsided character to the relationship. Although women's groups are automatically expected to endorse society-wide campaigns such as the 2000 Congressional Blacklist Campaign, whereby civil society groups identified and urged voters to reject National Assembly candidates tainted with corruption charges, this support is not necessarily reciprocated. Mainstream civic groups may express solidarity with gender-related causes, but until recently have been unwilling to do the "dirty work" (Cho H., 2002 interview). Moreover, although women activists are often "the hands and legs behind broader social struggles" (Chong, 2000 interview), they do not always receive credit for their efforts and remain poorly represented in leadership positions within civic coalitions.

Male civic leaders are slowly becoming conscious of the need for greater gender balance within, for example, public delegations, lobbying officials and conducting press conferences (Yoon, 2002 interview). Recently, for instance, female activist Park Young-Ran was elected codirector of the PSPD, one of the most influential civic groups, while steps to facilitate women's greater involvement in *shimin undong* activities (such as organizing more child-friendly events) have become topical in the *NGO Times*. There is a growing realization that the "social macho mentality among civil society activists [whereby] you have to work 24 hours a day and still have strength to drink beer late at night" hinders women's ability to join mainstream civic groups (Cho H., 2002 interview). Moreover, although numbers remain small, there is a trend toward increasing male involvement—primarily among the younger generation—in groups with a gender-related focus. Examples include supporting victims of Japanese military sexual slavery, prostitution prevention and support services groups, and efforts to overturn the family headship system.[3]

Labor

The post-transitional story of the labor movement has followed a different trajectory from the *shimung undong*, with the Federation of Korean Trade Unions (FKTU) in particular remaining closer to the radical roots of the *minjung* counterculture. Whereas the late 1980s saw a dramatic increase in unionization and labor unrest leading to significant gains in real income, the political influence of organized labor in the 1990s has been limited and unionization rates have declined markedly.[4] Despite the election of relatively progressive presidents Kim Dae-jung (1998) and Noh Moo Hyun (2003), until the Democratic Labor Party's (DLP) 2004 electoral breakthrough (see Chapter 5) labor organizations remained isolated from mainstream political parties as well as the *shimin undong*.

In response to democratization and globalization, the configuration of the labor movement underwent considerable change. In contrast to labor unions in other authoritarian late industrializers (e.g., Brazil and South Africa), Korean unions did not broaden their ideological frame to incorporate demands for socioeconomic justice voiced by low-income community organizations (Koo, 2001). Instead they became "more pragmatic and economically oriented," largely due to labor's particular historical evolution (216). Not only had the authoritarian state largely confined organized labor to the enterprise level, but superior economic performance also reduced the impetus for the development of active, urban poor community movements and close factory–neighborhood ties.

Heightened internal cleavages also played an important role. Whereas the growth of class-consciousness throughout the 1960s, 1970s, and 1980s was facilitated by relatively homogenous working conditions (e.g., semiskilled positions under despotic management practices (Cumings, 1997)), sustained economic development diluted working-class unity over time. Disparities in wages and working conditions in *chaebŏl* (business conglomerates) versus smaller companies became more marked in the 1990s, as did those between regular workers and the burgeoning ranks of irregular employees (Chong, 2000 interview). The 1997 financial crises, which saw unemployment rates spike from two to three percent to over eight percent in 1998, exacerbated these inequalities, as unions were unable to protect their members from the impact of a significant increase in labor flexibility.

On a more positive note, however, three progressive union groupings forged the Korean Confederation of Trade Unions (KCTU) in 1995 to counter the more conservative FKTU and to lobby more effectively for labor law reform in accordance with International Labour Organization (ILO) standards (Wang, 2000 interview). Although not legally recognized until 1998, 862 unions joined, and membership rose to 500,000 within a year (Koo, 2001: 197). Considerably smaller than the FKTU (with 1.2 million members), the KCTU nevertheless emerged as an important progressive voice in labor struggles, especially regarding temporary and part-time workers' rights (e.g., Choi, 2000 interview).

Nevertheless, labor's post-transitional influence has been largely disappointing. Although the movement has often lived up to its militant reputation, achieving fundamental improvements in labor laws has been constrained by the successful appeals of state and business associations to the "logic" of global competitiveness. For example, official recognition of the KCTU and the right to form multiple unions at the industry level were traded for employers' rights to lay off workers and the "no work, no pay" rule for full-time union leaders (Koo, 2001).

Securing legal political representation also proved a long hard-fought battle. Not until the election of Kim Dae-jung was labor afforded a legitimate political voice through a Tripartite Commission representing the government, labor, and business (Gills and Gills, 2000). Yet, although the FKTU proved willing to compromise in the context of the International Monetary Fund (IMF)-mandated restructuring, the KCTU rejected the Tripartite Commission's acceptance of mass lay-offs, setting the stage for a persistently antagonistic relationship between business and labor (Lee S., 2000 interview). Union leaders secured recognition as legitimate members of a national decisionmaking body, but were placed in the unenviable position of cooperating with business leaders and the state to maintain industrial peace in the midst of painful economic restructuring (Koo, 2001). An important silver lining, however, was the successful negotiation for labor's right to organize politically in 1999, leading to the launch of the DLP in January 2000. Although DLP leader Kwon Young-Kil polled poorly in the 2002 presidential elections, as most progressive voters settled for Millennium Democratic Party (MDP) candidate Noh Moo Hyun in order to deprive the more conservative Grand National Party (GNP) of the Blue House,[5] the party secured ten National Assembly seats in the 2004 congressional elections.

Gendered Interests

Labor's support for gender-related issues has been predominantly confined to equal employment concerns. Although shared ideological leanings and organizational histories have ensured largely cordial relations between the women's and labor movements, labor's rejection of the *shimin undong* paradigm as "bourgeois and right-wing" has retarded efforts by the women's movement to broaden unions' support of non-workplace gender issues such as sexuality, health, human rights, and political representation (Lee H., 2002 interview). As progressive MDP legislator Lee Mi-Kyoung laments:

> Union cooperation has been limited. Labor has many demands and is always so critical, but in practice they do not lend much support to progressive campaigns beyond their own concerns. I urge them to become better "community players." (2003 interview)

Moreover, in keeping with women's experiences in labor movements internationally (e.g., Jaquette, 1994; Craske, 1999), Korean labor organizations have been slow to integrate a gendered perspective into their own policies and programs. As former KCTU women's bureau vice-director, Lee Hye-Soon, explains, the movement remains profoundly patriarchal:

> Labor union leaders don't have much interest in women's issues . . . men put their own first . . . There are also cases of sexual harassment by male leadership. In comparison to other civil society groups, the leaders are less advanced in terms of gender awareness. (2002 interview)

Because labor's broader ideological framework remains premised on a male breadwinner model, during the 1997–98 crisis, unions were primarily concerned with protecting men's role as the head of the family and primary provider rather than supporting women workers who fell victim to a women-first lay-off strategy (Kim J., 2000 interview).

This male-centeredness is further reflected in low female representation within unions, particularly in decisionmaking roles. As of 2001, women filled only six percent of FKTU leadership roles, even though they represented almost twenty-five percent of the total membership base (Lee H., 2002 interview). Although the more progressive KCTU has informally supported the Korean Women Workers' Association United (Wang, 2000 interview), neither the KCTU nor the FKTU established internal women's bureaus until the late 1990s. Today there are two women employed in the KCTU women's bureau headquarters and since 2001 there has been a representative for women's affairs in all ten national branches. However, "women's affairs representatives" often hold this portfolio alongside other roles and thus gender concerns are seldom prioritized (Lee H., 2002 interview). As a result, women labor activists have established separate national umbrella organizations, as well as fully-fledged women's trade unions, in order to address gender-specific issues that male-dominated unions generally neglect—including both wage and employment stability concerns, as well as gender discrimination, sexual harassment, and childcare issues (Kim J., 2000; interview; Wang, 2000 interview).[6]

Strategies

Tensions aside, cooperation between labor and the women's movement has led to a number of important policy victories, which women's organizations would have been unlikely to achieve without labor support (Choi, 2001 interview). These include campaigns to abolish female appearance requirements (1995) and compulsory retirement for women after marriage or pregnancy (1989), the right to equal pay (1989), the mandatory establishment of childcare facilities within workplaces of 300-plus employees (1995), the right to three months paid maternity leave (2001), and sexual harassment prevention and redress regulations (1999) (e.g., SCCWA, 1998; PCWA, 2000b). Such joint initiatives have helped women activists to develop considerable expertise, while also encouraging labor groups to more proactively address gender discrimination through the legal system. As Korean WomenLink Women Workers' Center head Chong Kang-Ja notes:

> Originally equal employment reforms were pushed through primarily by elites and with assistance from lawyers and experts, but now much of the work is done by ordinary women in conjunction with unions and women worker organizations. (2002 interview)

For example, when more than 250 Lotte Hotel female employees complained of sexual harassment in August 2000, women's organizations and the Hotel Union persuaded 61 women workers to file suit against company executives on the grounds of "habitual sexual abuse" (Chong, 2002 interview). Although the case was initially spearheaded by women's groups to test the efficacy of the 1999 Gender Discrimination Prevention and Relief Act, the KCTU Service Industry Federation subsequently took responsibility for the legal proceedings (KCTU, 2000).

Conservatives

In contrast to the strong organizational histories, broad (albeit shifting) ideological similarities and a commitment to intra- and inter-movement solidarity that characterize progressive civil actors, Korean conservatives tend to be organizationally isolated and focused on a single issue. Although Korea's political culture remains profoundly conservative, the women's movement has faced less formidable resistance than its international counterparts as conservative voices lack representation within a cohesive organizational bloc. Cultural groups (e.g., nationalists, veterans, churches, right-wing political parties) and economic conservative organizations (e.g., conservative policy think-tanks, employers' federations) have opposed particular gender-related reforms at different junctures, but broader alliances have been tenuous at best, especially in the context of gender politics. Not surprisingly, though, because of an entrenched Confucian ideological framework, there has been a significant lag between legislative reforms and attitudinal changes.

Confucian Groups

Although Korea is often described as the most Confucian country of East Asia (e.g., Deuchler, 1992), only 1–2 percent of the population self-identifies as "Confucian" in surveys on religious affiliation (Koh, 1996), and Confucian associations account for just 4.7 percent of all religious associations (Cho H. Y., 2000). How are we to explain such an anomaly? The answer partly lies in the fact that Confucianism is a comprehensive social philosophy rather than a religion per se (e.g., Hahm, 1997). Confucian attitudes, including those concerning gender roles, are ubiquitous yet diffuse, perpetuated through the education system (via ethics classes or through textbook examples), via regular participation in family ancestor rituals, and through family clan networks headed by powerful patriarchs (Kim K. O., 1996). One need not be affiliated with a Confucian organization, such as a lineage association or *suwŏn* (Confucian academy), in order to subscribe to Confucian values and behavioral patterns (Duncan, 1997). A national survey designed to tap adherence to specific religious values and rituals found that key Confucian principles (e.g., filial piety, the three cardinal virtues, and the five ethics) strongly permeated the value systems of some 92 percent of respondents, while a substantial majority carried out important daily or ritual practices (e.g., ancestral memorial ceremonies, son preference, and avoidance of intra-clan marriages) (Koh, 1996).

Ideas, however, need organizational carriers for effective expression in the political arena (Steinmo et al., 1992). So when observers note "strong Confucian opposition" to a particular reform initiative, to what exactly are they referring? In contrast to Catholicism, for example, Confucianism lacks a centrally coordinated organizational structure. Although the *Sunggyunggwan* foundation is the symbolic heart of Korean Confucianism, tracing its roots to 1398, and often leads protests against threats to tradition (e.g., allowing *tongsŏng tongbon* or same-surname/same-clan marriages), it is only loosely affiliated with other Confucian groups. Local *Hyanggyo* (Confucian temples) are bound together as "imagined communities" (Anderson, 1991) through the practice of common ritual traditions, but are structurally independent and lack any formal organizational hierarchy (Kim K. O., 1996).

Given the social resonance of Confucian values, one might predict that Confucian organizations would enjoy considerable political clout relative to their official numbers. For example, the influence of *Yurim* (Confucians) is commonly blamed for the lack of progress in fully reforming Korea's anachronistic family and marriage-related laws. Despite such perceptions, however, the political strength of Confucian groups has declined significantly since the late 1980s. I would therefore suggest that "Confucian influence" has become convenient shorthand for status-quo oriented politicians' opposition to reforms.

Whereas the *yangban* (scholar elites) enjoyed culturo-political dominance during the Chosun Dynasty (1392–1910) (Deuchler, 1992), their relationship with the state has been considerably more complex during the twentieth century. Involvement in struggles against the Japanese notwithstanding, Confucian elites' postliberation relationship with the Rhee regime was strained due to tensions between former anti-Japanese fighters and the new government's anti-Communist policies (Kim K. O., 1996). Friction between the state and defenders of Confucian culture was initially heightened following the 1962 coup, as General Park denounced multiple Confucian cultural traditions and sought to regulate family rituals in the name of modernization (e.g., Kendall, 1996). Following protests by traditionalists, however, the junta selectively reincorporated Confucian practices and values such as *ch'ung* (loyalty to the state) and *hyo* (filial piety) into official public ideology and began to provide funds for the preservation of Confucian relics and scholarship (Kim K. O., 1996). As a result, although certainly not restored to their historical prominence, Confucian leaders came to enjoy a degree of renewed ideological and discursive legitimacy, facilitating formidable opposition to attempts to modernize family relationships (Moon, 1994).

The democratic transition, along with greater openness toward global influences, has largely stripped away this mantle of ideological legitimacy (Koh, 1996). Within a 15-year period Confucians have declined from a substantial political force, staging large protests outside the Congress, into a weak and increasingly anachronistic group of older men often reduced to issuing emotional threats (Lee H., 2003 interview). As political scientist Kim Sok-Joon noted:

> They are *very* weak. Their activities are exclusive traditional rites rather than activities of ordinary citizens. Because their ideology is too tradition-bound, they are isolated and have lost their popular support. (2003 interview)

This decline can be partly attributed to the elitist nature of Confucian organizations, which still cling to distinctions between *yangban* and ordinary folk. As Callahan notes:

> Scholar officials are patriarchs who have to lead the common people as children who cannot critically understand politics. In this sense, scholar-officials do not need to find out what the people want—via evidence of public opinion or discussion—but merely need to speak for the people. (1998: 303)

Attempts to modernize and popularize Confucian traditions in the 1990s had limited political impact, and generally belie the basic incompatibility between a hierarchical, corporatist Confucian worldview and democratic respect for individual rights (300).

The relatively weak institutional presence of Confucian organizations has been exacerbated by a general reluctance to forge alliances with economic conservatives. Whereas American protestants or the Latin American Catholic Church have broadened their political clout by aligning with economic conservatives and/or right-wing political parties (e.g., Lienesch, 1993; Haas, 2000), Korean Confucian organizations have largely shunned such connections (Choi, 2002 interview). Not only are there no natural shared class interests (i.e., Confucian association membership does not necessarily equate with economic prosperity) (Cho H., 2002 interview), but there is also little common ideological affinity because Confucian social thought values scholarly and cultural refinement over economic success:

> Confucians are against the market and global standards and even democracy . . . [they subscribe to a] hierarchy between jobs—the scholar is at the top and the businessman the lowest. (Kim S., 2003 interview)

Similarly, although the charitable wing of the Hyundai Asan Foundation has promoted traditional values via research projects and conferences as well as awards for "filial piety" (304), their impact has been limited. Both long-term Federation of Korean Industries (FKI) researcher Choi Sung-Soo and Lee Hye-soon, from the Korea Employers' Federation (KEF), for example, dismissed the Asan Foundation's activities as idiosyncratic rather than representative of the wider *chaebŏl* community (2002 interviews).

The weakening of Confucian organizations notwithstanding, it would be misguided to conclude that Confucianism no longer has an important sociocultural influence. Complicating analytical efforts is the fact that diffuse cultural values translate into some degree of political leverage through behind-the-scenes lobbying of congressional representatives with provincial constituencies. Because Confucian clans often exercise strong informal influence on smaller, rural communities, politicians have been generally reluctant to openly counter Confucian traditions for fear of alienating a potentially important constituency. Former MDP legislator and minister of Gender Equality, Han Myung-Sook, explained the dilemma as follows:

> Although both parties included the abolition of the family headship system in their [1997 and 2000] political platforms, Confucians . . . expressed their opposition so vehemently it was difficult for district legislators to carry out this promise . . . While not large in absolute terms, Confucian influence is still significant economically and politically— especially in rural areas where many powerful constituents are elderly. They don't rely on rational argument but wield votes as a stick. (2000 interview)

Gendered Interests and Strategies
Contrary to popular belief, the gendered interests of Confucian associations have been confined primarily to family law issues such as the preservation of the *hojuje* (family headship system) and *tongsŏng tongbon* (same-surname/same-clan marriage ban), and to restrictions on female participation in ritual ceremonies. Although the traditional family is the linchpin of Korean Confucianism and *the* institution Confucian groups have fought hardest to defend (Kim K. O., 1996), their concerns have rarely extended to broader morality politics. Confucian groups have been largely silent regarding signature feminist issues such as gender violence, women's political empowerment and equal employment rights, all of which could potentially destabilize

extant gender relations within the family (Nam, 2000 interview). Moreover, in the case of abortion, an issue so often championed by culturo-religious conservatives in other contexts, Confucian elders have been conspicuously mute, perhaps because their emphasis on perpetuating the male family line is at the root of Korea's high level of sex-selected abortions.

In terms of strategy, Confucian groups' elitist orientation has contributed to the decision to pursue their goals unaligned. They have relied on conventional collective action repertoires such as demonstrations outside the National Assembly, lobbying local politicians, and organizing public hearings and petition drives, as well as lawsuits to counter family law–related reforms (Yang, 1998; Moon, 2003). Additionally, and indicative of their declining sociopolitical voice and sense of desperation, some Confucian elders have resorted to threats and violence. For example, a 2001 feminist art project at *Chongmyo* (the most significant national Confucian shrine) provoked Confucianists to tear up the artwork and physically threaten project participants (Kim M., 2002 interview). Similarly, Ministry of Gender Equality (MOGE) officials and several women's NGOs endured ugly face-to-face confrontations after publicly supporting the abolition of the *hojuje* (Lee H., 2003 interview).

Religious Groups

Although Korean religious groups—both Buddhist and Christian alike—have considerable financial and human resources, religion has yet to become a politically salient cleavage. This is perhaps surprising given that Korean clergy are familiar with the U.S. model of religion and party politics on account of close linkages forged with the United States through post–Korean War missionary efforts. Moreover, a significant number of Korean pastors receive graduate degrees from U.S. theological colleges, where they have ample opportunities to network and observe first hand the political activism of American churches. However, as Clark (1997) points out:

> There is no organized political consciousness. No messianic leader has arisen to focus the energy of the Christian community on any purpose other than anti-Communism. Were that to happen the [Korean] Christian community would be formidable indeed. (194)

In everyday conversations, Koreans often suggest that "religion is just an individual matter," and "religion has never been a major political force in our country." Yet, although such observations contain only an element of truth, they provide a partial view of a more complex phenomenon.

Besides the ubiquitous Confucian values discussed above, over half the populace have separate religious affiliations, with about a quarter identifying as Christian and a quarter as Buddhist. Yet despite high levels of religious activity and religion's importance in the Korean social fabric (e.g., Duncan, 1997), religion has not emerged as a significant political mobilizational referent (e.g., Kim B., 1998).[7] Part of the solution to this puzzle no doubt lies in the sheer diversity of religious organizations in Korea. With over 300 smaller, new religions, including various Shamanistic, Christian, or Confucian-derived sects, Korea has the greatest number of new religions per capita internationally (Yoon, 1997). Thus, whereas the Catholic Church in Latin America is concerned about losing converts to rising Protestant and Pentecostal movements (Lowy, 1996), but enjoys the political sway afforded by a centrally coordinated institutional structure with a long organizational history, Korean Christianity is burgeoning and vibrant, yet lacks an institutional carrier to effectively channel believers' voices onto the political stage.

A second possible explanation relates to the nature of Korean religious traditions' political involvement over the course of the twentieth century. Despite participation in progressive struggles in the 1910s and 1920s, for instance, the traumatic confrontation with North Korean socialism led Korean churches to become strong supporters of the anti-Communist mission. "Because of its anticommunism it end[ed] up functioning in large measure as the handmaiden of the state . . . Anticommunism is what the churches and the state of South Korea have in common" (Clark, 1997: 183). As a result, whereas the Latin American Church's role as a protective umbrella during authoritarian rule often weakened the ability of progressives to criticize the increasing right-wing tendencies of the Church in the post-transition period (e.g., Garreton, 1996), mainstream churches (and temples) in Korea could not lay claim to the same anti-authoritarian ideological legacy. As political science professor Kim Sok-Joon notes:

> Most conservative groups didn't do their job during the dictatorship and lost their moral superiority to activist groups. Center-left oriented Catholics and Christians led the anti-dictatorship movement but they were a minority . . . Most religious groups didn't protest so today most important civil groups are pro-Noh [Moo-Hyun] and center-left. That's why Korea's religious groups lost their political influence. (2003 interview)

Accordingly, whereas the political opportunity structure of democratization allowed for the articulation of new social groups and interests, Korean religious organizations largely retreated from the political arena, turning their focus inward to concentrate on institution building and individual spirituality. As Korean Church Women United general secretary Reverend Lee Mun-Sook points out, for example:

> Church women were actively involved in Family Law reform and human rights concerns in the 1980s . . . but now we rarely lobby politicians—its left to the secular women's movement . . . We're focused inward because the Church never changes—we need to improve women's position within the institution . . . in leadership positions . . . and sexist language. (2001 interview)

This is not to argue that all religious groups have been unconcerned with social change. A number of religious-based organizations have been involved in environmental protection, antiprostitution and human trafficking legislative reform campaigns, antiwar and anti-U.S. presence on the peninsula movements.[8] Nevertheless, religion has not emerged as a defining characteristic of any politically significant post-transitional lobbying or voting bloc.

The third but equally important ingredient is the absence of partisan articulation of religious/moral values and interests. There is no major programmatic party actively courting religious groups along the lines of the U.S. Republican Party (e.g., Lienesch, 1993). Because of Korea's largely nonprogrammatic, catch-all type party system, there has been scant motivation for parties to actively mobilize the electorate along religious lines.

Gendered Interests and Strategies

Even in the realm of gendered morality politics, an area frequently manipulated by conservative leaders to bridge divergent class interests with the average voter (Stacey, 1999), Korean religious organizations have been conspicuously absent. Issues such as abortion, contraception, and sexual identity, which have become major campaign issues among religious conservatives in other countries, have generally not become politicized in Korea.[9] Although one would expect such matters to incite particularly fierce debate within a politico-cultural framework as conservative as Korea's, the populace has largely followed the state's pragmatic approach to reproductive issues and silence surrounding sex and sexuality. Abortion, for example, has remained illegal, yet widely practiced, and was in fact tacitly supported by the state to ensure the success of a two-child-only policy (Park S., 2003). Similarly, access to sex education has not attracted widespread attention, and only very recently have church groups (particularly Catholics) started to exert their position politically with regard to gay rights (Shin, 2004 interview). This is not to suggest that Korean religious groups do not care about morality politics or refrain from discussing it among their congregations (Lee H., 2001 interview). However, in terms of framing public discourses and particularly in contesting gender-related issues within the formal political arena, religious groups have not emerged as powerful opponents to the organized efforts of women's groups and their allies.

Economic Conservatives

Business or employers' associations and/or parties that represent their interests often play a significant role in countering efforts to push for legislative reforms regarding equal employment, the prevention of sexual harassment, and maternity rights (Escandon, 1994; O'Connor et al., 1999). In the Korean case, although no party explicitly represents business interests, a historical emphasis on economic growth rather than redistributive issues has rendered major political parties generally sympathetic to the interests of employers groups such as the Federation of Korean Industries (FKI) and the KEF.[10] Even so, the relationship between business and the state has proven more varied, and even conflictual, than one might expect. The unusually high "relative autonomy" of the state under the Park regime meant that whereas capital clearly benefited from the emphasis on growth, it did not control the process. Business owners who did not tow the government line often suffered for their asserted independence (e.g., Moon and Lim, 2001).

Business–state relations became increasingly differentiated following Chun Doo Whan's economic liberalization efforts (e.g., Kim E., 2000). The growth of the *chaebŏl* into economic titans, the emergence of alternative means of finance outside state control, as well as the increasing complexity of the economy, all conspired to reorient the balance of power between the state and capital. Simultaneously, the democratization process stripped away much of the government's control over an increasingly vocal labor movement. Accordingly, the state's insulation from both capital and labor in the economic policy formation process was generally debased by the time of President Kim Young-sam's 1993 inauguration (Kil and Moon, 2001).

Repudiation of the "dirigiste" past and the embrace of "free-market" policies were the hallmarks of the mid-1990s. Indeed, for the major *chaebŏl*,

> . . . [it] meant having their cake and eating it too—to be free of state monitoring and supervision without giving up politically connected loans or state control of labor unions while at the same time going global to escape rising wages and political demands from labor unions at home. (Kim, Samuel, 2000: 244)

Yet the state also acted against the expressed interests of business, for instance, through the introduction of the real name financial system, and labor opposition has at times tempered the Government's embrace of economic liberalization (Abdollohian et al., 2000). In fact, KEF international relations team manager, Sunny Lee, argues that employers' relatively limited influence is underscored by the fact that it was not until the nation faced economic collapse in 1997 that employers' demands for greater labor flexibility were realized:

> Although there is no good international comparative data, Korean employers do not see themselves as politically strong. Only the Asian economic crisis provided us with a window of opportunity to secure greater labor market flexibility. (2002 interview)

Channels of Influence

Post-transition, employers' organizations have utilized three main channels to influence labor policy: the Ministry of Labor (MoL), the Tripartite Commission, and lobbying/political monitoring. Because the MoL purports to tread a middle path between the demands of business and labor unions, business groups have sought to maintain close ties; as KEF official Lee Ho-Sun notes:

> The Ministry emphasizes partnership with labor and business and so they solicit both sides' opinions. They need to strive for balance—if they come down too strong on one side, they will spark fierce opposition. (2000 interview)

Similarly, employers' groups welcomed the establishment of the Tripartite Commission in 1998 due to its emphasis on conciliation. In reality, however, labor groups periodically boycotted the Commission when negotiations broke down, and resorted to more conventional demonstrations and protest to ensure their demands were met (Choi, 2002 interview).

More recently, employers have become concerned about labor's increasing political clout and have therefore initiated more specialized political monitoring activities. The combination of the election of a president sympathetic to labor (Kim Dae-jung) and labor's more aggressive foray into the political realm in the lead up to the April 2000 National Assembly elections, prompted employers' groups to establish a political candidate evaluation program. Employers' groups now prepare detailed evaluations on candidates according to their stance toward the market economy, issue press releases, and send policy suggestions to legislators and the Blue House. Whereas such systematic lobbying ensures that economic conservative voices are included in the policymaking process, the absence of a broader political or civic alliance significantly limits employers' broader social influence. For example, FKI researcher Choi Song-Soo insisted:

> We don't support any particular groups, whether religious, educational etc . . . If we formed an alliance wouldn't it give rise to a counter-alliance? There would have to be an ulterior political goal for us, and besides the economy, we don't have any broader goals . . . Historically some *chaebŏl* favored the extended family model—looking after employees like family—so in a way there were Confucian traits . . . Some conglomerates give money to religious organizations but that is an individual matter . . . Korean religious groups are simply not a major force of social change. (2002 interview)

Thus, in contrast to progressive civic groups, which provide mutual support on a broad array of political issues, conservatives' political activism remains narrow in scope.

Gendered Interests and Strategies

Employers' associations' gendered interests include promoting labor flexibility, minimizing costs, and maintaining a favorable domestic and international image, with employers often working to stall the implementation of gendered reforms, or to shift the costs back to the state. Interviews with employers' association members further suggest that a primary concern is to ensure that their voices are adequately represented and that gender policy is not formulated without also considering economic costs and corporate profitability. As KEF official

Lee Ho-Sun explains:

> Korean women remain underrepresented in the labor market vis-à-vis other countries. Employers are interested in why companies don't use women more and it's because women employees are burdensome to companies. My goal is to lobby the Ministry of Labor and work towards developing policies that will expand women's employment. (2000 interview)

Whereas women's lobbies have successfully pushed through legislation granting three-months' paid maternity leave and mobilized to retain the monthly menstruation holiday, employers' groups have argued that such policies increase the costs of hiring female workers thereby reinforcing the entrenched bias of business against women. Moreover, although companies are likely to be more willing to accept gender-related reforms when economic conditions are favorable, women are generally the first casualties of belt-tightening programs during periods of economic contraction. As long as hiring women entails extra costs, employers' representatives expect the current trend of hiring of women for peripheral, temporary, and no-benefit positions to continue:

> People complain that average wages for men and women are very different. But women are not really considered part of the core workforce because it costs so much more to hire women. Businesses are not volunteer social welfare foundations. Although we don't oppose policies that protect women in principle, the public sector doesn't take any responsibility and leaves it all up to companies. (Choi, 2002 interview)

This emphasis on maximizing profitability is, however, tempered somewhat by employers' desire to meet international standards and avoid negative press related to gender discrimination:

> Although national pressure is important, for us [KEF] the influence of international organizations has been more significant. We feel we have to match international standards. Because a measure internationally accepted it is easier for companies to understand, even if it is somewhat burdensome. (Lee H. S., 2000 interview)

In the case of the 2001 Maternity Protection Law, for example, employers' groups did not oppose increasing paid maternity leave to 90 days as this was part of the ILO Convention and deemed appropriate for members of the OECD countries. Indeed, employers shrewdly adopted the ILO's language of "social responsibility" and "burden sharing" with regard to maternity care, but strongly opposed and successfully thwarted demands by women's groups to provide paid leave for maternal health check-ups, miscarriages, and stillbirths, on the grounds that the costs were being transferred solely to business[11] (e.g., Lee H. S., 2002 interview). In such cases, employers also capitalize on Korea's relative late-comer status to the OECD to push for more graduated implementation of legislative reforms.

Domestically, however, economic conservatives appear less concerned with appeasing demands for progressive social policies. My interviews suggested that employers' groups expect largely conflictual relations with labor and women's groups. For example, when questioned on the KEF's relationship with women's organizations, Sunny Lee tried to sidestep the issue:

> We don't have much information or interaction with NGOs. The general sentiment of employers is that although these groups are called "civil," in fact they all stem from trade union backgrounds. (2002 interview)

In other words, due to the women's movement's *minjung* origins, employers are not surprised to be on the opposite sides of most policy debates.

Employers' associations are, however, committed to keeping individual companies abreast of gender-related legal changes in order to avoid litigation and bad press. Image concerns have led to a cooperative working relationship with the FKTU women's bureau and progressive women's groups. Cognizant of international cases where companies were compelled to settle expensive lawsuits that generated negative publicity, Korean employers' groups have become more aware of the importance of reducing sexual harassment and overt forms of discrimination against female employees (Choi, 2002 interview). Following the passage of the 1999 Gender Discrimination Prevention and Relief Act, for instance, employers established educational programs to prevent sexual harassment, and developed audiovisual materials in consultation with labor unions and women's organizations (Park, 2002 interview).

State Actors

State actors do not simply respond to women's movements' demands, but also have their own gendered interests (Scott, 1988). Whereas democratizing governments are less likely than their authoritarian predecessors to prescribe rigid gender roles and family models, historical ideologies may nevertheless have a significant residue effect. Particularly in polities with weak welfare states, rhetorical commitments to advance women's rights often coexist with the need to encourage the role of families and especially women in the provision of care for children, elderly, and the sick (Rosemblatt, 1997). The challenge then is to unpack these multiple and often contradictory ideological and policy directions as they evolve over the course of democratic consolidation.

In the Korean case, authoritarian era women's policies focused on the provision of assistance to marginalized women, with the paternal state stepping in to protect and remold women who had fallen from the protective realm of the family. Women's policies in the 1990s, however, increasingly focused on addressing broader, structural inequalities between men and women (e.g., Yang, 2002). Even so, the gender politics championed by the post-transition state are best characterized as an often conflicting hodgepodge of new policy emphases and enduring legacies. For example, the government continues to capitalize on women's disproportionate contribution to what Elson (1997) terms the "care economy," as well as domestic and voluntary community work that is "vital in developing and maintaining the health and skills of the labour force; and in developing the social framework" (8–9). As KWDI researcher Park Young-Ran explains:

> Everyone is confused . . . Although the Government played a major part in women-related legislation, it just set up basic frameworks in a hurry without cost-benefit analyses and understanding the impact . . . In terms of services for childcare, the elderly and disabled, they have mixed messages: women should work as that is what the times demand. But in terms of individual values or family relationships we are not yet prepared to meet these challenges. The Government needs to figure out whether women's policies really reflect the needs of women, men and children. Are they really listening to ordinary citizens? (2000 interview)

Harnessing women's volunteer labor constitutes a key example of the way that gendered arguments and policies are employed to further the state's broader political goals. Although the burgeoning of women's civil society organizations in the late 1980s/early 1990s meant that the government had to extend its relationship beyond support for pro-government groups such as the KNCW, successive democratic administrations have nevertheless sought to harness women's networks for political gain. The Ministry of Political Affairs No. 2 (MPA2), ostensibly set up to support women's increased participation in the public sphere, simultaneously drew upon reserve armies of women mobilized during the authoritarian era to implement community health projects, consumer rights campaigns, and to support the ruling party (Chang, 2000 interview). Even during the Kim Dae-jung administration, despite the discursive shift by the Presidential Commission on Women (PCWA) and MOGE away from "women and development" frameworks to an emphasis on "gender mainstreaming," the government has continued to focus on women's volunteer efforts to, for example, carry out electricity frugality campaigns or assist with 2002 World Cup logistics (Ha, 2000 interview).

State actors also employ gender-related policies to enhance their division's institutional power. A case in point is the conflict of interest between the Ministry of Justice and the PCWA over the far-reaching 1999 Gender Discrimination Prevention and Relief Act (GDPRA). Although the ministry had not been proactive in addressing gender discrimination within the legal system, ministry officials vocally opposed the PCWA-initiated Act. They argued that it was unnecessary as gender discrimination prevention was already provided for in extant legislation, and that the establishment of a quasi-judicial Gender Discrimination Complaint Center under the PCWA would exceed the Commission's boundaries (Yoon, 2001 interview). Yet, given the Ministry of Justice's poor record in addressing women-related concerns, the marginalized status of women bureaucrats, and the low budget allocated to its women's policy unit, officials were clearly as concerned about a perceived loss of authority as the logic behind the initiative.

Conclusion

The constellation of Korean state and non-state actors that contest gender-related issues and policy reforms are distinct from other Third Wave polities in several important ways. Progressive civic groups, bound together by close personal networks, a shared history, and common *shimin undong* paradigm, have forged loosely organized but sustainable alliances around a range of sociopolitical concerns, including gender-related issues. Although inter-movement tensions remain, civil society solidarity has lent the demands of women's groups a source of public legitimacy that appears unmatched in other regions.

By contrast, although historical constraints—especially a divided peninsula, truncated Left, and the postliberation revival of Confucianism as a nation-building tool—have contributed to a conservative political culture that continues to impinge upon current reform initiatives, the Korean case suggests that the political impact of conservative values largely depends on their institutional expression. This point is exemplified by the broad cultural resonance of Confucian values, but relatively weak institutional capacity of Confucian groups. Equally importantly, whereas economic and cultural conservatives, along with right-wing parties and international allies, have constituted a veritable power bloc in the contestation of gender politics in Latin America and Eastern Europe, cooperative ties among Korean employers' federations, veterans' associations, and Confucian organizations have been largely absent.

Finally, the state's conflicting institutional interests—the desire to appease domestic and international pressures for greater gender equality on the one hand and the need to continue to harness women's unpaid/cheap reproductive and productive labor power on the other—are not dissimilar from the gendered political calculations of other nascent democratic states. Problematically, however, Korean state actors have tended to pass ostensibly far-reaching reforms without ensuring that the corresponding infrastructure and policy frameworks required to implement such changes are in place.

CHAPTER 5

The Political Institutional Matrix—Identifying Access and Veto Opportunities

State structures and policies that regulate and mediate gender, race, and class relations of power in society are hardly immutable . . . Changes in political regimes—in the institutions that structure the relationship between State and society—may open up new opportunities for some women to influence policy formulation and implementation.

Alvarez, 1990: 272

The unique characteristic of our country is that there really is no significant policy difference between the ruling and opposition parties—there are no true conservatives or progressives in Korea, even in the case of women's policy.

Kang H., 2000 interview

Whereas scholars of democratic consolidation have addressed institutional change and the challenges it involves (e.g., Petras et al., 1994; Kang, 2003), analysts of the gender dynamics of democracy have tended to focus on problems of "institutional inertia" (Craske, 1999), "the return to politics as usual" (Jaquette and Wolchik, 1998), or even "masculinist politics" (Moon, 2003). Although such approaches make a valuable contribution to the democratic consolidation literature by (re)constructing citizenship as a fundamentally gendered process, they too often fail to unpack the state and provide a disaggregated analysis of the concrete problems that historically specific institutions represent.

Despite significant continuities with the authoritarian past, the potential for post-transitional dynamism is considerable: not just in terms of formal/legal reforms but also as a result of the emergence of a new generation of officials who shape and implement policies and shifts in citizens' willingness to utilize these channels to engage with the state. Accordingly, whereas a macro-level snapshot may suggest relatively pessimistic conclusions as to the potential for change, a more fine-grained analysis can allow us to recognize incremental yet important shifts over time. Moreover, whereas macro-institutional reforms such as a shift in the balance of power between the legislature and the executive may have a similar impact on policy formulation across diverse issue areas, the impact of other institutional changes can vary depending on the type of policy (e.g., recognition of political/civic rights versus fulfillment of socioeconomic rights) and the constellation of actors involved.

To better understand the dynamism of political institutions, I draw on the insights of New Historical Institutionalism, which emphasizes that "institutions constrain and refract politics" but never solely determine the outcomes (Thelen and Steinmo, 1992: 13). Although institutional legacies help explain policy continuities over time and diverse cross-national responses to common political or economic challenges (5), they are "sticky" rather than immutable. Institutional rules (both formal and informal) shape actors' strategies and goals, but do not preclude strategic maneuvering by political actors to influence the institutional parameters themselves:

> Groups and individuals are not merely spectators as conditions change to favor or penalize them in the political balance of power, but rather strategic actors capable of acting on "openings" provided by such shifting contextual conditions in order to defend or enhance their own positions. (17)

In the Korean case, it would be easy to assume that "access points" provided by specific institutional arrangements are limited as the "majoritarian [party system] and centralized-unitary elements of Korean democracy are the most pronounced compared with other Asian democracies" (Croissant, 2002a: 342). Yet because of the general immaturity of political institutions in nascent democracies, as well as Korea's idiosyncratic institutional architecture, I argue that civil society actors have enjoyed surprisingly broad access to the policy process post-transition. This chapter therefore maps the specific contours of Korea's political institutions—that is, the legislature, executive, bureaucracy, party system, and judiciary—the degree of post-transitional change, and the extent to which these changes provide new avenues for women, potential allies, or opponents to gain access to the state and effect social change.

Legislature

A well-functioning legislature should enhance the legitimacy and integration of a new government, while serving as a key mechanism to channel and represent civilian interests and manage potentially destabilizing social cleavages (e.g., O'Donnell and Schmitter, 1989; Diamond and Shin, 2000). The realities of fledgling democracies, of course, tend to fall short of this norm. Institutionally, legislatures frequently suffer from underdeveloped deliberation and policy expertise, and remain overshadowed by the executive and bureaucracy (e.g., O'Donnell, 1994). Moreover, the (re)emergence of the legislature as a key conduit of citizens' voices has often come at the cost of lowering the visibility of and limiting the political space available to social movements and grassroots groups (Chalmers et al., 1997).

In Korea, progress toward a mature legislative process has been partial and uneven. As seen in the April 2004 impeachment of President Noh, Congress has advanced considerably from its authoritarian era status as a "rubber stamp" and has developed more effective (albeit still far from ideal) oversight capabilities vis-à-vis the executive (Shin D., 1999). Yet, compared with advanced Western democracies, it remains an immature institution, plagued by limited policy expertise, disrespect for legislative procedures, under-resourced committees, and an underdeveloped culture of political debate on policy issues. New regulations on legislative proceedings, internal order, and discipline have ensured some degree of professionalism, but political parties continue to rely on obstructionist tactics to influence the legislative process. The majority party/(coalition) still adopts *nalch'igi t'onggwa* (extra-legal blitzkrieg tactics) to ram through controversial legislation (Lee Y., 2000), and in retaliation, minority parties often focus on uncovering scandals among rival party members, and resort to disruptive measures such as sit-ins, hunger strikes, and congressional boycotts (Shin D., 1999).

Similarly, existing rules and procedures often fail to ensure that policy proposals are thoroughly deliberated. Plagued by inadequate staff resources and frequent partisan skirmishes, the committee system remains rudimentary and limited in scope (Park C., 2000). Problems are further exacerbated by a cultural tendency to avoid public debate (Park S., 2000 interview). Deliberations are usually short and clustered at the end of National Assembly sessions, earning Korea the dubious title of "the world's fastest law-making machine" (Kim Y. H., 2000 interview). Strong party discipline throughout the 1990s, built around a regionally-based and personality-focused party system, has further hindered the development of ideologically-based party platforms and in-depth policy debate. Legislators are generally expected to vote in accordance with the party line on major issues, and face strong financial and electoral incentives to follow this mold (Park C., 2000).

> Like a father in a traditional Korean family who, alone, makes all the important decisions, every party boss exclusively controls the nomination of his party candidates for each and every electoral district of the National Assembly. (Shin D., 1999: 180)

Gendered Opportunities

These weaknesses notwithstanding, as progressive civic groups have altered their approach toward formal politics—moving from a rejectionist approach under Noh Tae Woo to state engagement under Kim Young-sam and to a civil society–state partnership under Kim Dae-Jung and Noh Moo Hyun—the legislature has become an important window to access the state. In the case of gender-related reforms, the tendency toward cursory deliberation has facilitated rapid legal reform as activists and policy practitioners have sought to negotiate this political environment to their advantage:

> The lack of political debate and rapid passage of laws is a joke but has some advantages. In Germany they spend years on one law and sometimes it will not get through; but in Korea, the Sexual Harassment Act, for example, took just a few hours. The trend is "let's make the law first, then amend it," otherwise you would never get through the barriers—especially the mentality of these conservative men. (Kim Y. H., 2000 interview)

Ironically, because legislative committees' scrutiny of bills tends to be superficial, the content of women's organizations' proposals (supported by progressive lawyers and legislators) has often been preserved, resulting in legislation that reflects more progressive attitudes than those held by the general populace. In the case of the family violence prevention law, for instance, an estimated 95 percent of the original bill, drafted by NGOs, was accepted:

> When we made the draft law all the political parties borrowed from our version and only slightly modified it because there were no other models. Content-wise it was all accepted. (Shin, 2000 interview)

The drawback, however, is that legislation is often passed without adequate consideration of broader societal implications, or whether existing infrastructure can accommodate such reforms.

> In other countries they make a law and a corresponding system, but in Korea first they make the law and then subsequently they have to make the system or infrastructure. (Byun, 2000 interview)

As a result, feminists have been compelled to organize a series of revision campaigns for laws such as the 1987 Equal Employment Opportunities Act, the 1995 Women's Basic Development Act, and the 1993 Act on the Punishment of Sexual Crimes and Protection of Victims to address important oversights (see chapter 6).

A second problem concerns public awareness. Whereas the very process of legal reform, involving vigorous multi-stakeholder debate, can facilitate broader awareness about social issues, Korean legislative initiatives regarding gender rarely spill over into wider community debates. As sociologist Kim Kyunghee points out:

> There are few instances where women's issues become major topics of social debate. When a law is being made, all sectors—NGOs, the government, ordinary citizens, schools—should debate the issues, but this kind of process is very new. We need training in the democratic process. (2000 interview)

However, there is a less obvious but important implication of a political culture that shies away from in-depth public debate over potentially divisive social issues. Although democratization provides new spaces for organized women to advance their gendered interests, in many countries this has been more than offset by the emergence of organized conservative groups that vigorously contest politics involving the family and sexuality. Democratic deepening may lead to the strengthening of voices across the ideological spectrum. Htun (2003), for instance, argues that Latin American proponents of gender equality ironically found it easier to push through reforms in presidential advisory committees during the authoritarian period under the rubric of "modernization," than push rights discourses through a democratic congress in the face of right-wing parties intent on fostering political cleavages along gendered lines. In Korea, by contrast, issues such as reproductive rights and sexuality have not become politicized, in part because right-wing parties have not attempted to mobilize Korea's largely conservative religious groups into a cohesive political bloc.

The Presidency

Excessive executive power is a common challenge facing nascent democracies. As O'Donnell (1994) argues in his work on "delegative democracy," executives in the initial post-transition period are often characterized by limited accountability, parliamentary subservience, and the election of populist candidates who utilize patron–client relationships to provide "strong leadership" in the face of socioeconomic and political instabilities. Inadequately checked executive strength post-transition can reduce the access points open to individuals and groups attempting to affect policymaking. As the point of transition recedes, however, and other branches of government mature, we should be alert to changes in the relative power of the presidency.

The Korean presidency has traditionally been conceptualized in terms of *taegwŏn* (great power) because of the executive's monopolization of economic and security policy formation throughout the authoritarian period (Lee M., 1990). Constitutional reforms in 1987, however, curbed executive privilege (Diamond and Shin, 2000), and electoral configurations exacerbated traditional regional cleavages and encouraged the institutionalization of *yŏso yadae* (ruling minority, opposition majority). Indeed, it was not until the April 2004 elections that the president's party was able to secure a congressional majority, and even then the ruling party secured just 152 seats out of 300. Successive presidents have been forced to either piece together coalitional majorities to pass legislation or to use alternative channels to push through policy reforms. As Lee Young-Jo (2000) notes:

> The façade of the all-powerful presidency concealed the reality of a weak presidency beleaguered by relatively strong social and political actors. If the presidency had been really strong, there would have been little need to bypass the normal channels of policymaking and implementation. Reliance on decrees signified that the president could not get reforms through normal legislative procedures. (120)

Post-transition, there has also been a shift in the basis of presidential legitimacy. Although the growth of progressive civic groups and the articulation of diverse citizen demands concerning issues such as social justice, the environment, and gender equality have galvanized presidents into taking a more active role in developing social and welfare policies, economic liberalization has weakened the state's control over the economic development process, which had been the executive's *raison d'être* during the authoritarian period (e.g., Kwon, 1999; Hahm and Plein, 1997).

How then can we reconcile these objective limits to presidential power with popular perceptions and scholarly emphasis on the "enormous powers of the Korean presidency"? (Kim, Samuel, 2003: 40). Part of the answer lies in traditional Confucian concepts of political leadership. Postindependence authoritarian leaders promoted the image of the president as the "father" of the nation whose wisdom in leading the country toward prosperity demanded "filial loyalty" from citizens. This "powerful legacy of personalizing and privatizing political authorities and powers" (Shin D., 1999: 262) continues to have a strong residual but mixed effect on the contemporary political stage. On the one hand, bureaucrats, ruling party legislators, and party officials are generally anxious to demonstrate acceptance of new policy frames or narratives endorsed by the president, whether it be globalization (Kim Young-sam) or human rights (Kim Dae-jung) (Kim, Samuel, 2003). On the other, because of high expectations invested in individual presidents, political society and the citizenry alike are quick to judge leaders when they fail to live up to these standards (Shin D., 1999). Both Kim Young-sam and Kim Dae-jung left office with only single-digit approval ratings, as a result of corruption scandals involving either close family members or aides. Similarly corruption in the Noh administration contributed to an early erosion of confidence in his leadership, especially as he had portrayed himself as an outsider fighting for clean politics alongside a new untainted generation of politicians.

Gendered Opportunities

As feminist historians have noted, political leaders may promote gender-related policies for reasons including nation-building, economic development, or a desire to distinguish a new regime from predecessors (e.g., Besse, 1996; Dore and Molyneux, 2000). Although limits on executive power preclude a neat correlation between presidential support and expanded political opportunities, My research suggests that if a president champions gender-equality reform, such support is likely to have an important spill-over effect in bringing gender-related issues on to the political agenda as well as increasing the intensity and pace of their deliberation. For example, a large proportion of the civil and political society actors I interviewed emphasized the symbolic weight of Kim's Dae-jung's backing for a broad set of gender-equality initiatives (e.g., Park S., 2000 interview; Kim Y. A., 2000 interview; Han, 2000 interview):

> Kim Dae-jung is the most progressive about gender issues among our democratic presidents. Because Korea is a very president-centered country,

the president's personal interest has a great influence. . . . The most frequent excuse used by legislators is that "the time is right but it is immature to implement the new system." But when the President intervenes and says "it is time to introduce the policy," no one says "no." (Lee M. K., 2003 interview)

Significantly, whereas advocates of gender equality in other Third Wave democracies have had to negotiate more uneven executive behavior (e.g., Feijoo, 1998; Vargas, 2002), Korean women have been able to take advantage of increasingly supportive and proactive presidencies.[1] In response to the shift in civil society–state relations from "patron–client" under Roh Tae Woo to "civil society–state partnership" with Kim Dae-jung and Noh Moo Hyun, women's organizations' modes of engagement with the executive branch have diversified and become increasingly professional.

In keeping with its authoritarian roots, the Noh Tae Woo administration's relationship with women's organizations was primarily one of patron and client. In return for loyalty and cooperation, government-friendly women's organizations, especially the KNCW, received funding and a sympathetic ear for moderate legislative reforms (Moon S., 2002). The transition, however, changed the pattern of politics surrounding women's policy development (Kwon Y., 2000 interview). In the wake of the 1987 "People's Uprising," Noh's anxiety to distance himself from his authoritarian roots and present a softer, more democratic image (Kang H., 2000 interview) coincided with the strengthening of civil society and the evolution of international norms on gender equality. He was therefore compelled to take a more proactive stance toward eliminating gender discrimination and violence:

> Even if President Noh was not personally particularly supportive of women's issues, he realized he should speak out to get women's votes. . . . many staff members around him said "you must promise X" and then he spoke up. (Chin, 2000 interview)

Yet, because policy changes were prompted more by a quest for domestic or international legitimacy than by a commitment to gender reform, measures were often top-down and cosmetic:

> The Government is passive . . . many women-related laws passed in the last ten years were launched by the women's movement. The Government accepts them two or three years later . . . acting out of paternal ideology. When the president changes, they want to show off what the country has done for X area . . . they need accomplishments. (Cho Y., 2000 interview)

Kim Young-sam's 1992 election and his administration's efforts to eliminate vestiges of authoritarian practices encouraged civil society actors to soften their opposition to the government (Cotton, 1995). For women's groups, the decision to provide project-based funding for NGOs in 1993 was particularly important (Yoon, 2000 interview). As KWAU's general secretary Nam In-Sun noted: "We all had to accept the need to transform our movement from an activists' task-force into a mass organization where ordinary people could participate" (quoted in Kim K. H., 1998: 210).

Although not a personal advocate of gender equality, Kim Young-sam's keen interest in improving Korea's international reputation prompted efforts to strengthen the government's record on women's rights, including a far-ranging set of reform goals drawn up by the *Segyehwa Hoeŭi* (Globalization Committee) in 1995 (Chang, 2001 interview; Kim S., 2003 interview). As historian Chung Hyun-Baek notes:

> The Kim Young-sam Government marked the beginning of true democracy in Korea, and because of its democratic nature it also had to address women's policy. . . . Kim didn't personally have a good handle on gender issues but because of the atmosphere of globalization, his administration tried to upgrade women's status. (2000 interview)

Strongly influenced by the 1995 Beijing Conference, "Ten Policy Priorities" aimed at expanding women's societal participation were drawn up, ranging from the provision of better childcare and maternal services through to utilizing mass media and information networks to increase gender awareness (e.g., Chang, 2001 interview). Implementation of these legislative reforms, however, was more problematic:

> In the case of the Women's Basic Development Act [1995] there was no preparation at all and suddenly they tried to make a special law but there was no infrastructure to implement it—how can you do that? (Cho Y, 2000 interview)

The transfer of power to opposition party candidate Kim Dae-jung in the December 1997 presidential elections represented a major step toward democratic consolidation and a watershed for civil society–state relations. Not only had Kim Dae-jung been a staunch opponent of authoritarianism, but having run for the presidency on three previous occasions, most people assumed his origins in marginalized Cholla province and status as an opposition candidate would prove too difficult to overcome (Kil and Moon, 2001). Voted in with only a 40 percent plurality and lacking support from the powerful business community, the Kim Dae-jung administration sought to cultivate a "partnership with civil society," including recruiting former activists to key positions within the ruling party, the bureaucracy, and the presidential advisory circle. The progressive women's movement was particularly optimistic, given his party's and his personal favorable track record on promoting gender-equality measures. As former KWAU corepresentative Shin Heisoo noted:

> If I compare individual presidents' own understanding of gender equality, DJ is much better [than YS]—probably the most excellent person in the whole Government. . . . DJ is the most progressive man I know and has a clear understanding of the comfort woman issue, for example, and of what gender equality involves. (2000 interview)

Whereas there was less support for movement leaders to enter political parties, an unprecedented number of former activists entered governmental women's agencies to work for change from within the state, giving rise to the emergence of "femocrats," or feminist civil servants with close ties to NGO circles (Na, 2000 interview).

Yet even Kim Dae-jung's supporters admit that having a gender-sensitive president had a more limited impact on legislative passage and implementation than they had initially hoped. Some analysts suggest that assigning too much weight to the president's personal agenda overlooks the key role of international pressure in shaping domestic policy:

> People say DJ is more pro-women—but I think the historical development of women's policies is more important. Although DJ's wife was involved in women's issues from an early stage, women's policies are also shaped by what has been going on outside Korea, like the UN women's movement agenda, etc. . . . Korea is strongly influenced by the international environment . . . not just leaders' personal interests. (Park Y., 2000 interview)

Others highlight the generally low priority accorded to women's issues. Even with genuine presidential support for addressing gender inequalities, a broad array of policy issues command executive as well as public attention. As former PCWA chairwoman Kang Ki-Won notes:

> Kim Dae-jung has real commitment but it's not the top priority. How can you expect the president to make [gender equality promotion] a top

priority? The only way is to have a very strong women's collective voice. . . . Women have to show [their voice] with their vote! (2000 interview)

Although Kim Dae-jung's successor, Noh Moo Hyun, did not share the same record of support for gender-specific reforms, his role as a long-term supporter of progressive social change and human rights, close contacts with progressive social movements, his status as a relative outsider in terms of established party politics, and his support base among the younger generation ensured continuity in the growing strengthening of relations between the state and women's movement circles. In particular, upon his inauguration in February 2003, Noh appointed long-term activist and KWAU president Ji Uhn-Hee to continue and expand Han Myung-Sook's progressive legacy as minister of Gender Equality, as well as the reform-driven Kang Kum-Sil as the Ministry of Justice's first female minister.

Political Parties

The development of a competitive, institutionalized party system is commonly identified as a key ingredient of democratic consolidation (e.g., Linz and Stepan, 1996). As conduits of citizens' interests, parties ideally play a bridging role between the public and the government:

> It is difficult to sustain modern mass democracy without an institutionalized party system. The nature of parties and party systems shapes the prospects that stable democracy will emerge, whether it will be accorded legitimacy, and whether effective policy-making will result. (Mainwaring and Scully, 1995: 2)

Successful party institutionalization depends on a combination of system level, and internal organizational and societal factors. At the party system level, key elements include: relatively stable patterns of interparty competition, limited party fragmentation (i.e., "the likelihood that the party of the president will obtain a majority of seats in the legislature and provide sustained legislative support for the executive's policy proposals" [Payne et al., 2002: 144]), and a limited degree of ideological polarization. At the same time, party organizations require established rules and structures, as well as reasonably stable and deep bases of public support whereby parties and elections are accepted as legitimate mechanisms for determining governance.

Korean parties score negatively on many of these indicators. Although not plagued by high ideological polarization, at the party system level key problems include electoral volatility and party fragmentation, while internal party weaknesses stem from weak party organizations and limited elite loyalty. Many of these shortcomings are rooted in the particular historical evolution of the Korean party system. Post–World War II, the North Korea threat thwarted the development of a diverse party spectrum: embryonic left-wing parties were crushed, thereby restricting domestic politics to a pro-American stance (Lee J., 2001). Subsequently, during the authoritarian era, because opposition parties were state-sponsored and represented in a largely powerless Congress, party organizations were unable to gain experience in public mobilization and remained without a grassroots membership base. Not until the political opening of 1983 did a genuine opposition party, the New Korea Democratic Party (NKDP), emerge. Unfortunately, because its symbolic leaders—dissidents Kim Young-sam and Kim Dae-jung—were unable to agree on a single presidential candidate in 1987, the opposition splintered and parties emerged along regional lines, connected to the so-called three Kims. Post-transitional party history has therefore been shaped by the political maneuvers of former Korean Central Intelligence Agency director and Park Chunghee's right-hand man Kim Jong-Pil; opposition leader Kim Young-sam, who later compromised and merged with Roh Tae Woo's ruling party; and Kim Dae-jung, the dissident leader with a more progressive platform (see figure 5.1).

This pattern of personality-centered politics was reinforced by the sudden post-transition loss of an overarching political paradigm. With the accomplishment of long-standing national goals of "economic development," and "electoral democracy," parties found themselves without an ideological organizational logic. Instead, regionalism, previously manifested only at the level of party factionalism, surfaced as the predominant cleavage within the party system. Unlike regionalist politics in Western Europe, for example, Korean regionalism did not overlap with other social divisions such as class or religion and was simply "an amorphous sentiment of belonging" (e.g., Kim B., 1998: 130), devoid of a specific policy platform or mass-membership due-paying organization.

> The anthropocentric cultural milieu of Confucian familism and Korea's history of bloody class conflicts before 1953 had deprived both Marxism and religion of mobilizational power and ideological potential. The regionalism of Korea [is] . . . an amorphous sentiment of belonging, with neither a specific program of policy action nor a sophisticated network of mass organization. (130–31)

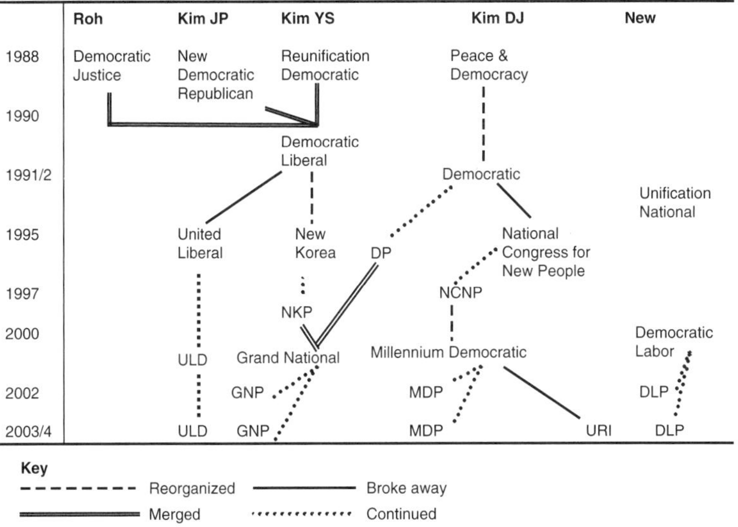

Figure 5.1 Evolution of Korean parties, 1988–2004.

Party System Dynamics

Parties have made arguably the least post-transitional progress among Korean political institutions, remaining far from Mainwaring and Scully's (1995) "institutionalized model," because of persistent structural, organizational, and attitudinal weaknesses. To be effectively institutionalized, party systems need low-to-moderate electoral volatility, a low level of party fragmentation (i.e., the ratio of congressional seats to vote share), and limited ideological polarization. Korea scores poorly on the first two counts, and only artificially well on the third. Because few parties have survived between electoral periods, the party system has been "breathtakingly turbulent" (Kim, Samuel, 2003: 39) and fits the "extremely unstable" score on Mainwaring and Scully's (1995) volatility index.[2] For example, in keeping with this pattern, the 2004 National Assembly elections saw a major realignment of political parties. The new progressive "Our Open Party (URI)" captured 52 percent of total seats, and the DLP an unprecedented 3 percent, whereas the MDP, which had served in various incarnations as the vehicle of President Kim Dae-jung, was unable to survive the final retirement of its founder (receiving just 3 percent), and the conservative GNP lost its position as the largest party (securing just 41 percent) (see tables 5.1 and 5.2).

Table 5.1   Sixth Republic presidential elections and vote share per candidate

Year	Party name	Party leader	Percentage of vote
1987	Democratic Justice Party (DJP)	Roh Tae Woo	35.9
	Party for Peace and Democracy (PPD)	Kim Dae-jung	27.5
	Reunification Democratic Party (RDP)	Kim Young-sam	26.5
	New Democratic Republican Party (NDRP)	Kim Jong-pil	7.9
1992	Democratic Liberal Party (DLP)	Kim Young-sam	42.0
	Democratic Party (DP)	Kim Dae-jung	33.8
	Unification National Party (UNP)	Chung Ju-yung	16.3
1997	New Korea Party (NKP)	Lee Hoi-chang	38.7
	Nat'l Congress for New Politics (NCNP)	Kim Dae-jung	40.3
	New Party by the People (NPP)	Rhee In-jae	19.2
2002	Grand National Party (GNP)	Lee Hoi-Chang	46.6
	Millennium Democratic Party (MDP)	Roh Mu Hyoun	48.9
	Democratic Labor Party (DLP)	Kwon Young-kil	3.9

Source: Croissant, 2002a.

Despite a mean number of just 2.95 parties post-transition, the country also scores poorly in terms of vote-to-seat proportionality (Croissant, 2002b). A combination of first-past-the-post and proportional representation electoral arrangements notwithstanding, the Korean system has largely reaped the negative features of both systems, not only scoring below the United Kingdom, where the electoral system is renowned for poorly representing voter preferences, but also failing to suppress factionalism, the key advantage of the Westminster-style electoral system (Park C., 2002).

Although Korea does not fare negatively on the third dimension of institutionalization—ideological polarization—the artificially narrow political spectrum stemming from the historical truncation of the political Left presents its own problems. On the surface, the parties of the three Kims can be loosely categorized as mirroring the ideological differences of their leaders—with Kim Dae-jung's party seen as progressive, Kim Young-sam's party as Center-Right and Kim Jong-pil's as conservative—but in practice parties have adopted catch-all centrist platforms in order to appeal to voters in the Seoul metropolitan area (representing 45 percent of the national total). There is therefore a much wider gap between the personal political commitments of respective party heads than is manifest in their respective party manifestos.

Table 5.2 Party names and leaders for National Assembly elections, 1985–2004

Year	Party name	Party leader	% of vote	Total seats
1985	Democratic Justice Party	Chun Doo Whan	35.3	148
	New Korea Democratic Party	Kim Young-sam and Kim Dae-jung	29.3	67
total seats	Democratic Korean Party	Govt. controlled opposition	19.7	35
276	Korea Nationalist Party	Govt. controlled opposition	9.2	19
	Minor parties		6.7	7
1988	Democratic Justice Party	Roh Tae Woo	34.0	125
	Party for Peace and Democracy	Kim Dae-jung	19.3	70
total seats	Reunification Democratic Party	Kim Young-sam	23.8	59
299	New Democratic Republican Party	Kim Jong-pil	15.6	35
(224 district +	9 minor parties		2.5	1
75 PR)	Independents		4.8	9
1992	Democratic Liberal Party	Roh, Kim Young-sam, Kim Jong-pil	38.5	149
total seats	Democratic Party	Kim Dae-jung	29.2	97
299	Unification National Party	Chung Ju-yung	17.4	31
(237 district +	3 minor parties		3.4	1
62 PR)	Independents		11.5	21
1996	New Korea Party	Kim Young-sam	34.8	139
	Nat'l Congress for New Politics	Kim Dae-jung	25.5	79
total seats	United Liberal Democrats	Kim Jong-pil	16.3	50
299	Democratic Party		11.3	15
(253 district +	Independents		12.0	16
46 PR)				
2000	Grand National Party	Lee Hoi Chang	39.0	133
	Millennium Democratic Party	Kim Dae-jung	35.9	115
total seats	ULD	Kim Jong-pil	9.8	17
273	Five minor parties		6.0	3
(227 district +	Independents		9.4	5
46 PR)				
2004	Grand National Party	Park Geun-hye	40.5	121
	Millennium Democratic Party	Chu Mi-ae	3.0	9
total seats	URI Party	Chung Dong-young	50.8	152
299	Democratic Labor Party	Kwon Young-kil	3.3	10
(243 district +	Independents		2.3	7
56 PR)				

Source: National Election Commission (www.nec.go.kr).

Relationships with Civil Society

The depth of linkages between parties and citizens and organized groups—measured by party longevity, stable patterns of societal support, and acceptance of parties and elections as legitimate mechanisms for determining governance—is an equally important dimension of party institutionalization. Korea scores poorly on party longevity—measured by the difference in the share of seats won by parties with ten plus percent of seats in the first and last post-transitional elections (Payne et al., 2002)—as none of the parties that contested the 1988 Korean congressional elections survived to 2004.[3] Part of the problem lies with the relatively weak presence of party organizations between elections (Kim W., 2003 interview), manifested in low party membership rates, the inability of parties to be self-financing, and heavy reliance on business elites for illegal donations (Kang, 2001).

A loss of public legitimacy due to elite domination and repeated scandals has also contributed to citizens' low levels of party identification.[4] Whereas 78–92 percent of respondents from Eastern Europe believed that parties "provide opportunities to participate in politics," just 57 percent of Koreans shared the same sentiment (Shin D., 1999: 191). There was an even larger cross-regional gap in citizens' assessments of party performance. Only 27 percent of Koreans agreed that parties "serve the interests of the public" compared with 46–69 percent in Eastern Europe, while 71 percent characterized Korean political party performance as either "non-democratic" or "mostly democratic" (181). Public affinity with particular political parties is similarly low. The Korean Barometer Survey found that a full 49 percent of the population had no party affiliation, and 52 percent of voters gave rankings of 0 or 1 on a scale of 0–4 (lowest to highest) in response to a question on party loyalty (Shin D., 2003). Importantly, though, despite widespread dissatisfaction with party practice, citizens have comparatively high levels of respect for parties and elections in principle. As many as 95 percent of respondents agreed with the statement "we need political parties if we want democratic development," which was higher than the response from Eastern Europeans (except for Bulgarians) (Shin D., 1999: 189).

Gendered Opportunities

The Korean party system's impact on gender politics has been more mixed than its poor overall ratings might suggest. Whereas male-dominated party structures have been slow to promote women to decisionmaking roles or nominate them as political candidates (e.g., Park K. A., 1999), the inchoate nature of the party system has paradoxically facilitated gender-related reform efforts. Notwithstanding the absence of a left-wing programmatic party—which the literature argues is highly corre-lated with the promotion of gender egalitarian policies (e.g., Stetson and Mazur, 1995)—the women's movement's lobbying efforts have secured the passage of a wide range of progressive legislation, even in the context of a broadly conservative political arena. How can we explain this success?

First, while Latin American women's movement organizations often fragmented post-transition around partisan loyalties (e.g., Jaquette, 1994; Waylen, 1996a), the Korean movement has largely avoided these divisions. Because parties failed to emerge as major conduits for policy preferences, feminist activists were reluctant to encourage movement leaders to stand for office, perceiving the electoral arena as a largely inef-fective channel through which to pursue social change (Yoon, 2002 interview; Cho H., 2003 interview). Although there has been an infor-mal division between the two major women's umbrella organizations along party lines,[5] these informal alliances have generally not extended to overt, institutional support for candidates of a specific party. Women's movement leaders have sought to avoid creating tensions among the movement's membership base, especially as political loyalties within branch organizations outside Seoul are often strongly influenced by regionalism (Yoon, 2002 interview). Indeed, fear of co-optation is so strong that leaders who toy with or accept invitations to run for political office often come under heavy criticism from colleagues, who are adamant that women's NGOs should not be seen as a springboard for individual political careers (Lee M., 2004 interview).

Despite organized women's distance from party politics, the introduc-tion of party competition and an associated desire to capitalize on women's rising voting rates provided a vital new political space—in terms of both women's party bureaus and women-related electoral plat-forms (Wade and Jin, 1996).[6] Given that Korean parties lack program-matic cohesion and primarily seek to maximize votes while avoiding alienating any particular voting bloc, they have been prone to passively accept the demands of women's movement lobbyists:

> The unique characteristic of our country is that there really is no signifi-cant policy difference, particularly in the case of women's policy, between the ruling and opposition parties—there are no true conservatives or true progressives. We either accept women's organizations' demands or do an

> opinion survey and because . . . all three parties generally rely on the same gender consultants, we tend to end up with the same policy direction. (Kang H., 2000 interview)

Particularly during elections, party leaders are susceptible to external pressures, being loath to give an advantage to the rival party or incur negative press (Kim W., 2003 interview). In the 1997 presidential elections, for instance, all candidates agreed to far-reaching maternity leave reforms, whereas in the 2002 elections each major contender supported revising the highly contentious *hojuje* (Yoon, 2003 interview). Women's NGOs continue to capitalize on this vulnerability throughout the election cycle, reiterating their demands through postelection fax and signature campaigns, and releasing annual evaluations to the ruling party detailing the extent to which it has delivered on electoral promises (Lee Y., 2000 interview). Such systematic lobbying has enabled the women's movement to influence party policy far beyond its actual numerical strength. Moreover, thanks to increasingly sophisticated movement demands and the entry of a small but increasing number of former activists into political parties, gender-related party platforms have become increasingly specific and oriented toward promoting gender equality rather than merely mobilizing women voters (see table 5.3).[7]

Although the party platforms for the 1997 and 2002 presidential elections were refined through negotiations with NGOs, public hearings, and televised debates on gender-specific policy issues with presidential candidates (Kim S., 2002 interview), the extent to which these pledges are indicative of fundamental rethinking within party organizations is more

Table 5.3 Major policy initiatives demanded by women's organizations in 2002 elections

Eliminate family headship system *(hojuje)* and develop gender egalitarian alternative
Expand rights for casualized workers
Increase national welfare budget by 50%
Reform legislation on sex workers and human trafficking
Implement 30% quota for district seats and 50% for PR party lists
Expand programs for single-parent families
Increase monthly stipends for one-year childcare leave
Increase women's representation in unification-related policymaking
Improve disabled women's rights
Provide greater support for maternity and childcare needs of women farmers
Implement gender awareness programs at all educational levels
Improve elderly welfare services
Expand Ministry of Gender Equality budget and staff

Source: WSPE, 2002.

questionable. As Kim Young-Ae, former vice-director of the MDP Women's Bureau, emphasized, the political will to implement pledges made in a bid to gain the support of women's organizations is too often lacking:

> The leaders at the party headquarters only give very wishy-washy support to gender equality. They have an authoritarian mindset and do not fully support the need to improve women's status . . . At election time they use rhetoric that endorses gender equality but that's really all. They still don't see that in order to have a strong society, it's important that women participate equally. (2000 interview)

In sum, moving party platforms on gender concerns from voter mobilization tools to genuine programs of social change will require longer-term pressure and monitoring from women's groups, feminist legislators, and femocrats.

Bureaucracy

Although typically not subject to the far-reaching changes undergone by elected bodies, a closer look at post-transitional political dynamics may reveal multiple new access points via the bureaucracy. An effective *civil* service necessitates that military era bureaucratic elites are brought firmly under control, ministries subjected to external monitoring (congressional and civic), and channels for civic participation developed. Depending on the extent to which authoritarian era bureaucrats are purged and/or new segments of the population are attracted to jobs within a democratic state apparatus, the overall tone of civil servants' social and ideological positionings may shift post-transition and be reflected in new policy directions (Petras et al., 1994). As Brock et al. (2001) argue, the "situated agency" of bureaucratic personnel is likely to have an important spillover effect on policy formulation and implementation:

> At once state actors and citizens, bureaucrats may have multiple and competing allegiances and identifications, [as] they are embedded in social, professional and political networks that span multiple sites and domains of discourse. The "inner life" of bureaucrats is a rich terrain of contestation in which career aspirations, departmental loyalties, unwritten rules and external pressures, as well as different normative constructions . . . come into play. (4)

Similarly, the development of new channels of civic participation, ranging from "invited forums of participation 'from above' " (1) (including representation on ministerial advisory committees or participation in semiformal consultation policy reform processes) through to the establishment of new infrastructure within the state, such as women's policy machineries, are likely to transform the state.

The Korean public sector is best characterized as hierarchical, rule-bound, and resistant to outside influence. Until the 1980s, bureaucratic elites played a substantial role in molding national development strategies (e.g., Evans, 1995). Not only did the majority of parliamentary statutes originate with the bureaucracy, but because of the legislature's weak oversight role, bureaucrats remained largely unaccountable to other branches of government (Park C., 2000). Moreover, whereas civil service personnel in other countries may accept positions in academia or the nonprofit or private sectors before subsequently reentering the bureaucracy, until as late as 1998, entrance into the Korean civil service was by competitive examinations only, with little value attached to alternative career paths. Given just two percent annual pass rates and considerably fewer bureaucrats per capita compared to their Western counterparts, Korean bureaucrats were (and continue to be) accorded considerable respect, representing a long cultural tradition of a merit-based bureaucracy that honors civil servants as social elites (Evans, 1995).

Moreover, because Korea's transition resulted from a "crisis of success," there has been limited impetus to overhaul the bureaucracy (Hahm and Plein, 1997). Unlike some authoritarian regimes that collapsed following economic crisis (e.g., Argentina), the Korean military lost power in part because its economic model became too successful, with middle-class citizens' interests shifting from more immediate survival needs to quality of life issues (Kim S. H., 2000). Accordingly, while the bureaucracy's direct micro-management of the economy has waned since the late 1980s (Kwon, 1999), its role in implementing social policy has risen, as exemplified by the launch of the National Health Insurance and National Pension programs in 1988. Additionally, because Korean legislation is often overly broad, the powerful role of interpreting new reform laws is left to bureaucratic officials, who decide whether to adopt an activist or conservative reading as they draw up the all-important bureaucratic implementation ordinances. As KWAU policy officer Cho Young-Sook explains:

> Sometimes the law is good but the implementation guidelines are bad—sometimes the meaning of the law vanishes. So although we first focus on the National Assembly, we have to immediately turn and monitor whether the government officials follow the meaning of the law fully or do they just

> ignore its real significance. . . . The *shihaengnyŏng* (enforcement ordinance)
> is sometimes more important than the law itself. (2000 interview)

In terms of personnel, although the Roh administration (1987–92) made relatively few civil service personnel changes, Kim Young-sam purged the *Hanuhoe* (secret military elite) and forced many of the *Taegu-Kyungbuk* (provincial political elites with ties to the military regime) to resign. The introduction of a "public official wealth registration system" that required high-level politicians to reveal illegally acquired wealth also contributed to the exit of remaining senior members of the authoritarian-era bureaucracy. As groundbreaking as these initiatives were, however, turnover among rank-and-file bureaucrats was relatively modest and largely due to natural attrition. In order to revitalize the bureaucracy, Kim Dae-jung therefore introduced contract-based expert appointments to encourage academics and nonprofit-sector workers to join the civil service. This allowed an unprecedented but admittedly still small number of activists (including women) to push for reforms from within the state. The administration also sought to replace seniority-based promotions with performance-based appraisals in an effort to promote policy innovation (Kim P., 2002).

Gendered Opportunities

Gender scholars have emphasized the bureaucracy's status quo, elitist orientation, and entrenched male dominance, particularly within the East Asian context (Craske, 1999; Ling, 2000). Although these barriers are an important concern, my research on the Korean case suggests that the gendered impact of post-transitional changes in the civil service has been more mixed, especially given the bureaucracy's relative influence, stability, and professionalism. As discussed in chapter 7, WPMs have grown in institutional strength and breadth, and have gradually developed closer, more cooperative ties with women's movement organizations. There has been limited progress, however, in shaping gender-related policies and budgets in mainstream ministries. For example, the former head of the Ministry of Health and Social Welfare (MHSW) Women's Focal Point, Soh Myung-Son, noted that although the ministry was formally responsible for implementing domestic violence programs, her colleagues felt no urgency to establish requisite infrastructure or fight for adequate budgetary resources because they saw that NGOs were already developing their own programs. Increasingly frustrated by this foot-dragging, Soh successfully sought international funding to develop her own project, albeit at the cost of "resentment and conflict" with mainstream coworkers (2000 interview).

Advances in securing women's representation in bureaucratic decisionmaking positions has also remained slow. In response to pressure from women's organizations, the Ministry of Home and Government Affairs initiated a quota system in 1996 for women civil servant recruits, as well as ministerial civilian advisory committees (see chapters 8–9). Although the system has increased the absolute number of women in the civil service, albeit from a low base, the quota system's focus on entry-level positions will delay the achievement of the critical mass necessary to re-orient bureaucratic policymaking for quite some time.

Judiciary

Establishing the rule of law has been identified as one of the minimum conditions for a democratic system. This process, however, is dependent on fostering a broader legal culture, including an independent judiciary (e.g., Yoon, 1990); citizens' internalization of respect for democratic procedures and notions of individual civic and human rights (Shin D., 1999); as well as constitutional protection for vulnerable groups (Linz and Stepan, 1996). How the "rule of law" is practiced within different democratic contexts can be especially important in determining whether new democracies advance women's rights to, for example, reproductive freedom and protection from violence (e.g., Jelin and Hershberg, 1996; Caldiera, 1998). Although far from optimal, the Korean judiciary has undergone significant reform since 1987 both in terms of formal infrastructure and (albeit to a lesser degree) personnel. In contrast to Korea's democratizing peers, change is also occurring in the way that the populace perceives and interacts with the courts (e.g., Prillaman, 2000). Even so, the overwhelming male dominance of the legal profession and its famed conservatism are retarding the speed of gendered social change.

The Revival of Judicial Review

In response to demands for greater judicial independence and more effective protection of civil and political rights (Kim S. H., 1997), the Constitutional Court was established in 1989, reviving the practice of judicial review, which was suspended during authoritarian rule. The Court has not only tackled a large volume of cases, but justices have also asserted their independence in an array of politically contentious fields, including national security, media censorship, and the *tongsŏng tongbon* (same-surname/same-clan marriage ban).[8] Youm (1994), for example, argues: "Judicial review is emerging as one of the most important institutions in a democratic Korea" (40). Similarly, West and Yoon (1992) maintain:

> In a cultural environment in which the legal system has long been viewed as an instrument of authoritarian governance. . . . the Constitutional Court has acquired more significance as an adjudicatory body than many Korean jurists and foreign observers expected. (115)

By overturning previous authoritarian practices and laws, and establishing the constitution as a "living document," the Court has accelerated the democratization process (Ahn, 1997). Between 1989 and 1995, many of the most egregious constitutional violations were overturned; for example, the parameters of the controversial National Security Act were restricted, the statute of limitations that had protected the perpetrators of the 1980 Kwangju massacre was overturned, and de facto press censorship was ended. Having established itself as an active defender of constitutional rights and as willing to resist political pressure from both the ruling party and its rival institution, the Supreme Court (Ahn, 1997), the Constitutional Court subsequently extended its activist work into social areas. In the words of Justice Kim Yong-Joon, "the Court has been instrumental in eradicating a number of unjust practices that had been defended in the name of 'tradition' " (1999: 2), directly challenging politically influential lobby groups such as Confucian and Veteran associations, which the National Assembly had been less willing to confront.

By promoting the rights to "the pursuit of happiness" and "equality," and strengthening individual freedoms versus the requirements of "public welfare" or "social order," the Court has also facilitated women's groups' gender-related legal change initiatives. Examples include overhauling legal prescriptions against adultery, the same–surname/ same-clan marriage ban, the Veteran Affirmative Action policy in the civil service entrance examination, the Nationality Act, which defined nationality according to the paternal rather than the maternal line, and most recently the *hojuje*.

Such landmark rulings notwithstanding, the enforcement mechanisms at the Court's disposal have been relatively weak until very recently. Although able to pronounce on the constitutionality of a lower court decision or piece of legislation, the Court has been unable to force relevant government functionaries (i.e., prosecutors, bureaucrats, or legislators) to redress the situation. In a number of cases where the Court overturned a significant law, for example, the same-surname/same-clan marriage ban, the National Assembly simply refused to revise the law and merely waited until the expiry of the Court's appointed deadline (Lee S., 2000 interview). Similarly, although the Veteran Affirmative Action policy was ruled unconstitutional in 1999, the ruling party effectively ignored the decision until after the spring congressional elections, in order to appease vehement public protests by veteran groups.[9] However, this relative balance of power is continuing to evolve as highlighted by the new public prominence of the Court following its involvement in adjudicating the constitutionality of the congressional decision to impeach President Noh Moo Hyun in 2004. The vote to impeach was rushed through Congress and perceived by broad swaths of the Korean electorate as illegitimate, bordering on a "legislative coup d'etat" and thus the Court's ruling—in favor of the President—was awaited with great anticipation. The Court also ruled on the constitutionality of moving the nation's political capital away from Seoul, one of the primary election pledges of President Noh, as well as on the controversial national security law. This unprecedented activity has led some analysts to fear the development of an "imperial judiciary" or "judicialization of politics" (Kim Sunhyuk, forthcoming).

Personnel Changes

The rapid expansion of the bar, which quadrupled in size between 1977 and 1996 and tripled again by 2003[10] (Ahn, 1997; KWDI, 2004), has not only broadened the types of law practiced to include consumer, labor and civil rights law but, perhaps more importantly, has helped to break down historical hierarchies. Although judges have traditionally been regarded as "expert clerks," owing to the more limited role afforded them within the civil law tradition, young judges are increasingly exercising their interpretative prerogative (Ahn, 1994). Similarly, a 300-strong collective of former political dissidents and civil rights lawyers called *Minbyŏn* (Lawyers for a Democratic Society) has emerged, and is actively promoting "full democratization" by assisting *shimin undong* organizations to draft reform bills and representing plaintiffs in court cases (Cho S., 2002 interview; Minbyun, 2004).[11]

These domestic changes have in turn been reinforced by the country's increasing integration into a globalizing world. Following entry into the

UN and ILO in 1991 and accession to the OECD in 1996, post-transitional administrations have taken considerable pains to present Korea as a state that respects international norms, including those pertaining to gender-related issues. Whereas critics have rightly pointed out that these measures are more often about image creation than substantive change (e.g., Cho Y., 2000 interview), we can nevertheless expect that ongoing pressure from various UN and ILO evaluation committees will contribute to gradual improvements in both the current gender imbalance within the judiciary and the level of gender sensitivity among legal practitioners.

Nevertheless, senior judges, lawyers, and prosecutors schooled during the authoritarian regime have benefited from their elite status and many are therefore resistant to opening up the profession. Legal scholar Yang Hyunah suggests that gender-related measures such as family law reform elicited particularly strong opposition because they involve deeply entrenched notions of tradition and nationalism, which continue to resonate with broad swaths of the population (1998). Accordingly, we need to be cautious about the propensity of the courts to adopt progressive interpretations of new gender-rights legislation. Recent examples of gender discriminatory rulings include a 1999 decision by the courts to waive an accused rapist's sentence after the parents of the perpetrator and the victim agreed to the couple's marriage, and the dismissal of an elderly woman's divorce petition because the judge argued that it was her duty to take care of her husband as promised in the wedding vows of her day (Lee M., 2002 interview).

Equally significantly, although increasing numbers of women have entered the judiciary over the past two decades, the gender ratio remains extremely unbalanced. In 2004, there were only 222 female judges (11.5 percent of the total), 82 female prosecutors (6.2 percent), and 369 female lawyers (5.4 percent). This pattern of male dominance is also prevalent within the Ministry of Justice, with women making up just 12.5 percent of the ministry's total staff, and less than 2 percent in deci-sionmaking ranks in 2002,[12] as well as in the country's law schools, where as recently as 2002 there were only 30 female law professors nationwide, with just a handful of feminists among them (Kim S., 2002 interview). To address this gender imbalance, a gender-sensitivity training program was introduced in 1998 for legal trainees, but as these programs target future rather than more senior legal professionals, it will take time for change to permeate the system (Lee O., 2000 interview).

Shifting Public Attitudes

Developing trust in the courts as the arbiters of justice and a willingness to resort to legal solutions in response to social grievances constitutes a crucial component of democratic consolidation (e.g., Helgesen, 1997). Korea's Confucian system of ethics has historically preferred nonlegal settlements to litigation, a bias further reinforced during the military dictatorship as the courts facilitated the government's repressive policies (Ahn, 1994). Citizens' attitudes vis-à-vis the law and courts as a channel of redress have nevertheless undergone considerable change since democratization. The results of the 1993 Korean Democratization Survey suggest that, conceptually at least, Koreans value justice and the law highly. Some 62 percent of respondents listed "fair justice" as an important feature of democracy: of the four political components of democratization—"political freedom," "political participation," "political competition," and "fair justice"—only the latter was cited by a majority of the 1,198 people surveyed (Shin D., 1999: 48). Admittedly, citizens continue to express some distrust as to the court system's neutrality, but judging by the rapid escalation of lawsuits filed over the last 15 years, as well as widespread use of constitutional petitions to redress personal grievances (Kim C., 2000), the populace's propensity to turn to the courts has increased markedly.

Gendered Opportunities

Although data on public attitudes toward the legal system has not been disaggregated by sex (Kim S., 2002 interview), attitudinal changes toward the judiciary can be seen in the number of ordinary women who are prepared to access the court to seek redress for private and public injustices as well as women's NGOs' increasing reliance on the courts to draw attention to gender abuses. The passage of gender-related laws, especially those relating to equal employment opportunities, family and sexual violence, and sexual harassment, has encouraged a gradual increase in lawsuits filed by working- and middle-class women alike (MOGE, 2001; National Police Agency, 2001).[13] This has been particularly pronounced in the case of divorce, with the crude divorce rate (recorded number of divorces per 1,000 people) rising from 0.6 in 1985 to 1.1 in 1995, 2.5 in 2000, and 3.5 in 2003 (Lee H., 2005).[14] Interestingly, it is wives who are turning to the courts in surprising numbers: in 1999, 64.2 percent of divorce petitions were filed by women (Kim C., 2000). Whereas the average age for divorce for women is 38.3 years (versus 41.8 for men), there has also been a rise in the number of elderly women filing for divorce in what has been dubbed the "silver divorce" phenomenon (Lee H., 2005).

Moreover, since the late 1980s women's activist groups have filed lawsuits on behalf of victims as a key strategy in promoting gender equality. As law professor Kim Sun-uk points out, "it is much easier for women to persuade nine or fewer justices than to win over the National Assembly" (2002 interview). Lawsuits have been used to raise awareness about discrimination and abuse—especially sexual and family violence, gender discrimination and sexual harassment in the workplace, or sexual harassment—as well as to "test" the efficacy of new laws. Two recent high-profile cases involving multiple plaintiffs that were supported by women's NGOs are excellent examples. In the first case, in 2000, female employees of Lotte Hotel filed a lawsuit against company executives, claiming "habitual sexual abuse." The verdict returned by the Seoul District Court ruled in favor of 40 plaintiffs and ordered the hotel and four defendants to pay damages. While the level of compensation was much lower than the 220 million won that had been sought (about US$180,000), the decision sent a powerful message to the business world "because it recognized management's responsibility for turning a blind eye to sexual harassment at work" (Chong, 2002 interview; Lee H. S., 2002).

The second case involved a dispute in 2000 between a feminist art collective, *Ibgim* (Puff of Breath) and the *Chonju Yi* clan over an avant-garde cultural event in Seoul's downtown Chongmyo Park, where the ancestral shrines of the royal Yi family are housed. After Confucian elders obstructed the event, which had received local government approval, eight artists supported by the KWAU filed a suit asking for 40 million won in damages (Choy, 2001). The Seoul District Court initially threw out the case citing insufficient evidence of illegal action, but a video documenting the clan's rampage persuaded a panel of four judges in 2003 to reverse the lower court's ruling in favor of freedom of expression (Dong K., 2003). As feminist photographer Park Young-sook noted:

> The court case shows the patriarchal and male-chauvinist nature of the Korean cultural environment where a purely cultural event can be turned into a social controversy. The court decision was only too right, and it will be like a breath of fresh air as it has set a good, albeit belated, precedent in moving towards a mature society. (Quoted in Dong K., 2003)

Conclusion

Post-transitional institutional changes have provided new but limited opportunities for Korean proponents of gender equality. At the level of institutional infrastructure, significant shifts have taken place in the balance of power between the executive and legislature with each successive democratic administration; the independence of the judiciary and its recognition of citizens' constitutional rights; and to a lesser degree the bureaucracy's enhanced openness and flexibility. By contrast, the political party system has made the least progress in moving toward the institutionalized ideal identified by many democratic theorists as a key characteristic of consolidated democracies.

Key gender-related institutional changes include the following: First, the immaturity of the legislative process has proven to be a double-edged sword, allowing for the rapid passage of surprisingly progressive gender-related legislation but at the cost of broader public debate and a deeper reshaping of cultural values. The limited politicization of gender issues has in turn been reinforced by a nonprogrammatic catch-all party system, which has deprived the Korean women's movement of a strong left-wing party to champion gender-equality reforms but at the same time thwarted the emergence of a politically articulate conservative bloc united around morality and gender politics. Second, the role of the president was found to be more constrained than popular images of *daekwon* (great power) might imply, but nevertheless important in terms of shaping decisions around resource allocation and institutional positioning for women's state machineries, as well as appointments of ministers and high-level judicial personnel. Third, in contrast to strong disillusionment in other Third Wave polities, the Korean judiciary has at times played a surprisingly activist role in overthrowing anachronistic gender laws.

At the level of institutional personnel, changes in the socio-ideological positioning of staff have played a significant part in fostering closer engagement between civil society groups and formal political institutions. In the absence of a widespread overhaul at the point of transition, a more reform-oriented and broadly representative generation of officials, legal professionals, and politicians has gradually gained in influence. Similarly, except in the case of political parties, which suffer from particularly low public approval, the Korean citizenry and especially civic groups have gradually become more willing to engage with and seek redress through political institutions, thereby also expanding subjective political opportunities.

CHAPTER 6

Policy Change: Differing Logics of Political Contestation

While legal advances alone cannot eliminate discrimination against women, laws expanding the rights of women interact with and reinforce broader processes of cultural change. The process by which de jure rights are translated into de facto rights may be frustratingly slow, but the latter is impossible without the former.

Haas, 2000: 1

Whereas women's movements in many nascent democracies continue to struggle to enact progressive legislation on, for example, divorce, sexual crimes, and access to contraception (e.g., Caldiera, 1998; Willmott, 2002), a wide range of gender-related legislative and policy reforms has been undertaken in Korea over the past 15 years. Women now enjoy a comprehensive range of formal rights encompassing bodily integrity, civic and political participation, and workplace equality (see Jones, 2003). Gender experts identified legislative change as the area in which the greatest progress has been made since the transition (Kim Y. et al., 2001), while the UN Commission on the Status of Women singled out Korea as a model case for advances in formal gender equality in 1999 and 2000 (Lee H., 2003 interview).

These advances are all the more impressive, given the low baseline in the 1980s from which the women's movement has had to struggle. Although women's workplace participation and access to higher education rose dramatically over the 1960s–1980s period, Korean women remained subject to strict Confucian gender roles and prescriptions on the eve of the 1987 democratic transition. They had no right to equal inheritance or to a public pension in the case of divorce, lacked child custodial rights, were subject to harsher penalties than men for adultery and remarriage after widowhood, and could not pass on their nationality status to their children if married to a non-Korean. In the workplace, women lacked any guarantees of equal employment rights or wages, and were without redress for either sexual harassment or discrimination in the case of marriage and childbirth. In the sphere of education, women were excluded from conventionally male fields, ranging from taxation policy to volunteer service abroad to the police academy. In terms of human rights, sexual violence was recognized as a crime against family honor rather than against individual women, and family violence was largely ignored. Antiprostitution laws penalized providers rather than buyers or profiteers, just as the government continued to tacitly support the industry. Furthermore, although women had been granted suffrage rights in 1948, upper limits remained on women's representation in the civil service, and early governmental agencies for women were weak and without enforcement powers. In short, women did not gain full citizenship rights until well after the democratic transition.

The importance of the eradication of these discriminatory regulations notwithstanding, some observers offer rather negative assessments of Korean gender-related legislative reform efforts because of disparities between legal passage and implementation (e.g., Kim S. H., forthcoming). Although such concerns are certainly valid and are addressed here, I nevertheless argue that it is important to recognize the significance of the breadth of reforms achieved in the Korean context. Most basically, although the Korean *ppalli ppalli* (quick-quick) mentality tends to foster a "glass-half-empty" approach when assessing policy advancements, it is important to take stock of recent history and acknowledge the dramatic post-transition changes that have occurred. Moreover, if we place Korea within a broader comparative perspective, the range of reforms secured is particularly striking (e.g., Friedman, 2000; Johnson, 2002). Such progress signals that Korean women and their allies enjoy sufficient influence on the political stage to prevent conservative opposition groups from silencing public debate on a diverse array of issues, while effectively cajoling gender-blind (or even reactionary) politicians to vote for advances in women's rights.

Bearing in mind Haas's (2000) observation that "while legal advances alone cannot eliminate discrimination against women, laws expanding the rights of women interact with and reinforce broader processes of cultural change" (1), it is important that we unpack the cluster of actor- and institution-centered variables that account for Korea's success. I begin by mapping the overarching dynamics of gender-policy development. I argue that key ingredients in improving women's rights have included the strength and flexibility of organized women and their ability to forge coalitions with civil society and state actors, the relative weakness of institutionalized opposition, coupled with Korea's rapid legislative process, a nonprogrammatic party system, activist strands of the judiciary, and a national eagerness to "catch up" internationally.

Yet while this pattern of interaction between actors and institutions helps us understand the enactment of a wide range of policy reforms, it is less useful in explaining the underlying dynamics of the passage of laws in specific issue areas. Through process tracing, my research suggests that the passage of legislative and policy change followed distinct sub-logics. I draw on three separate case studies to illustrate my argument: the negotiation processes leading to the enactment and subsequent revisions of the 1987 Equal Employment Act (EEA), the passage of the 1989 and 2005 Family Law revisions, the 1993 Sexual Violence Prevention Act, the 1997 Special Law on Punishment of the Crime of Domestic Violence, and the Law on Protection of Domestic Violence Victims.[1] The most prominent difference to emerge is the degree of opposition and its institutional articulation. Although the case studies show some variation in the intensity of campaigning, the relative organizational capacity of leading women's groups, and the type of conjunctural coalitions that women activists forge, these are insufficient to explain the timing and content of resulting legislation. Similarly, although institutional factors are certainly not uniform across cases, the degree of deviation in bureaucratic or congressional support/resistance, presidential commitment, the level of political influence held by WPMs, or international pressure do not neatly correlate with differential success across policy issue areas. I conclude that the ease with which women's groups are able to secure legislative change is determined to a significant degree by whether the opposition to particular gender reforms is represented by an institutional carrier or is more diffuse and embedded in everyday cultural practices and values.

Besides the powerful symbolic effects of legislative reforms, the extent to which new laws are implemented is a key indicator of the impact of democratization on gender equality. Political leaders may agree to enact gender-related laws so as to enhance their legitimacy with voters, distance themselves from more authoritarian predecessors, or improve their country's democratic kudos in international forums. However, international experience suggests that implementation remains patchy at best, and sanctions for offenders are largely tokenistic (e.g., Johnson, 2002). Likewise there has been insufficient effort to address broader infrastructural barriers, including the marginalization of WPMs (e.g., Waylen, 1996b) and limited gender awareness among civil servants and judicial personnel charged with enforcement (e.g., Macauley, 2002; Gideon, 2002). In order to assess the implementation of gender policies in Korea, this chapter therefore discusses, where possible, the level of resources allocated to carry out new prescriptions, the bureaucracy's and judiciary's enforcement record, and whether legislation stipulates penalties for violations.

Equal Employment Rights and Maternity Protection Legislative Reforms

1987	*Equal Employment Act*, revised 1989, 1995, 1999
2001	Revisions to maternity leave–related legislation: *Labor Standards Act, Equal Employment Act, Employment Insurance Act.*

Employment-related reforms capture an area in which, on the eve of the democratic transition, women had few legal rights and faced obviously unequal treatment compared with their male counterparts. Yet today, formal legal protections have been established against direct and indirect gender discrimination (including wages, benefits, working conditions, appearance requirements, and promotion procedures) as well as sexual harassment. Moreover, women are entitled to 90 days' paid maternity leave and (along with men) one year partially paid childcare leave. Successive reforms over the course of each democratic administration allow us to trace the evolution of the balance of power among civil society and state actors, as well as the ways in which the institutional framework, international norms, and the global economic environment have shaped the contestation of equal employment–related policies.

I argue that the passage of increasingly sophisticated revisions to the EEA can be attributed to a well-coordinated coalition of women's and labor movement activists, sympathetic scholars, and progressive women legislators, as well as influence from international organizations, especially the ILO, the UN, and the OECD. The demands of the pro-reform coalition have been watered down, however, by the opposition of employers' federations focused on preserving labor flexibility and a lower wage bill. Changing perceptions as to the costs of labor unrest, as well as the increasing importance of being seen to meet international standards, have served to temper opposition from business groups over time. Given the state's own interests in maximizing women's human resources, political elites have sought to mediate between the two camps, while ensuring that broader national imperatives—maintaining Korea's competitiveness in global markets, the reproduction of a healthy workforce, and minimizing costs—are met. The following discussion is organized thematically, beginning with changes in state interests and international discourses, and then turning to the evolution of women's conjunctural civil society/state coalitions, their multidimensional strategies, and discursive tactics.

Evolving International Norms and State Imperatives

At each juncture of the EEA reform process, the political opportunity structure for women's mobilization was shaped by a new configuration of international and domestic influences. In the case of its original 1987 passage, the international diffusion of the Women in Development (WID) paradigm and the imperatives of domestic economic restructuring were of primary importance. Emerging from the economic crises of the early 1980s, and faced with rising international competition, Korea was forced to accelerate industrial-sector reform, particularly in labor-intensive industries in which women were concentrated. With real wages rising amid general labor scarcity, calls to better utilize women's human resources were accepted by the military junta and business groups (Paik J., 2002), and addressed in the Sixth Five-Year National Development Plan (1982–87). Accordingly, the Korean Women's Development Institute (KWDI) produced a draft equal employment bill in 1985 (Kim K. H., 1998), but business was vocally opposed to it and it was not passed until October 1987 (e.g., Kang H., 2000 interview).

Although progressive women's organizations were not the primary initiators of the original EEA, the expansion of civic groups calling for greater substantive democracy in the immediate post-transition period facilitated both its original passage and the subsequent reform process. Recognizing that women's economic inequality was a major source of their wider societal subordination, women's activists argued that the EEA did not go far enough, and called for better enforcement mechanisms and sanctions for violations. The political turmoil of the transitional phase proved conducive to these organizational efforts, leading to the 1989 EEA reform. As long-term women's labor activist Chong Kang-Ja noted:

> In the late 1980s, the Government feared labor strikes because of the country's experience of massive strikes in 1987. They were therefore very cautious . . . and were much more concerned about labor-business relations than the gender dimensions. (2002 interview)

The patterning of institutional and political factors that facilitated women's mobilization for the second major EEA reform (1995) was quite distinct. As democratic governance became more habituated and civil society–state relations less antagonistic, the political environment proved more conducive toward women's advocacy than ever before. In particular, the "hype" surrounding the 1995 Beijing Conference encouraged state officials to pay greater attention to their gender-relations record, as illustrated, for example, by the 1995 ban on appearance requirements in the employment recruitment process.

Concurrently, however, rising labor costs, accompanied by increased competition in traditional light industries, had once again placed business concerns with labor "flexibility" back on the political agenda. In response, women and labor activists lobbied against the proposed Dispatch Law due to its potentially negative implications for women,[2] while stepping up demands for EEA reform that would provide for more substantive improvements in gender equality. In this instance, however, business groups were able to carry the day, as the state elected to prioritize global competitiveness:

> The government views the utilization of the unused women's labor force, including married women, [as a way to] increase women's participation in society, mitigate the shortage of human resources . . . [and] strengthen the competitiveness of Korean industry. (Prime Minister Yi, 1995, quoted in Yang, 2002: 77)

During the Kim Dae-jung administration, labor-related reforms were significantly broader in scope; ironically, not because of pressure from below or the president's close historical ties with labor, but rather in response to the 1997/98 economic crisis. Mass bankruptcies resulted in a sharp spike in unemployment as highly indebted corporations responded to a collapse in regional demand, massive foreign exchange instability, and a quadrupling of interest rates. Women's workplace rights underwent a significant reversal following the crisis, in turn giving rise to pressure by WPMs and civic groups for legislative support and more substantive state aid (e.g., vocational training programs, unemployment counseling, and shelters for impoverished female heads of households). Officials were compelled to respond affirmatively to these demands, given the absence of meaningful social safety-net mechanisms (Wang, 2000 interview).

Perhaps surprisingly, in light of still high unemployment rates and the sharp decline in household income, the third EEA reform campaign initiated in 1999 did not make material demands but called for the prohibition of sexual harassment and indirect gender discrimination. Building on a longer-standing struggle to provide women with legal recourse against rampant workplace harassment,[3] the campaign demanded assurance that women would not disproportionately bear the costs of reform, although it did not oppose labor restructuring per se.

Having witnessed first-hand the high costs of indirect discrimination during the 1997/98 economic restructuring, the women's movement was highly motivated to secure legal redress for women who had been fired because of their collective disadvantageous positioning within the labor market (Pak, 2002). Whereas employers argued that women were fired because they happened to be employed in more expendable sectors, feminists countered that the very fact that women were concentrated in less valued areas was the result of endemic gender bias in recruitment and educational processes. A ban on "indirect discrimination," they hoped, would raise public awareness about this basic inequality and provide women with the legal tools needed to take action against lay-offs of this nature (e.g., Cho S., 2002 interview). Activists were able to take advantage of the fact that Kim Dae-jung was "in debt" to labor/civic groups because of his introduction of rather draconian restructuring measures. They also benefited from less intense opposition from the business community as the policies in question would not entail significant monetary outlay.

The political environment that facilitated the most controversial and influential of the five employment-related reforms, the 2001 Maternity and Childcare Leave revisions, combined the ruling party's need to deliver on election campaign pledges, demographic concerns, an emphasis on effective human resources utilization, as well as a desire to meet ILO and OECD standards. Further, the fact that Korea by mid-2000 appeared to have entered a period of sustainable economic recovery fueled by consumer credit and domestic demand also made it possible to refocus on material benefits for women workers. In response to complaints by women's groups about the difficulties women face in (re)joining the paid labor force, the ruling MDP included extended paid maternity and childcare leave in its 2000 congressional election platform. But why were state actors willing to support what could only be a highly contentious issue, especially given legislative gridlock and the fact that *chaebŏl* reform and economic restructuring were only partially complete?

Most immediately, the ruling party was responding to declining popularity rates and the need to reaffirm its reputation as being responsive to civic demands and broader welfare goals. Similarly, MOGE was under pressure to quickly demonstrate achievements after its 2001 establishment. Broader state goals were also at stake. This included a growing concern that the absence of state support to help women balance childcare and labor force responsibilities had contributed to Korea's plummeting birthrate:

> How long do women have to suffer disadvantages due to pregnancy, childbirth and child care? Why isn't the cost of the child-care and maternity leave shared with society? Discrimination against women has led them to choose late marriages or no marriage at all, and diminished women's desire to have a child . . . This seriously low birthrate could hamper national competitiveness or national security from the very foundation. (Legislator Yi Mi-gyeong, quoted in Yang, 2002: 77)

A second concern was human resource maximization and, in particular, the importance of women's full participation in an increasingly knowledge-based society. As MoL Equal Employment Policy Bureau Chief Shin Myung noted:

> Only 55 percent of women work versus 95 percent of men. From the state's perspective it's a waste . . . We don't just approach unequal employment from a human rights paradigm but focus on how to upgrade women's abilities, develop training programs, and resolve maternity and sexual harassment issues. (2002 interview)

International competitiveness was a final motivating factor, particularly after Korea joined the OECD:

> If we want companies to become outstanding internationally, we need women. I call these laws "male protection laws" for effect and ask men "How can you earn enough by yourself to cover living costs? . . . In Western countries they average $30,000 but Korea averages just $10,000." It's also important for companies' image. (Shin, 2002 interview)

In this regard, meeting the ILO yardstick of 90 days' maternity leave served as an important incentive for the state and an internationally accepted standard against which business groups found it difficult to lobby aggressively. As the Special Congressional Committee on Women's Affairs ((S)CCWA) concluded:

> By comparing Korean policies and statutes with internationally recommended standards and trends . . . we came to the conclusion that

> maternity protection needs to be strengthened and the costs . . . shared by
> society. (1999, quoted in Yang, 2002: 79)

Women's Conjunctural Coalitions

The ability to form alliances among women across ideological lines, and from within and outside the state, as well as solidarity efforts with mixed-sex progressive movement organizations, represents a core strength of the Korean women's movement. In the case of employment issues, women activists have forged coalitions with intra- and inter-movement groups, femocrats and party sympathizers, depending on the specific political juncture and relative strength of their conservative opponents.

Because the origins of the first EEA bill (1987) were state-driven, direct pressure by a broad-based coalition of civic groups was unnecessary. By contrast, the first EEA reform campaign, which was launched immediately after the original law came into effect in 1988, was spearheaded by a coalition involving the newly formed KWAU in tandem with legal experts and scholars. This alliance marked a

> watershed in gender politics in Korea . . . [Whereas] there had not been
> any formal channel to represent women's interests, the progressive
> Women's Movement's strong involvement in the EEA revision campaign
> made gender-specific issues visible in Korean society and played a signifi-
> cant role in establishing KWAU's status as a representative of women's
> organizations. (Kim K. H., 1998: 160)

Organizations such as Korean WomenLink and the Korean Women's Political Research Center held public forums to criticize the shortcomings of the EEA, and in 1989 the KWAU established the "Special Committee for the EEA Revision" to coordinate their lobbying strategy. The Korean National Council of Women (KNCW) was excluded because of considerable ideological differences and their support for the original 1987 Act (Kim K. H., 1998).

The second reform initiated in 1993 reflected the growing maturity of the movement, especially progressive women's organizations' increasing engagement with both the state and the KNCW. The main campaign initiators were the KWAU (representing 24 member groups) and the National Labor Union Coalition as well as the Hyundai Labor Coalition and the Office Workers Union, both of which shared a high percentage of female members. In keeping with warming relations between conservative and progressive women's groups, the KNCW also lent support despite lingering misgivings about the progressive wing's strategies vis-à-vis business groups.[4] On the state side, the MoL's comparatively progressive Women's Bureau endorsed at least some of the campaign's demands, while the KWDI provided background research and policy proposals (e.g., Kim E., 1995).

Notwithstanding this multisectoral display of solidarity, and considerable public awareness stemming from the high-profile "appearance requirement" lawsuit brought against major companies by women's organizations in 1994, the coalition's efficacy was constrained by employers' concerted lobbying efforts and a lack of National Assembly support. Relatively few movement allies had entered formal politics at the time, and the newly established SCCWA had yet to develop an active lobbying stance (Park S., 2000 interview). As former Korean Confederation of Trade Unions women's bureau vice-head Lee Hye-Soon noted: "[In 1995] the Government wasn't very proactive—now they are certainly more progressive and sympathetic. Only women's groups worked really hard at that point" (2002 interview).

The third reform of 1999 drew on a similar array of civic groups but included more industry-specific unions and professional educators' associations, together with greater support from like-minded legislators and government officials (SCCWA, 1998). In contrast to the disappointing outcome of the 1995 EEA campaign, which had dampened activists' enthusiasm for legislative reforms (Chong, 2002 interview), the presence of more supportive congressional allies and especially the 1996 appointment of long-term women's advocate Lee MiKyong to the Committee on Labor and Environment, encouraged the movement to launch a new campaign focusing on sexual harassment and structural forms of gender discrimination.

The sexual harassment issue attracted widespread support from scholars, legal experts, and educators. Moreover, although employers' groups downplayed the women's movement's demands in media interviews, there was a general recognition that addressing sexual harassment was demanded by the times, and in light of shifting public sentiment, vocal opposition would only harm business groups' reputation (Lee H. S., 2000 interview). Meanwhile, a broad coalition of feminist scholars, women's groups, the KWDI, and the PCWA, was involved in advocating indirect discrimination provisions. The MoL was somewhat reluctant to endorse the revision (Shin M., 2002 interview), but passage was secured via targeted lobbying by a broad cross-section of women in both civil society and state agencies, and ironically facilitated by limited awareness on the part of most legislators.

Finally, efforts to secure extended paid maternity and childcare leave in 2001—a formidable task in a polity with a noticeably underdeveloped welfare state—marked a pinnacle in Korean women's organizational solidarity (e.g., Chong, 2002 interview). Although the Women's Association United for Reformation of the Labor Laws alliance did not call on the same degree of assistance from scholars and legal experts, the women's bureaus of the two national labor umbrella organizations, the new Korea Women's Trade Union and the MoL's Equal Employment Promotion Bureau were markedly more proactive than in past reform efforts (e.g., Shin M., 2002 interview). The coalition was further strengthened by the newly established MOGE, which prioritized the revisions as its principle policy goal in 2001, and the lobbying efforts of recently appointed gender experts in the ruling and major opposition parties. As MDP gender expert Kim Young-Hee pointed out, efforts to secure the requisite budget to expand maternity leave from 60 to 90 days was only possible because there was a broad coalition in favor:

> I had to convince MPs that this money was very necessary . . . I argued that if we didn't reform we were going to lose women voters and so it got through. I also worked with women MPs—most were newly elected and very eager to enact new laws . . . Male politicians' assistance was important too. For example, I couldn't get the budget through with the help of women members alone as there were too few in decision-making positions. (2000 interview)

Multidimensional Strategies

The history of the equal employment legislation reforms is an exemplary case of the power of a multipronged feminist strategy that flexibly combines grassroots mobilization and education, media campaigns, lobbying of political society, action research, and litigation, as well as internal efforts within political parties and state agencies. Although early reform strategies were not especially innovative, reflecting the embryonic state of the women's movement in the late 1980s/early 1990s, the 1992 campaign built on five years of organizational experience and involved a wider range of lobbying strategies. In addition to public hearings, demonstrations, street theater, and nationwide signature campaigns (KWAU, 1998), women's groups mobilized around two high-profile lawsuits in conjunction with scholars and lawyers. In the first case, a solidarity committee supported a teaching assistant whose contract had been terminated after she had rejected the sexual overtures of her Seoul

National University (SNU) professor employer. Although the plaintiff initially won damages, the defendant subsequently retaliated with a defamation suit. To the consternation of the women's community, the defamation case was decided in the professor's favor on the grounds that sexual harassment should be defined according to the standards of "reasonable women" rather than from a feminist perspective, which the ruling equated with a combative perspective on gender relations (Kim K. H., 1998). In response, activists picketed the courthouse, petitioned the judge, and subsequently publicized the case in the 1995 Beijing Women's Conference. Seeking to counter tradition-bound interpretations of appropriate gendered behavior, feminists insisted that the law be revised to include a definition of sexual harassment that included any form of unwelcome sexual conduct that created a hostile working environment, whether physical, verbal, or visual. Such reforms, however, would not be accepted for another four years.

The second lawsuit involved the appearance requirements that employers stipulated for female recruits. In an effort to eradicate corporate requirements that women employees be "attractive" and of a specific height and weight, Korean WomenLink and the KWAU launched a lawsuit against 44 major companies. The case attracted support from teachers and professors and served to raise public awareness, particularly after Harvard law students testified as expert witnesses. As feminist activist and scholar Cho Soon-Kyung explained:

> For the courts the presence of the Harvard law students was quite intimidating—"how will they look in front of foreigners?" . . . We really need international networking . . . To say it wouldn't happen in other countries is often used to embarrass people here. (2002 interview)

After the Prosecutor's Office indicted only 8 of the 44 companies, citing that appearance requirements were "a problem of competition among women rather than gender discrimination," women lobbyists drew on the U.S. Continental Airlines case that has ruled that weight requirements were gender discriminatory to call for further EEA revisions (Kim K. H., 1998; Chong, 2002 interview). These demands fell on more sympathetic ears in the legislature and a clause was inserted that prohibited discrimination based on appearance in hiring practices, as well as in bonus and promotion decisions.

In 1999, key tactics included research by academics and the KWDI, public discussion forums, efforts by femocrats in the MoL and PCWA, as well as the now established pattern of joint lobbying by the KWAU,

KNCW, and labor organizations. As early as 1996, the civic solidarity committee for the third EEA reform presented a bill to Congress calling for prevention efforts as well as the criminalization of sexual harassment and indirect discrimination. Whereas MoL officials and mainstream politicians had opposed the inclusion of these concepts in 1995 on the grounds that the public was insufficiently aware of their significance,[5] continued education efforts by women's organizations and scholars, combined with the much-publicized Supreme Court's favorable ruling on the SNU sexual harassment case in 1998, reduced the salience of public ignorance in the political equation. Femocrats were also aware of the government's need for international legitimacy and actively supported the revisions in advance of the 2000 Beijing Plus Five review, which would be an important litmus test of their efficacy in front of international peers (PCWA, 1999).

Because of the general success of the third reform initiative, the strategy adopted in the case of the 2001 maternity and childcare leave revisions was largely unchanged. Femocrats in the MOGE and MoL were firmly behind the proposed changes, as were the MDP and GNP party gender experts and their respective women's bureaus (Park S., 2000; Kim K., 2000 interviews). Accumulated policy expertise, meant that women's and labor groups required fewer consultations with outside experts, and attention shifted to media and public education campaigns (Kim J., 2000 interview).

Discursive Sensitivity

The ideological resources deployed by women's organizations in their efforts to secure equal employment rights have combined international human rights–oriented discourses with language specific to the Korean context. Although their discursive tactics have almost always been in opposition to those of business lobbies, women's linguistic frameworks have increasingly converged with state discourses over time.

In the case of the first two revisions, activists focused on "women's lifelong right to work," "equal employment rights," and the "right to healthy motherhood" (Kim K. H., 1998: 170–71). Arguing that ending differential treatment between men and women is a prerequisite for gender equality, feminists broke with the *minjung* framework of the 1970s–1980s, which had prioritized class struggle and national reunification over gender issues. Without questioning the need for protective legislation per se, women's organizations demanded the exemption of women from dangerous and overtime or night work, as well as paid maternity and monthly menstruation leave (e.g., Chang, 1994).

This line of reasoning was in stark contrast to the economic rationalism and formal equality arguments advanced by employers' groups. Economic conservatives sought to capitalize on the call for "equal employment" to cut special rights for women regarding paid vacation and overtime, arguing that protective legislation discouraged hiring female employees. In particular, business leaders were anxious to end the monthly one-day paid menstruation leave and even offered greater maternity leave allowances in exchange (Lee H. S., 2000 interview). Despite the appeal of the offer to some feminist groups, women workers' organizations refused to compromise, as menstruation leave was seen as a means to improve chronically underpaid factory workers' incomes. Sociologist Cho Sook-Kyung, however, suggests that:

> Menstruation leave tends to augment differences between men and women when strategically we should be trying to reduce differences. While the reason for keeping it is to compensate women workers' low wages, I believe it would be better to focus directly on low income itself . . . For example, it would be better to convert menstruation leave to a paid healthcare leave. (2002 interview)

The campaigns leading up to the third EEA reform and the establishment of the GDPRA in 1999 moved away from issues specific to the Korean context and drew more heavily on the international language of women's human rights. Activists maintained that women should be free from all forms of unwanted sexual attention in the workplace as it "disrespects women's humanity" and "causes shame and humiliation" (Hahn, 2001b). Moreover, they argued that it was the responsibility of the government and employers to educate employees about sexual harassment and to prevent not only violations of "women's right to work but also the general human rights of women" (KWAU, 1998: 20). Similarly, in the case of indirect discrimination, women's organizations sought to pressurize the government using the rationale that: "It is an international trend to define discrimination not only as direct discrimination, but also as any act that results in discrimination against workers of a specific sex" (10). They also called for the ratification of all ILO conventions relevant to enhancing women's rights.

Whereas the PCWA generally concurred with this human rights framework, the MoL, while endorsing tougher measures against sexual harassment and gender discrimination, relied on references to improving the "utilization of human resources," the promotion of a "harmonious workplace," and hence "greater productivity" (Park S., 2002 interview).

Specifically, MoL officials contended that it was important to eradicate sexual harassment because the higher stress levels suffered by female employees as a result, diminished their work ethic and lowered productivity levels. "We tell employers: 'If the working atmosphere is poor because of sexual harassment, production will fall—surely this isn't your preference? Don't let the atmosphere turn negative' " (Shin M., 2002 interview). Employers' groups acceded to this logic, but nevertheless called into question the public perception that sexual harassment only occurs in the workplace. As FKI official Choi Song-Soo noted:

> Sexual harassment can have a huge impact on a company's image but we think the public needs to have appropriate awareness that it occurs in all realms of society, not just business . . . . (2002 interview)

Finally, the discursive tools employed to promote the 2001 maternity and childcare leave extension were less academic than those used in the 1999 EEA reform, perhaps explaining why they resonated so effectively with the public. The rhetoric of both activists and state officials converged on the need for society to take collective responsibility for facilitating citizens' ability to balance paid and family work (Paik J., 2002). Equal Employment Promotion Bureau head Shin Myung framed the core issues as follows:

> There are three main burdens facing women: housework, economic activities and childcare. How we divide these burdens is a joint societal issue because society is spurring women's participation in the labor market. We originate from mothers and reproducing a healthy workforce is important work . . . Just as societies have a collective economic responsibility, it is exactly the same with reproductive responsibilities. (2002 interview)

Women activists also emphasized that despite formal provisions in the EEA stipulating women's right to take maternity leave, sociocultural attitudes and a lack of childcare infrastructure effectively rendered maternity and childcare responsibilities an individual rather than societal concern. New legislative provisions were necessary, they argued, to expand childcare leave options to male as well as female workers, and to provide guaranteed income during the leave period. This was deemed especially important in light of the government's inadequate provision of affordable childcare facilities, which forces families with two wage earners to choose between expensive private care services and care by other family members (Yang, 2002).

Business endorsed the "social responsibility" rhetoric, but argued forcefully that the costs should be shared throughout society rather than "shouldered by business alone" (Choi, 2002, interview). Employers' associations maintained that although it was acceptable to extend maternity leave from 60 to 90 days to meet ILO standards,[6] the proposal to cover the additional costs from the national employment insurance fund would send business costs spiraling.[7] They alleged that the proposal would not only have

> a negative effect on the nation's economic recovery, [but] that pursuing maternity protection law patterned after advanced countries, without considering corporations' paying capacity, would result in . . . the decrease of job opportunities and women's unemployment proportionately . . . . (Paik J., 2002: 61)

Yet because the state's implementation costs would be limited, and support for the revisions would enable the government to curry favor with women's and labor groups while simultaneously fulfilling a major electoral pledge, complaints from employers' associations constituted a moderate political risk. Moreover, legislators and business leaders were realistic as to the limits of the new policy's implementation potential: passing a progressive law in the context of Korea's weak legal enforcement culture does not neatly translate into effective enforcement. For example, director of the Legal Investigation Bureau at the KEF Yi Seung-gil admitted:

> As for child-care leave, since the extension of the period of leave or the scope of application is likely to be ignored in a practical sense, it is recommended that the current regulations remain unchanged . . . In the present situation, in which even the sixty days of maternity leave is not fully granted in many cases, it is necessary to reexamine if it will be practically beneficial for women to extend maternity leave to twelve weeks. (SCWA, 1999: 27–30 quoted in Yang, 2002: 80–81)[8]

Similarly, during related National Assembly debates, lawmakers conceded, "while most of the large companies in which many women work tend to follow maternity leave regulations, it is difficult to expect small companies to follow them. There seems to be a discrepancy between law and reality" (ibid, 81).

Impact

Although the multistaged campaign to secure greater legal workplace rights for women has criminalized overt forms of gender discrimination and given recognition to the structural impediments women face in competing with their male counterparts, enforcement of these rights remains tentative at best. Full implementation will not only entail considerable costs for employers' and governmental coffers, but will also necessitate that female employees overcome their historic reluctance to expose violations within a competitive, male-dominated workplace (Lee H. S., 2002 interview). Limited public debate and hence weakened spillover effects in the case of earlier revisions (i.e., until 1995) has led to a tendency for employers to accept the passage of legislation in a bid to avoid negative press, while subsequently neglecting or postponing implementation. Newly legislated rights are not yet firmly embedded in the social contract, but are rather fragile and subject to reversals in the context of broader national dictates. For instance, not only did the 1998 collapse in employment hit women harder than men (-7.3 percent versus -5.1 percent), but most women who lost their jobs were not counted as unemployed, but simply disappeared from the labor force (NSO, 2002).

> During the crisis we witnessed that the Equal Employment Opportunity Law is an insufficient means for protecting women. Restructuring targeted women first but our society called upon women to "cheer up their depressed husbands" . . . Moreover, in the Government's unemployment policy, women are still marginalized . . . their job training programs are narrower than men's both in terms of training period length and the range of occupations for which training is offered. (Yoon, 1998 interview)

The exposure of the less-than-robust nature of women's employment rights has nevertheless had an important silver lining, encouraging new campaigns to introduce more comprehensive legal protections. The PCWA's increasingly proactive stance against gender discrimination; considerable media attention directed at the social implications of the "IMF crisis," and rising concerns that the new regulations would directly impinge on men's daily office interactions (Hahn, 2001b) all contributed to widespread debates around the introduction of legal measures to define and address sexual harassment. This in turn led to significant attitudinal shifts. Indeed, according to survey research carried out by the KWDI one year after the law's passage (1999), general levels of awareness had increased significantly as shown in table 6.1.

Table 6.1   Change in workplace sexual harassment levels since the 1999 EEA reform

	Total %	*Male %*	*Female %*
Improved	54.3	56.8	52.2
No change	43.3	40.7	45.6
Deteriorated	2.4	2.4	2.3

Source: Hahn, 2001b: 3.

However, although survey respondents were generally aware that sexual harassment is now a crime, detailed knowledge of what this entails or available avenues of redress was less widespread. Some 31.3 percent were aware that sexual harassment is a prosecutable offence and 18.2 percent had some knowledge of the legal regulations, but fewer than 10 percent were familiar with definitions of harassment or could list realistic preventive actions. Further, whereas 82 percent of respondents disagreed with the notion that "[t]he best settlement method for sexual harassment is ignoring it," 66.3 percent still agreed that "[w]hen confronting the issues of sexual harassment, victims' relationship with colleagues will be debased" (Hahn, 2001b: 9–10). This suggests greater education is needed to remove the social stigma associated with speaking out against unwanted sexual attention. Moreover, whereas those who had attended educational sessions reported that the frequency of sexual harassment incidences had decreased following the implementation of the law and the majority (88 percent) said they now viewed sexual harassment in a more serious light (6), only one-third of the organizations covered by the law had held compulsory education sessions. Measures taken to sanction offenders in the workplace also seem to undermine the issue's gravity. A 2004 survey found that the largest percentage (37 percent) were only lightly cautioned, while 26 percent had to apologize publicly, 16 percent were required to undergo education about sexual harassment, and just 5 percent suffered a pay cut (*Seoul Yŏnhap Shinmun*, July 2, 2004).

Debates concerning maternity leave revisions sparked considerable interest among ordinary citizens, especially as the original version proposed leave for obstetric appointments, miscarriages and stillbirths. Yet, reflecting the informal power of employers, a year after the law's passage the number of women who had taken advantage of the new regulation was significantly lower than MoL predictions, whereas in the case of male spouses, the rate of those opting for paternity leave was miniscule (Shin M., 2002 interview). Nevertheless, by the first half of

2004 the number of female employees taking leave before and after childbirth had risen to 19,198, and the number taking "temporary retirement" for childcare purposes had risen to 4,290. The number of male employees taking advantage of this system remained very low, however—just 78 nationwide (MoL, 2004).

Civic and Family Rights

1960	Korean Civil Code, Books IV ("relatives") and V ("succession")
1962 revision	Married sons able to start own family registry
1977 revision	More egalitarian inheritances for daughters/wives; Amnesty on marriage ban for same surname-same clan couples (tongsŏng dongbon)
1989 revision	Power of family heads diluted
2000 revision	Same surname/ same clan marriage ban eliminated
2005 revision	Family Headship System (*hojuje*) eliminated

The Family Law has been the most emotionally charged gender-related law debated over the past 15 years. The *hojuje* (family headship system) constituted both the ideological and substantive backbone of male supremacy within the family. Patrilineal succession served male interests by providing for the transfer of economic, political, and ritual power from father to son (Nam, 1995). Although a broad coalition of women's organizations, building on efforts of early feminists from the preceding three decades, secured important revisions of the family law in 1989, subsequent efforts to eliminate the patriarchal family headship system were not successful until 2005.

The 1989 Revision

Women leaders initially hoped that postindependence American influence and spillover effects from the International Declaration of Human Rights would encourage the introduction of more egalitarian legal rights for women (Moon, 1994). However, nation-building efforts instead focused on reviving Korean traditions that had been brutally suppressed under Japanese colonialism. Conservative family values and practices were enshrined in the 1960 Civil Code, including the patrilineal family headship system and bans on intra-clan marriages. Ostensibly in the name of tradition, many of the more conservative practices embodied in the 1960 Code were, ironically, remnants of Japanese imperial rule (MOGE, 2003; Moon, 1994). Beginning in the mid-1950s, women's groups led by Korea's first female lawyer, Lee Taeyoung, embarked on a frustratingly slow struggle to revise the *hojuje*, with family law reform dominating the agenda of middle-class women's groups until the transition to democracy in 1987. Like their 1990s successors, this early generation of feminists tried to leverage evolving political openings so as to eliminate the legal basis for women's domestic subordination.

The first of these historical moments was the "transitional chaos" of the early 1960s, when the Park junta agreed to limited reforms under the guise of streamlining family law in accordance with the logic of modernization and the nuclear family (Yang, 1998). A second juncture conducive to reform emerged in the mid-1970s with the creation of the Pan-Women's Group for Women' Reform (PFLR), which included 62 member organizations. In an effort to capitalize on the international community's focus on population concerns, the PFLR argued that "the succession of patrilineage in the family [and resulting son preference] had been the major obstacle to family planning" and by extension to national development (Kim, 1983).

On the domestic front, feminists took advantage of the record 12 women legislators in the *Yushin* National Assembly to push for the 1977 revision, including more egalitarian inheritance provisions for wives and daughters. Meaningful change was precluded, however, by vociferous opposition from politically influential Confucian scholars, clan associations, and some segments of the bar (Nam, 1994). In the context of the 1977 revision, an amendment proposed by the PFLR attracted a mass outcry from Confucian leaders, including a petition of 340,000 signatures and a strongly worded opposition paper presented to Congress by *Yudo Hoe* (Confucian Way Association). Cultural conservatives claimed that abolishing the *hojuje* would "destroy tradition" and "respect for one's ancestors," sacrificing the "spiritual happiness of the Korean family" in favor of "Western material happiness" (Yang, 1998: 146). Similarly, efforts in 1984 by the reconfigured Women's Union for Revision of Family Law were thwarted by lobbying from Confucian loyalists, especially in rural constituencies (153). Finally, in 1986, over 5,000 traditionalists (largely unhindered by the police, who were usually deployed to control demonstrations) turned out to protest against yet another reform bill (Moon, 2003).

In short, despite strong coordination and diverse public awareness and lobbying strategies, the balance of civil society power before the transition enabled women to secure only piecemeal revisions. Reform initiatives were blocked by Confucian groups, who deployed arguments of "tradition" and "national uniqueness" to hold sway over the legislative process. Substantive progress, however, was realized in the immediate

Table 6.2 Main contents of the 1989 Family Law Revision

Definition of relatives (*ch'injok*) revised to ensure equality on paternal and maternal sides
Mandatory legal relationship between mother and stepchildren abolished
Permissible reasons for divorce expanded
Married couples' residence determined by mutual consent, rather than husband alone
Living expenses deemed a couple's joint responsibility
Right to child custody for either parent following divorce introduced
Marital property divided upon divorce according to post-marriage contribution
Adoption system revised; adoption for the sake of continuing the family lineage eliminated
Property inheritance rules revised to ensure equality among family members

Source: Nam, 1995: 117; Yang, 1998: 165–66.

post-transition period, with the passage of a comparatively extensive set of reforms in December 1989. This shift reflected the sudden importance of electoral politics and the heightened public resonance of new discourses on human rights, democracy, and modernity. Armed with a petition of almost 500,000 signatures and systematic lobbying of legislators, women's organizations succeeded in shifting the terms of the debate from that of "legislative revision" versus "family preservation" to "full" versus "partial revision" (Moon, 2003) (see table 6.2).

Not surprisingly, the most divisive issue was the question of whether to fully eradicate the *hojuje*. Although supporters argued that democratic ideals demanded a complete overhaul, conservatives were able to water down proposed reforms by focusing on the practical difficulties entailed in reorganizing the family registry system (Kim R., 1994). For feminist activists it was a bittersweet victory; as noted by Lee Tae-Young:

> Today, thirty-seven years of tenacious women's struggles have abolished the long and high barriers of human discrimination! [Nonetheless] I regret very much that the heritage of the marriage ban of *tongsŏng donghon* and the system of the family head remain. (Lee 1992: 379, quoted in Yang, 1998: 166)[9]

A Protracted Path to Success

Although activists had failed to eradicate the two tenets of family law most central to Korea's Confucian family system, that is, the headship system and the same-surname/same-clan marriage ban, women's organizations did not launch new reform initiatives until the mid-1990s. Having achieved significant improvements in women's rights within the family, the movement reoriented its focus to concentrate on the implementation of the 1987 law as well as other issue areas where women's rights were notably lacking (e.g., employment, protection from violence, maternity/childcare leave, etc.). Moreover, in keeping with Lukes's (1974) notion that power comprises both the ability to thwart policy developments and the capacity to keep issues off the political agenda, my interviews with activists suggest that the residual power of Confucian organizations was sufficient to preempt reform initiatives. Regardless of their objective organizational strength, subjective perceptions of Confucians' political influence was enough to discourage women's groups from instigating a new campaign (Han, 2000 interview).

By the late 1990s, the political opportunity structure had been sufficiently transformed for women's groups to make another push at abolishing the *hojuje*. Government reservations on clauses relating to family equality in the Convention on the Elimination of All Forms of Discrimination Against Women (Article 16) had become increasingly embarrassing, especially after the U.N. Commission on Human Rights concluded in its 1998 and 1999 reports that the family headship system "reflects and strengthens patriarchal society" (Kim S. U., 2005). Moreover, existing family law was incompatible with the government-advocated goal to "endeavor to establish family relations based on democratic and equal values and norms" (PCWA, 2000a: 25) as embodied in the Women's Basic Development Act (WBDA) and the Gender Discrimination and Relief Act (GDPRA).

These favorable dynamics provided momentum for a wider reform initiative launched in 1999 led by the Citizens for Abolition of the Family Headship System (CAHF), representing Korean WomenLink, the Korea Legal Aid Center for Family Relations, the KWAU, and KNCW. Realizing that successful reform would depend on broad public support, CAHF initiated a diverse nationwide public awareness campaign, including press conferences, public opinion surveys, signature petitions, a popular Internet campaign, and a survey on "Legislators' Awareness of the Family Headship System Issue" (Yoon, 2003 interview). They also prepared lawsuits to challenge the constitutionality of the *hojuje* in 2000 and 2002. Significantly, whereas early family law reform efforts had been viewed as a "women's issue," this new phase attracted support from a broad cross-section of progressive civic groups under the banner of "societal democratization" (Moon, 2003). A total of 113 organizations worked with the coalition, including religious-based groups, major environmental associations (e.g., Green Korea), political reform groups, such as the PSPD and CCEJ, disabled people's rights advocacy groups (e.g., Korea Differently Abled Federation), and Lawyers for a Democratic Society.

Table 6.3 MOGE's family policy objectives

Current system	MOGE's vision
Patriarchal family relationship	Democratic family relationship
Standardization of nuclear family	Support various family types
Women-oriented family and labor protection	Society's partial responsibility toward family protection

Source: Data from the Ministry of Gender Equality (www.moge.go.kr).

On the institutional front, WPMs became increasingly supportive of reform efforts. In 1999, the PCWA endorsed the CAHF's mission, incorporating family inequality into its annual Women's Week activities and cosponsoring a nationwide public opinion survey with the Korea Legal Aid Center for Family Relations (PCWA, 2000b). Similarly, MOGE actively promoted the "realization of horizontal family relationships" via policies such as paid maternity and childcare leave and the introduction of old-age pensions for divorced couples based on the number of years of marriage. Under the second (2003) minister of Gender Equality Ji Eun-Hee, MOGE began to actively lobby for the eradication of the *hojuje* (see table 6.3).[10]

Even so, this broad conjunctural coalition of NGOs, femocrats and feminist legislators, combined with more vocal presidential support, met with considerable opposition. Although Confucian organizations have become increasingly marginalized post-transition, the concerted attack on the *hojuje* by women's groups and their allies ironically fostered a limited revival of Confucianists, who forged their own issue-specific counter-organizations. Having suffered a significant blow when the same-surname/same-clan marriage ban was ruled unconstitutional in 1998, the Korean Clans United and the Sunggyunggwan Confucian Association formed the "All Citizens United for Protecting the Traditional Family System" to protect the *hojuje*, the last remaining pillar of the Confucian family structure. In tandem with the Korean Association for the Elderly and the Association of Bereft Families of Persons of National Independence Merit (Moon, 2003: 133), the alliance of conservatives maintained that "abolishing the *hojuje* will completely destroy the Korean family system," and, harking back to *saek kkal nonjaeng* (Cold War rhetoric), accused the government of "trying to follow North Korea's civil law" (Baek, 2003). While this movement was narrower and less well coordinated than that of its pro-reform counterpart, the continued resonance of Confucian values among the older

generation and particularly rural populations, allowed it to enjoy disproportionate influence over policy debates.

> [T]he legacy of the Confucian normative system of meaning, although not
> highly discernible in urban, capitalist, and industrialized Korea, underlies
> this landscape of (historically Western) modernity as an integral part of
> Korea's hybrid modernity. Political, economic, and cultural elites in con-
> temporary Korea, still dominated by the older generation, share the inter-
> pretive system with those conservative social groups. (Moon, 2003: 133)

Despite this slow progress, family law reform emerged as one of the
top three demands of progressive civic groups in the 2002 election season, and presidential candidates felt compelled to state their positions in
their electoral platforms. With public support for reforming the *hojuje*
rising to nearly two-third, partly thanks to the success of the CAHF
campaign (Nam, 2004), only GNP candidate Lee Hoi-Chang was
unwilling to endorse fully eradicating the headship system (WSPE,
2002). Following the election, incoming President Noh appointed progressive women ministers Ji Uhn-Hee and Kang Kum-Sil to head
MOGE and the Ministry of Justice, respectively, both of whom were
publicly committed to eliminating the headship system. With the political space available to progressives widened, women's groups found a
more encouraging political environment for the realization of democratization and equalization of the family.

In order to facilitate this process, the Noh administration established
a coordinating committee involving five key ministries and the KWDI,
and organized public hearings between May and September 2003 to plan
an alternative family registry system (Yoon, 2004 interview). Similarly,
in response to demands from civil society, the National Human Rights
Commission released an investigatory report in March 2003 that concluded that the *hojuje* violated the Constitution and women's human
rights (NHRCK, 2003). These efforts culminated in a cabinet decision
to support revising the Civil Code in May 2004.

In parallel to these executive initiatives, family law reform was also
being debated in the National Assembly. A bill proposing to abolish the
family headship system was introduced in May 2003 by Representative
Lee MiKyoung and signed by 52 legislators from the two major parties
at that time, the GNP and MDP (Lee M., 2003 interview). However,
despite cross-party platform election pledges, the Legislation and
Justice Committee remained intransigent during the 16th Congress. The
Committee not only stalled for time until November, waiting for the

outcome of the government's inter-ministerial investigations about the feasibility of reforms, but ultimately rejected the bill, sympathizing with conservative arguments that the Civil Code was "not discriminatory as females could assume the position of family head" and that moreover, "ending the headship system would lead to the dissolution of the family unit" (Nam, 2004).

As discussed in chapter 5, however, the dramatic political reconfiguration that characterized the 17th Congress resulted in surprisingly favorable political openings. Although the GNP had opposed abolishing the *hojuje* in the run-up to the April 2004 elections, their relatively poor performance led to a change in party leadership. After Park Gyun-Hee, who personally supported the reforms, took over the helm of the GNP, all four major parties were united in their support for changing from a family to an individual registry system. The unprecedented number of women legislators in the 17th Congress was a second key factor. Whereas women's 5 percent representation in the 16th Congress had limited their involvement in congressional committees and hindered the ability of feminist legislators to push for reforms, the presence of 39 women in the 17th Congress, a large majority of whom were united in support of family law reform, had a powerful symbolic impact. Despite concerns about women's divergent levels of commitment to gender equality, all but two women who were present voted for the bill (Korean National Assembly, 2005).[11]

Even so, conservative opposition proved tenacious. Several conservative GNP legislators in the Legislation and Judiciary Committee opposed the bill out of concern for the impact on their rural constituents and the "longevity" of Korean families (Seo, 2005). Ultimately, it was only after the Constitutional Court ruled in February 2005 that the Family Law violated the principles of human dignity and equality enshrined in the Constitution that the reform bill finally passed at the standing committee level (11–15) on March 1, 2005, and the National Assembly plenary on March 2.[12] Perhaps fittingly, the *hojuje* was finally abolished on the last day of the special National Assembly session with 161 supporters, 58 opponents, and 16 abstentions. The law stipulated that the new system would take effect in January 2008 and would entail three key reforms: a personal registry system to replace the family registry tradition, a redefinition of the family to allow for multiple family types, and the ability for children to take their mother's surname following agreement with both parents. Progressive civil society welcomed the decision as a victory for democratization, human rights, and equality after 48 years of struggle. The KWAU highlighted the end of "patriarchal family order" whereas CCEJ representative Kim Sang-Kyum praised the change in terms of equal citizenship rights as it "acknowledges both patriarchal and matriarchal lineages" in defining Korean nationality, and a *Sarangbang* Group for Human Rights official hoped it would pave the way for a broader recognition of minority and gender rights (Lee K., 2005).

Impact

Although the 1989 Family Law reform did not eradicate the family headship system, the revisions nevertheless had a far-reaching impact on gender relations within the family (Cho M., 1998). Until the democratic transition, married women had no right to exert control over the family income or choose the family residence, had very limited access to marital property in the case of divorce and no child custody or even visitation rights,[13] were unable to transfer their nationality to their children, and were discriminated against with regard to the grounds on which they could file for divorce (e.g., Lee K., 1995). Moreover, women were only able to succeed as family heads if there were no male descendants and they were not entitled to an equal share of the parental inheritance.[14] In other words, the family headship system was a device "to perpetuate men's succession of lineage and their control over family resources" in the fullest sense (Nam, 1995: 116).

However, these inequalities have been significantly diluted post-transition. As public and judicial attitudes gradually evolved in response to legal revisions and changing demographic realities (especially escalating divorce rates), women have gained a more equal footing in family and marriage matters (Kim R., 2000). Although daughters will continue to be transferred to their husband's family registry upon marriage and retain the lowest status in terms of family head succession until 2008, this discrimination has fewer consequences partly because over time the role of the family head has become more symbolic/ceremonial with fewer economic ramifications. Moreover, while still impeded by traditional notions of male and female contributions to the household, recognition of female rights in divorce and child custody decisions has improved markedly.

Unlike the old law, which was firmly stacked in favor of the husband, the 1989 reform offered six grounds for divorce within a fault-based system, including infidelity, extreme cruelty, and if a spouse was missing for three years (Lee K., 1995). Within months of the new law entering into effect in January 1991, a number of petitions had been filed for equitable property distribution, resulting in "tradition-breaking deci-sions" whereby the courts acknowledged women's right to a share of household property for the first time (Lee K., 1995: 496). The rapid escalation of divorce over the past decade, and the fact that the majority of these are initiated by the wife, indicates that women are utilizing these legal rights (Kim C., 2000).

Nevertheless, traditional notions of women's contribution to the household economy embedded within the law, as well as the mindsets of the judiciary, limited the reform potential of these regulations. Specifically, the definition of marital property included only assets jointly acquired after marriage in both partners' names, and excluded " 'special property' acquired prior to marriage and that acquired during the marriage in the husband's or wife's name" (497). Yet, given that the husband has tended to be recorded as the official representative in business/property transactions, women's legal access has been considerably less robust than it appeared on the surface (Nam, 1995).

Widespread social biases as to women's worth continue to contribute to unfavorable property division decisions, with women often granted "token awards." In fact, equitable division was so rare in the early 1990s that the 1993 Korean Yearbook included as a noteworthy item a decision in which a woman received 50 percent of a divorce settlement (498). In an effort to set fair standards for property division, and in conjunction with the United Nations Development Programme, MOGE initiated a project in 2001 to assess the financial value that women's domestic labor contributed to the national economy. The study concluded that women's unpaid labor was equivalent to between 0.92 and 1.65 million won per month and contributed 13–23 percent of total GDP per annum (Kim T., 2001: 9). The results, however, have yet to be incorporated by the courts in any systematic manner.

A third major change that women have enjoyed post-transition is the right to participate in child custody decisions. Divorce for Korean women no longer necessarily entails abandoning their rights to maintain contact with their children. Whereas the courts gave prima facie prefer-ence to fathers until the 1980s, by the early 1990s the emphasis was already shifting toward greater consideration of child welfare and a mother's role therein. Even so, the law's recognition of joint custodial rights remains premised on "the property status of the father and mother, and any other circumstances thereof," which disadvantages women in the context of unequal distribution of marital resources (Lee K., 1995: 501). For example, a 1994 Seoul High Court case granted the father custody rights because of his superior financial circumstances, even after recognizing that the divorce was the husband's fault (ibid.). In sum, to ensure that women are granted de facto as well as de jure familial rights, both the laws themselves and the judicial personnel that implement them need to recognize more explicitly the particular sociocultural contexts in which family life is played out.

The Right to Bodily Integrity

1994, revised 1997, 1998	*Act on Punishment of Sexual Crimes and Protection of Victims*
1997	*Special Law on Punishment of the Crime of Domestic Violence*
1997, revised 1998	*Law on Protection of Domestic Violence Victims*
2000	*Act for the Protection of Adolescents from Sexual Crimes*

Efforts to legislate women's right to bodily integrity, especially freedom from sexual and family violence, constituted a major focal point of the Korean women's movement throughout the 1990s. Employing creative research, awareness-raising, and service provision initiatives, women's organizations worked with a broad coalition of progressive civic groups to successfully lobby the state for change. The accomplishments achieved to date, especially in terms of legislative initiatives, have been impressive.

Deeply entrenched conservative Confucian family and sexual mores meant that concerted efforts were needed to change public attitudes and secure women the legal right to protection from violence as well as access to channels of redress. Specialized progressive women's organizations that emerged post-transition played a pivotal role, as did the return of scholars from study abroad who introduced human rights discourses (Shin, 2000 interview). With the weakening of the *minjung* paradigm in the late 1980s, women activists were afforded the discursive space in which to problematize the patriarchal underpinnings of Korean society and focus specifically on issues of gender and sexuality.

> In the 1980s there was gender blindness among women workers and activists—partially because violence by men was viewed as violence by the regime rather than by men per se . . . However, once the women's movement developed some distance from the lens of the democracy movement, they could really focus on sexual violence and problems associated with the male-dominated sexual culture. (Min, 1999: 37)

An important catalyst was a spate of sensational cases of violence in the late 1980s/early 1990s. These individual tragedies underscored the social costs of gendered violence and called into question conservative chastity-focused sexual ethics that implicitly condoned sexual and domestic violence. The case of a labor activist, Kwon In-Sook, who was sexually tortured by the police while under arrest for participation in pro-democracy demonstrations in 1996 was the first case to attract media attention around sexual violence. Although Kwon downplayed the gender-specific nature of her abuse, the incident nevertheless served as an important rallying point for women's groups on violence issues (Kim K. H., 1998). Civic (and media) attention was further heightened in the early 1990s in response to three high-profile cases involving violence committed against male aggressors by their victims (Cho Y., 2000 interview). In the first case, the boyfriend (Kim Jin-Kwan) of an incest victim (Kim Bo-Eun) killed the latter's stepfather (a high-ranking official) to avenge her repeated rape as a child. A solidarity committee was set up to appeal their case, resulting in a surprisingly lenient sentence for the perpetrator. The second case involved a woman (Kim Bu-Nam), who killed her childhood rapist, a neighbor, whom she blamed for her subsequent inability to sustain a regular heterosexual relationship. Lastly, a solidarity committee was formed to protest against the imprisonment of Byun Wol-sun for having bitten off part of her rapist's tongue. These cases became inscribed in public memory. Even congressional records of legislative debates relating to gendered violence include a detailed chronology of related incidents (SCCWA, 1998: 84, 130), suggesting that public emotion provided an important impetus for the passage of these new laws.

Similar *causes célèbres* served to erode social taboos against airing experiences of domestic violence. In one poignant case, a woman (Lee Hee-Soon) wrongly confessed to murdering her violent husband in order to protect her mother, who had actually killed the son-in-law as she could no longer bear to see her daughter's suffering (Cho Y., 2000 interview). As KWDI researcher Byun (2000) noted:

> When battered women murdered their violent husbands, it raised awareness concerning the seriousness of male violence in the home. Society, including the government, had [previously] disregarded the seriousness of the issue, so that [battering husbands] had never had to face the law. (5)

Aside from these individual dramas, concern with violence against women was strengthened by a series of research campaigns that sought to lift the traditional veil of silence surrounding the issue. In the academy, the completion of three women's studies postgraduate theses on rape at Ewha Womans University in 1989 had a considerable impact on activists' and scholarly awareness (e.g., Chang, 2000 interview). The studies contributed to a heightened interest in research on sexuality and gendered forms of violence (e.g., Shim, 1998), as well as the establishment of the Korean Sexual Violence Relief Center (KSVRC) by women's studies graduates who adopted a high-profile lobbying approach (Lee M., 2000 interview). International data, including from Interpol, suggested that Korea had the third-highest rate of sexual offenses in the world, with approximately 13 percent of women having experienced actual or attempted rape, and helped confirm that the *causes célèbres* mentioned above were not exceptional but rather part of a disturbing social trend. Surveys conducted in the early 1990s showed a similarly high level of gendered family violence (Shim, 1998).

Against this backdrop, the Korean Women's Hotline and the newly formed KSVRC, in conjunction with the KWAU, embarked on a lobbying campaign to explicitly criminalize violence against women and recognize the state's responsibility toward protecting women's human rights. Prompted by an absurd case in which the police were called by a male abuser to intervene in the alleged "kidnapping" of a domestic violence victim by the Korean Women's Hotline (Shin, 2000 interview), the KWAU adopted violence against women as a priority in 1992.

Sexual Violence Legislation

Whether to push for legislation explicitly focused on sexual violence or for legislation with a broader conceptualization of gendered violence provoked heated debates among movement groups (Lee M., 2000 interviews; Shin, 2000). Although these discussions led to intra-movement tensions, their key contribution was the framing of violence from a women's human rights perspective. Once a decision was reached to campaign to secure a law specifically against sexual violence, activists sought to broaden the mere physical definition of rape found in the Criminal Code to include the notion that rape is a "crime against a person's decision-making power about sexual matters" (Shin, 2000 interview) and may include both heterosexual and same-sex rapes. Although this feminist content was unfortunately diluted in the 1994 bill, these debates marked the beginning of a discursive shift away from a focus on chastity toward an understanding of violence against women as a human rights issue (Kim K. H., 2002).

Cognizant of a dearth of strong supporters in the legislature—at that time there were just six women National Assembly representatives— activists initiated a range of media and networking strategies to raise public awareness. Examples included a well-publicized self-defense whistle campaign, press conferences, poster campaigns, the celebration of International Violence against Women Day, and solidarity movements with *causes célèbres*. Perhaps most significantly, whereas Latin American women drew on regional networks to pressurize national legislators (e.g., Johnson, 2002), Korean women's groups organized domestically to coordinate a mass signature campaign, attracting support from a broad cross-section of progressive movement organizations such as the PSPD or CCEJ and Buddhist organizations. As KSVRC activist Lee Mikyung stressed:

> I realized at that point that women's groups and other groups have to do this together . . . they supported this campaign based on the attitude that sexual violence is not just a women's problem but a societal problem . . . We demonstrated that it affects men too, whether it be a potential threat to their daughter or wife. Therefore, we can't but see it as an issue that affects us all. (2002 interview)

In contrast to the EEA and family law reform processes, advocates of the sexual violence law did not have to contend with an institutionalized opponent. Although the Act on the Punishment of Sexual Crimes and Protection of Victims Thereof met with resistance from judicial professionals and legislators with a legal background (Lee H. and Jong, 1999),[15] there was no vocal, coordinated civil-society–based opposition. Moreover, the women's movement capitalized on the political opening presented by the 1992 presidential elections to ensure that all parties agreed to the passage of a sexual violence law.

> The [presidential] election was in 1992 and so that was why the sexual violence law passed so quickly [in 1993]—all parties agreed in order to get our votes. They all looked at our proposed bill and despite being pretty conservative, they accepted our demands—only revising it a bit . . . This change of attitude was so sudden—the KSVRC was only a small organization (of course we didn't do it alone) but it only took a year. (Lee M., 2002 interview)

Subsequent struggles were to be over the breadth of the law (e.g., whether to include marital rape and stalking) as well as enforcement issues.

Family Violence Legislation

The divergent dynamic of the family violence law reform process (1994–97) reflects the shifting contours of democratic consolidation and institutional reform more broadly, as well as the impact of increasingly proactive WPMs and the process of movement learning. Domestic violence was initially more difficult to address owing to its cultural invisibility and potential threat to the "sanctity of the family." However, by 1997 shifts in societal attitudes and greater receptivity to international norms resulted in significantly less congressional resistance (Shin, 2000 interview). An increase in sympathetic legislators as well as the expansion of cross-movement support (including a congressional petition of 85,000 signatures) further assisted the process.[16] In fact, activists estimate that around "95 percent" of their demands were incorporated into the final bill (Shin, 2000 interview).

On the basis of the women's movement's accumulated experiences at the legislative level, in the courts and in the field, activists had become more adept at framing their demands in culturally resonant ways and also more attuned to ordinary women's needs. In order to alleviate public fears that the introduction of such a bill might decrease family stability, activists couched their demands in terms of preserving "family health" rather than women's individual rights. This approach included efforts at family rehabilitation rather than a focus on supporting women to divorce an abusive spouse. Although such a shift in emphasis appeared more conservative than feminists' earlier demands, experiences in the field subsequent to the 1994 passage of the Act on the Punishment of Sexual Crimes suggested that for women to benefit, any legal tool would have to provide them with protection (such as police intervention and restraining orders) from abusive partners, and wherever possible avoiding the husband's incurring a criminal record. Many women would be unwilling to contact the authorities if it would entail a social stigma and/or loss of family income. As a result of this sensitive packaging, and despite still considerable public resistance, including protests on the part of some Confucian groups who raised the specter of family disintegration, the political space available to naysayers contracted, with the law passing largely intact.

Impact

To assess the impact of these laws on sexual and family violence, it is imperative to recall the baseline from which feminist efforts were initiated. Despite rapid economic development, notions about gender and sexuality in Korean society were by all accounts highly conservative at the point of transition. A women's body was not viewed as her own, but rather was largely controlled by her male relatives. Family violence was viewed as a typical pattern of domestic life, as reflected in the well-known proverb: "Women and dry fish should be beaten every three days." Moreover, it was deemed a personal issue with no room for outside intervention (Cho Y., 2000 interview).

In the case of sexual violence, the importance of lineage in a patriarchal society (played out in symbolic terms through regular ancestor worship ceremonies) meant that chastity was highly valued and rape was considered a crime because it threatened "the purity of blood" (Shim, 1998: 112). Rape was perceived as an offense against the husband or father rather than the victim herself. Indeed, this mindset was so deepseated that even until the late 1980s, the rape of a wife by an unknown intruder was chillingly dubbed a *kajŏng p'agoe pŏmjoe* (family-destroying crime) because of the husband's inability to live with his wife following her loss of chastity. Given this social climate, burglars adopted a deliberate strategy of raping the women of the house in front of other family members to avoid having the crime reported (117).

Today, by contrast, although the chastity ethos and notions of the "father-as-king" still linger (Chang, 2005; Lee M., 2002 interview), survey findings suggest that attitudes have changed dramatically. Following the passage of the family and sexual violence prevention laws and the considerable public awareness efforts surrounding their passage, gendered violence is increasingly seen as a violation of the right to sexual self-determination or of women's human rights more generally (Shim, 2002: 151).[17]

Similarly, activists' efforts to call attention to the gravity and pervasiveness of family violence were initially rejected as "anti-men" (Cho Y., 2000 interview), KWDI researcher and violence against women specialist Byun Whasoon emphasizes that:

> In raising the issue of wife battering, [the family violence prevention movement] challenged the ideology of the family and exposed the poison of a patriarchal family structure held together only because wives endured violence from their husbands. (2000: 10)

A 2001 survey, for instance, showed that 90 percent of the population was aware of the family violence law, and, by extension, that such behavior is a criminal offense (Kim Y. et al., 2000). Similarly, the limited statistical data available indicates an increased willingness among women to break taboos surrounding family and sexual violence, and to seek help from the justice system.[18] For example, in the six months after the Family Violence Law went into effect in July 1998, some 3,685 cases resulted in arrest, and 8,928 arrests were made over the following nine months (Kim E. et al., 2000). By 2003 that figure had risen to 16,408.[19]

Changing public attitudes about sexual violence have similarly been identified as an important accomplishment of the 1990s legal reform initiatives. Although comparable public opinion survey data is not available, scholars and activists point to significant attitudinal shifts. For instance, Shim points out: "With the increase in self-reflexivity and women's consciousness-raising, sexual violence is now defined as a human rights violation, a violation of women's right to sexual self-determination" (1998: 126). KSVRC director, Lee MiKyong, concurs. At the time of the 1997 revision of the sexual violence law, attitudes were "much better" and in the 2000s they are "much better again, social awareness is much higher" (2002 interview). Moreover, in accordance with Article 3 of the law, which mandated that central and local governments implement sex education programs, the Ministry of Education has significantly increased the number of classroom hours spent and sought to revamp the curriculum to provide more practical education (Nam, 2001 interview).

There is still considerable room for improvement, however, in terms of both the content of the law and its implementation. The symbolic significance of the 1994 passage of the sexual violence law notwithstanding, the limited scope of the final version was bitterly disappointing to the KWAU drafting committee. As the former committee chair noted:

> Our fundamental feminist perspectives were washed out when the legislation passed because the Government just took existing penal code provisions and combined them, which was terrible. That's why we have tried to revise it and still need to make changes. (Shin, 2000 interview)

Most seriously, until 1997 the law only allowed for the reporting of abuse by the victim in the name of "protecting the victim's honor." It failed to provide for stronger penalties against sexual abuse of minors and disabled people (added 1997/98), and omitted (as it still does) specific references to marital rape or stalking.[20]

More problematic than the content of the law (which was revised in 1997 and 1998 to address some original weaknesses[21]), has been its implementation by the courts. The KSVRC estimates that just 6 percent of total victims report their abuse to the authorities, which they contrast with an estimate of 35 percent in Wisconsin, United States[22] (Lee M., 2002 interview).

> The implementation record is very discouraging. The 6 percent reporting
> rate means that some 94 percent of women don't come forward, and sug-
> gests that they don't want to use the law . . . Even among the women we
> provide phone counseling to, the majority don't want to press charges . . .
> We need a broader cultural movement before the law will really prove
> effective. (Ibid.)

Although sentences for sexual violence have been lengthened as judicial personnel better understand the gravity of sexual offenses, the overall rate of sentencing remains low. The imprisonment rate among offenders was 58 percent in 1994 and only slightly better at 61 percent in 1997 (Kim E. et al., 2000). Moreover, the available statistical data regarding sexual violence crimes is woefully inadequate, suggesting an insufficient allocation of resources by the Ministry of Justice and the National Police Agency for monitoring progress. Figures on reoffenders, sentencing rates, and types of sentences passed are either not available or suffer from a lack of consistency among agencies or across time (e.g., Lee K., 2002 interview). Furthermore, typically absolute numbers rather than percentages are provided (e.g., National Police Agency, 2001; NSO, 2002), hindering researchers' ability to detect rates of change over time.

Insufficient gender awareness among judicial personnel also remains problematic. Women's groups have successfully lobbied police stations and the Judicial Research and Training Institute to introduce gender-sensitivity education programs, but these initiatives remain on a relatively small scale (Shim, 2000 interview). Moreover, a recent pilot survey by the KSVRC found that among 480 lawyers and police cadet respondents, a majority still blamed the victim, attributing sexual assault and rape to women's clothing and appearance (Lee M., 2002 interview). Perhaps most disturbingly, a backlash of countersuits by male defendants for loss of reputation has effectively transformed the victim into the perpetrator, further discouraging women from coming forward to the authorities (Cho L., 2002).

State funding for counseling and protective facilities has risen, however, in accordance with the sexual and family violence laws and the WBDA, and most recently as a result of the MOGE's specific mandate to address gender violence. An extensive network of counseling and legal aid services, information centers, and shelters for women and children have been established. Television, print media, and Internet campaigns have been organized by the PCWA/MOGE to raise awareness of the problems of abuse and advertise available services, including the government-funded national hotline for violence against women: "1366"

(Lee K., 2002 interview).[23] This said, the service delivery infrastructure remains far from optimal. Problems include the limited number of women utilizing these services, a relatively short maximum period of stay, inadequate resources to cover legal aid and medical expenses, and, as yet, weak linkages between governmental and voluntary networks on the one hand, and prosecutors' offices, medical services, and legal aid on the other (Park Y. and Hwang, 2000).

The significant increase in violence-related facilities also disguises issues of quality. In keeping with the general observation that state actors are often motivated by legitimacy concerns rather than a genuine commitment to advancing women's status, the government advertises the number of facilities established and victims served as a sign of success (MOGE, 2001; Kim S., 2000 interview), rather than the quality of service offered. As a result, although women's groups campaigned for the sexual and family violence prevention bills on the basis of a human rights framework, activists now find themselves competing for funding to operate shelters and counseling services alongside religious or private for-profit organizations whose operating principles may be antithetical to feminist concerns of empowerment and individual rights (Park Y., 2000 interview). For example, religiously informed shelters for women victims tend to prioritize reconciliation and family preservation (e.g., Lee M., 2002 interview).

Conclusion

Securing far-ranging formal rights and gender-policy reforms represents the most important benefit of democratization for Korean women. The discrimination that women faced 15 years ago is now scarcely imaginable for younger generations:

> In socialist countries the most serious problem is that the women's revolution was just given to them—that's why they don't view women's issues as their own. We know how hard we worked but the younger generation don't understand how they came to enjoy their freedoms—it's just a given. They don't know about the long historical struggle and what women's organizations have been doing to improve society. Our experience is enormous but how can we make people remember? How can we make people implement [these achievements] and sustain and advance them? . . . This is our challenge now. (Cho Y., 2000 interview)

The comprehensive civil, human, political, and socioeconomic rights that Korean women enjoy today have been achieved through women's movement organizations' savvy lobbying, coalition-building, and awareness-raising tactics, in tandem with the increasingly proactive approach of WPMs. As clearly played out in the successive EEA and violence against women reforms, women have successfully maximized shifting political opportunity structures and forged conjunctural coalitions, combined diverse pressure tactics both within and outside the state, and adopted discursive strategies that carry international legitimacy but remain culturally resonant. Importantly, as the content of gender-related legislation has become more detailed through the refinement process of multiple revisions, political leaders and those charged with enforcement have found it increasingly difficult to be equivocal about their implementation efforts.

To account for the micrologics of legislative reform in specific rights–based areas, however, the configuration of the conservative opposition emerges as the most significant explanatory factor. In the case of the sexual and family violence laws, although the proposed changes were antithetical to deeply ingrained sexual and family mores, without a specific organization to counter its demands, the women's movement was able to secure relatively rapid legislative passage. Resistance from conservative legislators, especially those with legal backgrounds, served to weaken the content of the first law on sexual violence, but was insufficient to present a credible threat to the introduction of a specific legal tool to protect women's right to sexual bodily integrity.

Similarly, although well-coordinated business associations have diluted efforts to improve women's workplace rights and necessitated that the movement compromise on legislative content and engage in multiple reform struggles, this resistance has moderated over time, thanks largely to the growing importance of international norms on the Korean political stage. Moreover, whereas employers' groups enjoyed increasing freedom from the state from the late 1980s/early 1990s, the relative strength of labor post-transition as well as the state's ambivalent role and mixed policies vis-à-vis business served to limit economic conservatives' capacity to contest policy, affording women and labor groups some political openings.

By contrast, although the Confucian opposition weakened significantly over the course of democratization, neither the state nor international pressure was able to effectively counter their appeals to tradition, stability, and preservation of Eastern values in the case of the Family Law until 2005. Despite a gradual liberalization of social values and a rapid shift in demographics, Confucian organizations were able to maintain the most cherished pillar of the Confucian family model, the family headship system, because of their sustained influence in rural constituencies, and the compatibility of their values with the senior political establishment and an older generation of the public. Moreover, whereas the government in the 1970s/1980s was able to counter Confucian demands (albeit to a limited degree) on the basis of appeals to population control—preoccupations with lineage and son preference were seen as impediments to smaller families—there were no equivalent national imperatives post-transition.

Finally, each of these reform cases highlights the persistent disparity between women's de jure and de facto rights. Notwithstanding the women's movement's growing professionalism, WPMs increasing political clout, and the introduction of gender-sensitivity training programs for various state actors, implementation of gender policy is far from optimal. Key hindrances include resource constraints, a dearth of longitudinal statistical data and reliable policy indicators, and the limited monitoring capacity of women's organizations and femocrats. Additionally, shifts in conservative grassroots attitudes often lag behind the introduction of new legislation. To realize the transformative potential of Korea's impressive legislative reform record, gender-equality advocates will need to reorient their strategies to concentrate on implementation and monitoring. In this regard, civic assessments of the legislature's annual review of the bureaucracy, the preparation of shadow reports for major international bodies (especially the UN, ILO, and OECD assessment committees), gender-budget analyses at the central and local government levels, as well as strengthening gender-sensitivity training in all branches of government will be of central importance.

CHAPTER 7

State Transformation: Creating a Women's Policy Machinery Infrastructure

Before ordinary officials could not understand what we [femocrats] were talking about, but after the establishment of the Women's Focal Points they try to listen and even ask for ideas . . . I think women's leadership in the focal points is essential . . . Men cannot understand women's issues as women do because they do not lead women's lives. We have our own experiences and that kind of experience makes a person persuasive.

Nam, 2001 interview

Feminist theories of the state are broadly divided between those that conceptualize the state as "a masculine construct, which offers nothing to women," and those who view the state "as the primary terrain in the struggles for the advancement of women" (Craske, 1999: 84). Whereas some studies emphasize the resources the state can offer women (e.g., women's refuges, health clinics, childcare facilities) (e.g., O'Connor et al., 1999), others focus on the constraints women face within male-dominated bureaucracies, especially their concentration within caring-related ministries and in lower professional ranks (e.g., Staudt, 1997; Stevenson, 2000). As Rai suggests, "the state is a fractured and ambiguous terrain for women, needing complex negotiation and bargaining by those working within its boundaries, as well as those on the outside" (2003: 19). Straddling this complexity, WPMs have been identified as an important tool for advancing women's status and challenging gender hierarchies:

In contrast to the structures of the welfare state or of the liberal state, which have excluded feminist policy from political debate, those [WPM

> structures] established with a mandate to focus directly on women's status have the capacity to turn leaders' attention, in some cases for the first time, to laws and regulations that can change the status of women in relation to men. (Stetson and Mazur, 1995: 272)

Moreover, in successful cases, WPMs have utilized public resources to help nongovernmental feminist and women's advocacy organizations advance their own policy agendas (e.g., Honculada and Ofreneo, 2003).

However, research from both advanced Western polities and nascent democracies has also shown that efforts to "take feminism into the state" (Alvarez, 1990) are largely dependent on the broader political milieu in which they are located (Sawer, 1998; Waylen, 1996a). In the Latin American context, for example, analysts have emphasized the contradictions and tensions inherent in pursuing a feminist reform agenda within patriarchal, status quo–oriented states. Since the democratic transition, women's state agencies have followed a checkered path, emerging strong but often waning in influence (Alvarez, 1990; Waylen 1996a). For example, in Brazil, although Women's Councils established at state and federal levels enjoyed considerable visibility and policy influence in the immediate post-military period, in subsequent administrations feminists were often replaced by partisan appointments, budgets were cut, and the efficacy of the Councils undermined by a lack of elite political will (Caldiera, 1998: 77). Similarly, although the establishment of the Chilean *Servicio Nacional de la Mujer* (SERNAM) in 1990 was heralded as an important indicator of women's potential political clout post-transition, the agency's efficacy has been hampered by rivalries between Socialist and Christian Democrat staff (Valenzuela, 1996 interview), the Catholic Church's overt opposition to women's reproductive rights, and by right-wing parties who view SERNAM as "a threat to the family" (Waylen, 1996b).

Critics also contend that a distancing of middle-class femocrats from grassroots organizations and their concerns are "evidence of the co-optation of some of the more acceptable demands of the women's movements" (Waylen, 1996a: 130). Given a drain of activist leaders into the state, there has been a tendency for WPMs to replace "women's movements as the interlocutor in the public discourse on women" (131), thereby muting feminist criticism. This uneasy relationship has been exacerbated by a shift in international funding away from civil society toward state agencies, which has compelled women's organizations into clientelistic relations in order to secure access to funds (Vargas, 2002). In short, the Latin American experience confirms the thesis that "the maintenance of a feminist agenda and the achievement of policy transformation depends less on the existence of an institutional space per se than on the relationship of this space to autonomous feminist organizations" (Caldiera, 1998: 77).

My research, however, suggests that the particular political opportunity structures of Korean democratization have contributed to a distinct WPM trajectory. Although initially institutionally weak and limited to a welfarist approach, there has been a gradual strengthening in institutional positioning, presidential commitment to gender equality reforms, and civil society–state linkages since the establishment of the first WPMs in the 1980s. Today a full-fledged Ministry of Gender Equality (MOGE) is embedded in a broader infrastructure that includes women's policy offices in key ministries and all provincial/metropolitan governments,[1] a government-affiliated think-tank for women's issues, the Korean Women's Development Institute (KWDI), and a Congressional Standing Committee on Women's Affairs (CCWA). Moreover, this WPM infrastructure is guided by a five-year Basic Women's Development Plan and related annual implementation plans, which encompass strategic gender issues such as sexual harassment and gender-discrimination prevention in the workplace, the incorporation of women's domestic labor contribution into national budget analyses, the promotion of a social consensus whereby childcare is seen as the shared responsibility of men and women, and reform of the *hojuje* (MOGE, 2002a; Kim J., 2002 interview).

The central question addressed by this chapter is therefore: to what extent have Korean advocates of gender equality been able to bring about policy reforms and secure access to policymaking channels by exploiting fissures within the state and prising open new "women's spaces" (Alvarez, 1990: 268)? For analytical purposes, I divide the discussion into three parts:

- The KWDI (1983–current).
- Ministerial women's bureaus, which have evolved from (i) the Ministry of Political Affairs No.2 (1988–97), a mini-ministry, to (ii) the Presidential Commission on Women's Affairs (1998–2000), a hub–spokes organization directly under the President's Office to (iii) the MOGE (2001–present), a bona fide ministry.
- The CCWA (1994–present), which was upgraded in 2002 from a special to a standing committee in the National Assembly.

Employing a modified version of Stetson and Mazur's (1995) state feminism framework, I address two broad questions: what factors led to the establishment of WPMs and what accounts for their relative success or failure? To explain WPM emergence, I consider the constellation of actors involved (proponents and opponents), executive political will, and international influences. To assess whether or not a WPM is successful, I analyze the machinery's institutional positioning and resourcing, the quality of monitoring and accountability mechanisms, its policy capacity and achievements, as well as civil society linkages—especially the level of access afforded to autonomous women's organizations to influence the policy agenda and decisionmaking processes.

The Korean Women's Development Institute

The KWDI was established in 1983 as part of a larger public relations blitz by the Chun Doo Whan regime to overcome its legitimacy crisis. Chun was seeking to improve his standing with civil society groups, including women's organizations, as well as responding to international pressure in the context of the UN Decade for Women (1975–85) and the 1979 UN Convention on the Elimination of All Forms of Discrimination Against Women (CEDAW), which called for the creation of national machineries to address discrimination against women (Kim Y. C., 2000 interview).

In response to women leaders' demands for the establishment of a research institute on women's status to inform gender-related governmental policy frameworks, the government established the KWDI with a mandate combining policy-oriented research with leadership training, vocational guidance programs, and support for women's civic organizations (Kwon, 1995).[2] Initially operating under the auspices of the MHSW because of its welfare-oriented research focus, the KWDI's institutional positioning has evolved over the last two decades. It was rehoused in the MPA2 in 1988 and then spun off as a semi-autonomous think-tank under the Social Sciences and Humanities Council in the Prime Minister's Office during a wider restructuring of government-affiliated research institutes in 1998 (Park Y., 2000 interview).

Prior to 1987, despite generous funding and staff resources and the intentions of some reform-oriented staff,[3] the KWDI's role was largely symbolic. As women's studies professor Chang Pilwha notes, its role in reshaping gender relations was constrained by a research agenda rooted within a "Women in Development" (WID) paradigm:

> If you look at the KWDI constitution, there is no word for "equality"—only "development," "utilization of human resources." They have a tradition of

making remarks on gender without commitment to a change in power relations. (2000 interview)

Moreover, the KWDI lacked the requisite power to ensure that its policy proposals were accepted, much less implemented, and on occasion it faced censorship (Kim Y. C., 2000 interview). For instance, the government banned the release of a draft equal employment bill in 1986 because of pressure from business groups, who were wary of the far-reaching implications of a similar bill in Japan a year earlier (Kim K. H., 1998).

Post-transition, however, the KWDI has played an important role in shaping the gender-related policy agenda, providing the bulk of the research used to draft a wide range of women-related legislation. As KWDI researcher Park Young-Ran emphasizes:

> The gender policy we have today is in no small way what the KWDI has worked to create since 1983. It has provided most of the research on women's economic situation, welfare, health, etc. that provides the basis for amendments or new laws. So we really have been influential . . . Even though [non-governmental organizations—NGOs] have been very skeptical and critical—they sort of acknowledge the contributions of the KWDI. (2000 interview)

Admittedly, the Institute's research agenda has traditionally been restricted to the politically feasible and by its need to sustain long-term relationships with other bureaucratic agencies. However, it has been particularly influential in promoting political quotas for women, drafting the Ten Women's Policy Priorities under the *Segyehwa Hoeŭi* (Globalization Committee) and the Women's Basic Development Plans, conducting national surveys on shifts in gender attitudes, particularly vis-à-vis gender-related legal reforms (e.g., Chang, 2001 interview), as well as evaluating women related policies, including childcare facilities, single mother provisions, violence shelters, and elderly women's care (Park Y., 2000 interview).

Success, though, has not been linear as the KWDI was "downsized" following the 1997–98 economic crisis in the name of "smaller government." Although affording greater autonomy, the 1998 reforms narrowed the KWDI's mandate and increased reliance on project-based funding.[4] Moreover, its status as the chief source of governmental women-related policy research was eroded as the government broadened its research pool to include university-based and independent women's studies research units that had proliferated in the 1990s (Lee H., 2003 interview).

Nonetheless, an increasingly cooperative relationship with women's organizations has emerged since the late 1990s. Not only have a number of feminist researchers entered the KWDI, but informal linkages between research staff and women's NGOs have also improved, including participation in seminars and conferences and representation by KWDI researchers on NGO committees in an advisory capacity (e.g., Kim K., 2000 interview). Formal institutionalized mechanisms for women's organizations to influence the Institute's agenda and provide feedback on its research findings are still lacking. Despite the KWDI's enviable resources (especially relative to chronically underfunded NGOs), scholars and NGOs have rarely lobbied for greater access or influence over its research endeavors. In this sense, the KWDI constitutes a potentially important, but underutilized, institutional space.

Ministry of Political Affairs No. 2

Taking advantage of the relative flexibility of the transition period, civic leaders and women legislators urged presidential hopefuls in the 1987 elections to increase women's presence in decisionmaking roles and establish a permanent women's bureau within the executive. As former legislator Kim Yung-Chung noted:

> Our ideal was to create another vice-prime minister of social issues that would deal specifically with women's affairs or if not, a special adviser on women's affairs to the President. The third option was this ministry [MPA2]. (2000 interview)

Given the minimal costs entailed, all candidates accepted the proposal so as to avoid politicizing the issue. In particular, victor Noh Tae-Woo was motivated by a desire to distance himself from his own military past, and appease a rapidly expanding civil society (Kang H., 2000 interview).

However, because Noh's commitment to advancing gender equality was more tokenistic than substantive, the obliquely named MPA2 (originally established to oversee the 1988 Seoul Olympics) did not enjoy full ministerial status and suffered from low funding and staffing (only 20 staff in 1988 and 56 by 1995) (Kwon, 1995). Designed as a coordinating body, it was not empowered to propose legislation, and although located within the Prime Minister's Office, MPA2 ministers often lacked the political commitment or leverage to call upon the prime minister to exert pressure on other ministries (Park W., 2000 interview). As women's studies professor Chang Pilwha explained:

> As the name suggests, the MPA2 was concerned with political affairs, rather than committed to women's advancement. It was concerned with how to utilize women as voters to further government interests and promote national development. (2000 interview)

Its relative longevity aside, the MPA2's efficacy was limited. Its institutional positioning and resources were low, its mandate prior to the passage of the 1995 Women's Basic Development Act (WBDA) unclear, and political commitment to addressing gender inequalities on the part of the first two post-transitional presidents and ministerial officials was half-hearted. Under Noh, the Ministry carried out long-overdue domestic reforms: increasing women's participation in all levels of government, improving access to vocational training and educational facilities, and overseeing legislative reforms concerning equal employment, childcare, and family law. Critics, however, charged that the Ministry's approach centered around public relations efforts to advertise a "series of firsts," including the first ministry dealing with women's affairs, and the opening of once exclusively male educational institutions (e.g., military, tax office) to women. (Kim Y. C., 2000 interview).

Under the Kim Young-sam administration, the MPA2 took on a more active role, in keeping with the broader expansion of reform opportunities. As part of Kim's globalization campaign and in response to the 1995 Beijing Platform for Action's call to mainstream gender issues, the *Segyehwa Hoeŭi* (Globalization Committee) drew up a set of ten gender-related policy priorities, ranging from better childcare provision to incentive programs for private- and public-sector employers to recruit more women. Capitalizing on this new space, MPA2 officials drafted the 1995 WBDA, which legislated the government's commitment to time-bound affirmative action policies for women and required both central and local governments to develop annual women's policy plans and implementation reports (Kwon Y., 2003 interview). MPA2 officials were also able to augment the financial resources at their discretion through the creation of the Women's Development Fund, which the WBDA earmarked for programs to advance women's social, economic, or political status (PCWA, 1999). Although initially under-appreciated by activists and not implemented until 1998, the WBDA marked an important turning point in the trajectory of Korean WPMs and has subsequently emerged as an important tool for activists and femocrats to push for policy changes within a gender-mainstreaming paradigm (Yoon, 2002 interview).

In general, however, the MPA2's record as an initiator of policy proved rather weak. Policy programs were usually developed in reaction to pressure from women's NGOs rather than generated internally (Lee K., 2002 interview). Part of the problem can be attributed to leadership: although several ministers—Kim Yung-Chung (1989–90), Kwon Young-Ja (1993–94) and Lee Yon-Sook (1997–98)—had feminist politics and enjoyed linkages with the women's movement, other appointees had only limited gender-related expertise or movement ties (Lee K., 2002 interview). This was in turn reflected in the MPA2's policy orientation, which was more concerned with national development and social order than with gender equity (Kim K. H., 2002).

Civil society–state linkages were also relatively weak as the formal channel of access, the Women's Policy Evaluation Committee (WPEC), held infrequent meetings and selected civilian participants largely on the basis of social prestige rather than linkages with women's advocacy organizations (Kang K., 2000 interview).[5] Moreover, as discussed in chapter 3, the women's movement only began to engage with the state in the mid-1990s, with femocrats first emerging in significant numbers under the Kim Dae-Jung administration and the MPA2's successor agency, the PCWA.

Presidential Commission on Women's Affairs

Although the inauguration of Kim Dae-Jung in 1998 constituted an important watershed for gender relations, activists were initially disappointed with Kim's compromise decision to dismantle the MPA2 and establish the PCWA. As former director of the PCWA's Gender Discrimination Prevention Office Chang Song-Ja notes: "We voted for President Kim because we believed he would establish a ministry. So when only a commission was set up, many women felt they were cheated" (2001 interview).

Nevertheless, the PCWA's organizational structure—which was more in line with the women's national machinery advocated in the 1995 Beijing Platform for Action—was met with cautious optimism. In recognition of the crosscutting nature of women's concerns, the PCWA provided for a hub–spokes coordinating mechanism, with a central body directly under the president and "Women's Focal Points" (WFPs) in six key ministries with women-related policy mandates (i.e., Education, Health and Welfare, Labor, Home and Government Affairs, Justice, and Agriculture and Forestry) (PCWA, 2000b). Even so, officials and NGOs continued to discuss possible methods to arm this machinery with greater authority. PCWA officials and especially its first chairwoman, Yoon Hoo-Jung, sought to take advantage of Kim Dae-Jung's rhetorical commitment to equalizing gender relations and his administration's awareness of women's organizations' dissatisfaction with the PCWA. As activist Shin Heisoo noted:

> When the DJ government came up with the PCWA, it was a sort of sacrifice within a government power struggle. The IMF crisis meant his administration had to downsize all government agencies, and because women were powerless, the MPA2 was modified into a commission, which in theory has more power but in reality could be a powerless umbrella. (2000 interview)

In particular, they campaigned to win presidential and ruling party support for a new law specifically addressing gender-discrimination prevention:

> If we were going to address women's issues, I realized we would have to address core societal structures and change conservative mainstream ideas. So as PCWA head I prioritized developing the Gender Discrimination Prevention and Relief Act. Our Constitution guarantees gender equality but in reality it has depended on interpretations [of male officials]. So we needed a more systematic way of defining gender discrimination and gender equality. (Yoon H., 2001 interview)

Constituting an important advance in the protection of women's human rights, the GDPRA (1999) afforded the PCWA a more concrete mandate and a specific sphere of jurisdiction, as well as equipping it with limited enforcement powers. Whereas WPMs could previously only encourage companies and public agencies to follow antidiscrimination regulations, the GDPRA legislated the establishment of a formal complaints procedure, the investigation of victims' cases by PCWA staff, and adjudication by the PCWA-affiliated Council of Commissioners (PCWA, 1999).

Significantly, the GDPRA was largely promoted from within the state, marking an important juncture in the maturity of Korean WPMs as proactive proponents of gender equality. In contrast to the passage of the WBDA which had encountered little opposition from political elites, PCWA officials' commitment to this reform initiative was tested by the need to struggle against considerable opposition from the Ministries of Justice and Labor and more conservative legislators. Mainstream bureaucrats questioned the need for a law that specifically addressed gender discrimination, arguing that the MoL already had its own gender-related complaints office, and furthermore that the then-pending Human Rights Law also incorporated gender discrimination. Similarly, the Ministry of Justice opposed assigning the PCWA with quasi-judicial status (Lee O., 2000 interview; Kwon Y., 2003 interview).

On the congressional front, the PCWA also received a cool reception when its draft bill was presented to the ruling party (Kwon Y., 2003 interview). Objections were raised to the proposed expansion of the PCWA's role as a coordinating body to an agency with investigatory powers over complaints from ordinary citizens. Detractors also asserted that public awareness of sexual harassment issues was insufficiently high to warrant the establishment of a special investigative body. Nevertheless, thanks to a combination of PCWA persistence, executive support, active lobbying by the (S)CCWA, and international demonstration effects (especially the Australian gender-discrimination prevention model), the Act eventually went into effect in July 1999.

Policy Capacity and Civic Access

Whereas activists had called for a strengthening of WPMs, the PCWA was perceived as a sideways step from its predecessor, the MPA2. Despite PCWA rhetoric concerning the importance of being "directly under the President's Office," its institutional status was technically lower than that of the MPA2, and it was still unable to independently propose legislation. Staff numbers were slightly lower (down from 57 to 51) in the Commission itself, though compensated for by six staff appointees in each of the WFPs. Similarly, budget resources increased only marginally in 1998 vis-à-vis that of the MPA2 because of belt-tightening during the "IMF period"; though in subsequent years funding increased exponentially (Chang S., 2001 interview).

The PCWA, however, was structurally innovative and provided women's organizations with considerably improved access to the policy process. The hub system facilitated coordination with women's policy units in specific ministries and provided the infrastructure for the government's gradual (but still incomplete) shift from a WID perspective to a gender-mainstreaming paradigm. It also enabled advocates of gender equality working within the state to influence a broader range of policy issues. For example, in the Ministry of Education, the WFP played an active role in reviewing the gender content of school textbooks, introduced a more comprehensive sex education program, and advocated hiring targets for women in schools and universities

(Nam, 2001 interview). In the Ministry of Agriculture and Forestry, the WFP oversaw the implementation of a labor-substitute program for pregnant agricultural workers (Park S., 2001 interview), while the Ministry of Health and Social Welfare WFP succeeded in introducing a "gender sensitive checklist" to which all ministerial policy decisions were subsequently subject (Soh, 2000 interview).

The WFP directors I interviewed universally bemoaned the marginal status of their offices within their respective ministries, but at the same time were cautiously optimistic that their offices could help change the attitudes of their male colleagues toward gender issues in general and their female colleagues in particular (e.g., Hwang, 2000 interview; Soh, 2000 interview; Park S., 2001 interview). As former head of the Ministry of Education WFP Nam Sung Hee explains:

> Before ordinary officials could not understand what we [femocrats] were talking about, but after the establishment of the Women's Focal Points, they try to listen to what we are saying and even ask for help . . . I think women's leadership in the Focal Points is essential . . . Men cannot understand women's issues as women do because they do not lead women's lives. We have our own experiences so that kind of experience makes a person persuasive. (2001 interview)

Similarly, given the particularly low representation of women in decisionmaking roles in the Ministry of Justice, two former WFP heads noted that the unit's establishment was in itself an achievement (e.g., Lee O., 2000 interview). Moreover, attention to gender concerns has gradually improved through overseas study tours for officials, the organization of seminars with international agencies such as the UN Commission on Human Rights, and strong lobbying efforts to secure more appointments of women within the Ministry (Cho H., 2000 interview).

The capacity of these offices was also enhanced by the recruitment of outside experts to head the WFPs. Hailing from academia, the NGO community, and the legal profession, these women brought new expertise and perspectives to their respective ministries by drawing on existing networks to assist in the development and implementation of new policies. Their appointments also contributed to a more positive view of women's state machineries among the movement community, encouraging more cooperative relations. For example, Korean Women's Hotline director Shin Heisoo noted that in the case of violence against women, activists discussed with the WFP heads in the Ministries of Justice and

Health and Social Welfare how to make the CEDAW optional protocol more applicable to the Korean situation, and worked with the Ministry of Education WFP director to set up gender-sensitivity education programs (2000 interview).

The innovative potential of the WPM system notwithstanding, femocrats, activists, and scholars all acknowledge that its practical policy influence was hampered by the relatively weak institutional status of WPMs within their respective ministries, a dearth of funding and staffing, and the PCWA's limited coordinating powers. In theory the hub–spokes system approximated what Stetson and Mazur (1995) describe as "centralized cross-sectoral approaches" or "administrative nerve centers for inter-ministerial policy correspondents [units]" (288), which they argue are most conducive to integrating gender issues into formerly gender-blind policy areas. In practice, however, the PCWA had insufficient clout to pressure ministers with gender-related portfolios to fully carry out their mandates. Moreover, as members of a young organization engaged in carving out its own territory (especially campaigning for the introduction of the GDPRA), PCWA officials often lacked the energy and resources to stay abreast of detailed developments in individual ministries. For example, Kang Ki-Won, the second of three PCWA Chairs, evaluated her experience quite negatively:

> I attended all cabinet meetings, but besides the 30 percent quota for women in ministerial committees, no special changes on women's issues were discussed . . . Although Cabinet members are the best of the Korean constituency in terms of gender sensitivity, they don't initiate women-related programs. They realize that now we're in an age where you can't discriminate against women in public, but they are not active. (2000 interview)

Linkages between the PCWA and the WFPs have therefore been more important in terms of personal networking and support than endorsing concrete policy initiatives. As Nam Sung-Hee, Ministry of Education WFP head, noted:

> We just exchange information, share our experiences and give advice. The basis of our relationship with the PCWA is private friendship, but in terms of public relations, it's limited. Outside the Ministry of Education it is very difficult to understand what is going on inside so I don't think the PCWA can play a big role in terms of policy direction. (2001 interview)

In addition to the PCWA's role as a coordinating body, the GDPRA provided it with "some teeth" to investigate and enforce antidiscrimination measures (Yoon H., 2000 interview). The number of cases handled was comparatively small,[6] but along with the revised EEA (1999), the GDPRA contributed to the integration of the concepts of *sŏng hŭiryŏng* (sexual harassment) and *sŏng chabyŏl* (gender discrimination) into the everyday lexicon of the Korean public (Han and Kim, 2001). In the name of fostering "genuine equality between men and women in the business world" and "contributing to national economic development" (PCWA, 2000b: 59), the 1999 Act on the Support of Women-Owned Enterprises was another important mainstreaming initiative. Its central aims were to develop programs to support women-owned start-ups and business incubators, as well as to prioritize products supplied by women-owned firms in government procurements (Kim J., 2002 interview).

Access to the policy process, both formal and informal, also improved under the PCWA. In contrast to the relatively inactive WPEC, the PCWA-affiliated Council of Commissioners (composed of the vice ministers of the six WFP ministries, seven civilian experts, and the PCWA Chair) met monthly. Charged with debating and approving the PCWA's policy initiatives, the Council had the right to revise or veto policy proposals, thereby ensuring greater civilian input into policy development (Chang, 2000 interview). In addition, under the GDPRA, the Council was charged with adjudicating cases of gender discrimination that could not be resolved through the PCWA's Gender Discrimination Prevention Office. Although decisions were not legally binding, in cases of non-compliance the PCWA was authorized to publish the results of its investigations in newspapers, which served as a deterrent for companies and public agencies loath to attract negative publicity (Chang, 2001 interview). Informally, the PCWA also encouraged greater consultations with the women's movement community. As activist Shin Heisoo pointed out: "We have more friends in the Government now and can therefore talk more freely" (2000 interview).

Ministry of Gender Equality

In February 2001, Korea became one of just a handful of countries to establish a ministry specifically devoted to women's affairs.[7] Because of femocrats' and activists' dissatisfaction with the PCWA, the Council of Commissioners had persistently lobbied for the establishment of an independent women's ministry (Chang, 2000 interview). In response to these pressures and in an attempt to better the women-related affairs record of his long-term rival Kim Young-sam (Kwon Y., 2003 interview),

Kim Dae-Jung announced the establishment of a ministry charged with promoting gender equality in his 2000 New Year's address. Although the women's community warmly welcomed the news, there was considerable debate about whether the Ministry should focus solely on gender-related issues or combine gender as well as youth affairs. Whereas a combined policy focus would result in more resources and thus political clout within the Cabinet, progressive women's group leaders generally argued that a joint agency would dilute a gendered approach to policymaking (Park S., 2000 interview).

Not surprisingly, MOGE's establishment was not unanimously supported, with some political elites and conservative groups claiming that it was unnecessary and constituted reverse discrimination. For example, at one public hearing I attended prior to the Ministry's establishment, some male audience members asked, "Why don't we establish a ministry for men?" and argued, "We need a ministry for the elderly more than we do for women." Such criticisms notwithstanding, MOGE was granted full ministerial status in 2001, including the power to initiate legislation, and was equipped with an expanded (albeit still small) staff of 120 with greater budget resources.[8] Mandated to promote gender mainstreaming, MOGE oversees the implementation of the Women's Basic Development Plan and coordinates the policy efforts of the WFPs.[9]

Policy Capacity and Civic Access

Although MOGE's institutional status was clearly still that of a minor ministry, presidential commitment to advancing gender equality was evident in Kim Dae-jung's appointment of veteran political dissident and women's movement leader, Han Myung-sook, as its first minister. Given that the executive had previously shied away from appointing the leaders of either of the two major women's umbrella organizations to ministerial positions for fear of alienating the other (Shin, 2000 interview),[10] Han's appointment (and retention over the course of two subsequent cabinet reshuffles) was a bold move. In contrast to a series of political appointment blunders during the Kim Dae-jung administration, Han's tenure proved successful on the basis of the respect she came to command within the ministry (e.g., Lee H., 2003 interview), the Cabinet, and activist community (e.g., Yoon, 2002 interview). President Noh followed suit by appointing former KWAU president Ji Uhn-hee as MOGE head in 2003.

In addition to its coordinating role, MOGE's responsibilities extend to developing policies targeting violence against women, some equal employment programs, and, most recently, childcare services (Kim S., 2003 interview). These substantive policy directives, formerly subsumed under the MHSW and MoL respectively, were transferred to MOGE as a result of intra-bureaucracy lobbying. Not surprisingly, although neither the MHSW nor the MoL had prioritized the gendered components of their mandate, they strongly criticized the restructuring because of the loss of staff and resources it entailed, and what they contended was MOGE's "lack of expertise" (Kang, 2004 interview).[11]

To date, the Ministry's achievements have been considerable. It played a significant role in passing the landmark Maternity Law reforms in 2001, which provide for three months' paid maternity leave and one year of partially paid parental or family nursing leave (see chapter 6), and was at the forefront of efforts to address the country's rampant sex industry and sex trafficking problems. This campaign culminated in the much publicized 2004 Act on the Punishment of Procuring Prostitution and Associated Acts and the Act on the Prevention of Prostitution and Protection of Victims Thereof. These laws took a selective noncriminalization approach to prostitution, providing for rehabilitation programs for "victims" and special protection for foreign trafficked women on the one hand, and introducing stiff penalties for purchasers of sex and brothel owners on the other. In addition, MOGE has launched initiatives to accelerate gender mainstreaming, including the introduction of a gendered perspective into the national budget planning process and the development of a national IT policy framework that "consciously integrates a gender equality agenda" (Ramilo, 2002); established a national one-stop women's emergency hotline, "1366," for victims of violence;[12] and launched a cyber mentoring program for women to promote knowledge exchange and networking (MOGE, 2002b).

In terms of providing channels of access to the citizenry, MOGE has built upon the relations developed under the PCWA. At the formal level, the Council of Commissioners was renamed the Committee of Gender Equality Promotion and has come to focus more specifically on gender-discrimination cases, while the discussion of policy issues has been taken over by a separate advisory committee. Informally, avenues of communication were strengthened following the appointment of Han Myung-sook and Ji Uhn-hee, given their high standing with the women's movement community (e.g., Yoon J., 2002 interview). Much improved public relations efforts, including the establishment of an interactive website and database, have similarly increased civic awareness of the Ministry and its activities (Kim J., 2002 interview).

The Congressional Committee on Women's Affairs

The third prong of the Korean WPM infrastructure is the CCWA, which functioned as a temporary special committee from 1994 to 2002 before being elevated to the status of a standing committee in February 2002.[13] Faced with a dearth of allies in the Congress, the KWAU campaigned for the establishment of a special congressional women's committee from 1993, arguing that developing legislators' expertise in women's policies was crucial to effectively addressing widespread gender inequalities (Kwon, 1995: 54). After a petition in June 1994 by 61 women's organizations, the Special Congressional Committee on Women's Affairs Establishment bill was quickly passed by both parties, motivated at least in part by a desire to showcase the government's commitment to advancing gender equality at the forthcoming 1995 Beijing UN Women's Conference (Cho Y., 2000 interview).

As a special rather than standing committee, the SCCWA was institutionally weaker and smaller than other Congressional committees, had a correspondingly smaller research staff, and significantly more limited functions. Although able to present opinion papers on women-related laws, and monitor and file reports on the extent to which bureaucratic women's policy agencies fulfilled their assigned duties, it was unable to deliberate on or suggest new bills and could not participate fully in the National Assembly process (Lee Y., 2000 interview). Moreover, not only did committee members generally fail to take their work seriously, but their lack of expertise was exacerbated by the appointment of non-specialists to the (S)CCWA's affiliated expert committee until the late 1990s (Park S., 2000 interview).

In a concerted effort to improve the Committee's profile within Congress and to maximize its potential, the CCWA now writes opinion papers on all bills relating to women, including maternity leave, equal employment, education issues, family law, and sex trafficking. It also liaises regularly with the heads of women's organizations, enjoys a close working relationship with the gender experts of the major parties (Kim Y. H., 2000 interview), and produces a bimonthly newsletter to keep legislators and NGOs informed of the Committee's activities (Park S., 2000 interview). Although too little time has elapsed to evaluate the impact of the twofold increase in women legislators in 2004, given that more than half hark from a progressive civil society background, we can also hypothesize that the (S)CCWA's influence will benefit from the presence of an increasing number of gender-sensitive representatives in a broader array of congressional committees.

Yet, although formal impediments to the Committee's status were removed after its elevation in 2002 to the status of a standing committee—which included an expanded research staff—its influence has improved less than hoped (Lee M., 2003 interview). Part of the problem is that although male legislators viewed membership in the SSCWA as a means of attracting female voters' support, they prioritize participation in more powerful standing committees over active follow-up (Park S., 2000 interview).[14] Perhaps more importantly, though, the (S)CCWA still lacks an adequately articulated and systematized monitoring mandate. Whereas equivalent committees in Australia and Canada, for example, are responsible for monitoring gender accountability in budget reporting to Parliament (i.e., the degree to which state agencies provide disaggregated data on the impact of their mainstream programs on women and men) and for gender-impact analyses of state agencies' policies (Sawer, 2003), the CCWA's work is still undertaken on a comparatively ad-hoc basis. Unless its role is institutionalized, progress toward gender mainstreaming will continue to be evaluated on the basis of "inputs and promises" rather than "institutional outcomes" measured by "gendered summary outcomes about poverty reduction, assets and incomes, and good governance" (Staudt, 2003: 60–61).

Conclusion

The gradual evolution of a multi-institution WPM infrastructure can be seen as an important step toward realizing gender equity in Korea. In contrast to the experiences of a number of other countries, women's agencies have not emerged as the terrain of partisan rivalries, and a conservative backlash has been largely avoided. Feminist activists, WPM officials, and sympathetic legislators have made use of shifting political opportunities—especially executive support and international conferences and demonstration effects—to consolidate the institutional positioning of WPMs and expand the state's legal and resource-related responsibilities to address gender inequality. In particular, the 1995 WBDA and 1999 GDPRA constituted important shifts from a largely reactive to an increasingly proactive state approach.

Formal changes in WPMs have also been reflected in civil society attitudes. Public awareness of the state's gender-policy initiatives is growing (see chapter 10), and relations with civil society groups have become markedly more cooperative. Not only are women's voices increasingly articulated within state apparatuses through the appointment of femocrats, but activists and grassroots organizations are becoming more willing to work alongside the state to improve women's welfare.

Nevertheless, several organizational and attitudinal problems will have to be addressed if WMPs are to realize their full potential. Most fundamentally, the budget and staffing resources allocated to WPMs will have to be significantly augmented if MOGE and affiliated agencies are to fully carry out their mandate to eliminate gender discrimination and mainstream gender. The capacity of WPM personnel and general level of gender awareness within the bureaucracy also necessitates concerted attention. Thanks to the recruitment of former activists and academics, the introduction of basic gender-sensitivity programs, as well as the need to respond to women's organizations' increasingly sophisticated policy demands, the level of gender expertise in the bureaucracy is improving. Even so, overall gender awareness among public officials remains low. Korean WomenLink activist, Yang Hae-Kyung, for example, explains that although she was "delighted" at the time of the MOGE's foundation,

> the lack of gender expertise among officials is problematic . . . I feel especially annoyed when working with officials on sexual violence policies because of their ignorance about these issues. (2001, interview)

Moreover, given the rotation system of bureaucratic staff, even WPM personnel who develop a gender perspective in their work over time (e.g., Cho H., 2000 interview; Soh, 2000 interview) usually are not in their posts long enough to build an adequate level of gender expertise in specific areas.[15] It is therefore all the more important that bureaucrats posted to MOGE or WFPs are given intensive gender-sensitivity education to equip them with the skills and conceptual background necessary to develop and implement gender-sensitive policies. As Sawer (1996) puts it, " 'bilingualism' is required in both the dominant and gender discourses" (23).

A third organizational weakness concerns the less-than-optimal coordination among multiple WPMs. Although infrastructural breadth has considerable promise, relationships and information sharing between agencies have not been as cooperative as formal appearances suggest. Aside from personal relationships between MOGE and WFP staff, there is a dearth of formal channels of communication between these agencies and the KWDI, SSCWA, and the Blue House Secretary, thereby hindering synergy effects. Moreover, having been established in a piecemeal fashion, the ideological underpinnings of respective WFPs diverge considerably. As former PCWA Cooperation and Liaison Bureau director Park Woo-Keon explains, ministries with sizeable women-related portfolios, especially the MoL and MHSW and the central WPM agency, tend to have "different ultimate goals about women's status" (2000 interview). While the MHSW is focused on underprivileged women and views women as targets of social services, the MoL approaches gender concerns from a human resources maximization perspective, which is in turn distinct from the PCWA/MOGE's emphasis on protecting women's human rights.

Perhaps equally as troublesome are the relatively skeptical attitudes among movement groups as to the utility of WPMs. Whereas activists have become more willing to engage with and pursue change via the state over time, overall attitudes remain quite critical. For example, scholar and activist Chon Hyun-Baek notes:

> In reality ex-activists who joined government organizations haven't helped us so much, but by doing cooperative work, our critical voice has been weakened. The problem is that now we do not have an opposition party that will listen to NGO demands so we have no choice in terms of the political map but to be close to the Government. (2000 interview)

Similarly, Korean WomenLink activist, Lee Hyun-Kyung, confessed that she does not have "any expectations or interest in government policy. Like my friends, I don't have anything to say about what the Ministry should do or how it should change" (2001 interview).

Although these critiques are reassuring in so far as suggesting that fears of movement co-optation or "beheading" have not been borne out in Korea, such relative pessimism toward the state may prevent activists from recognizing the considerable potential that Korea's broad WPM infrastructure holds. In part because of comparisons to the better-established machineries of Western Europe and Australasia, (relative to which Korea is likely to underperform in the short to medium term), activist leaders continue to criticize bureaucratic agencies in broad brushstroke terms rather than engaging at a more specific level and identifying concrete micro-opportunities for intervention. As Staudt (2003) argues, however, WPMs necessitate "connections to outside constituencies, which themselves understand the institutional structures, pressure points in budget cycles and procedural issues" (59). Accordingly, now that activists and femocrats have successfully fought for the infrastructural tools to shape gender policy, only by expanding civil society scrutiny and developing detailed gender audit and policy monitoring programs (ideally in partnership with the (S)CCWA) will it be possible to make WPMs more responsive.

CHAPTER 8

Women's Political Representation: Accounting for Gradualism

I was very active in the cabinet—I talked to every minister about what they were not doing for women. What is your plan for women? What proportion of women do you have in X division? They couldn't answer well and tried to avoid me . . . That was my negotiating power . . . When I suggested something they just said "let it pass."

Lee Y., 2000 interview

At its core, democratization involves the equitable representation of civic identities and interests. One important contribution of the gender and democratization literature has been a rethinking of how democracy is practiced—do elected officials fairly reflect the composition of society in terms of gender, class, and ethnicity? Have concepts of "the political" been broadened to incorporate everyday life and community politics? (e.g., Alvarez et al., 1998). During the struggles against authoritarian rule, a general optimism prevailed that democratization and women's involvement in pro-reform social movements would contribute to a broader reconceptualization of politics and power relations (e.g., Radcliffe and Westwood, 1993). Post-transition, however, not only have women's inroads into formal political institutions been less significant than hoped, but female representatives have often conformed to, rather than challenged, traditional gender stereotypes (Craske, 1999). Even in the case of successful entry into public office, feminists' capacity to affect change has been hampered by weak institutional positioning and inadequate gender sensitivity on the part of male colleagues (Craske and Molyneux, 2002). Similarly, the everyday life issues they fought to have revalued by the political mainstream have often remained sidelined in the name of neoliberal economic imperatives (e.g., Schild, 1998; Montecinos, 1999).

Given these concerns and the diversity of women's socioeconomic, cultural, and ethnic positionings and priorities, there has been widespread debate as to how best to define "representation for women" or "women's interests" (e.g., Basu, 1995). Indeed, the very ". . . category of 'women' itself is a contested idea . . . as a women's body does not guarantee gender consciousness" (Chant and Craske, 2003: 21). Whereas feminists in power may strive to reduce gender inequality, other women may be as conservative as their male colleagues. Indeed, conservative politicians often recruit women candidates of a similar political persuasion in order to disarm criticisms of gender bias (Feijoo, 1998).

These problems notwithstanding, women activists in nascent democracies have employed diverse strategies to counter their underrepresentation and augment women's demands for equality. In order to evaluate such efforts in the Korean context, this chapter examines post-transitional change in women's formal political representation, as well as the extent to which greater representation has advanced gender equality. In keeping with the cautious tone of recent literature, I do not assume that higher numbers of women will necessarily be correlated with gender-friendly policy development. Although data limitations preclude a broad assessment of the ties between legislators and women's groups, as well as their voting/policy record on gender-related issues, I draw on anthropological studies and my own interviews with political actors to provide a picture of the degree of support for feminist initiatives within Korean political institutions. Finally, this chapter addresses the introduction of quotas for women over the last decade in the nomination of legislative candidates, civil service recruits, and ministerial advisory committees. It analyzes the key players involved in promoting quotas, their strategies and framing methods, as well as those of their opponents.

Legislative Representation

Understanding the pathways by which women legislators came to power provides important clues in assessing their likely commitment to advancing gender equality. There are four broad possible routes through which women may be nominated for elected office: on the basis of their professional standing; on the strength of their reputation as influential women's movement activists; as a reward for loyalty to a particular party;

or by being related to powerful male politicians (e.g., Ling and Bunch, 1999). Although Korean women legislators from 1948 to 1988 belonged to the social elite, they achieved office by virtue of activist careers or professional expertise in nonpolitical fields rather than via the popularity of a male relative (Soh, 1994).[1] The so-called first generation entered politics as a result of personal experience during periods of major political upheaval (i.e., the 1919 March First Independence Movement or the postliberation period) and all but one were imprisoned for their political commitments (ibid). By contrast, most women representatives during the military dictatorship were selected and appointed on the basis of their accomplishments in socially prestigious fields (Kim Y. C., 2000 interview). The trend of nominating prominent professional women to party lists has persisted post-transition, although over time more progressive women with gender-related expertise have been selected as candidates.[2]

Women's representation did not improve significantly with democratization, with women comprising only 2 percent of elected legislators between 1988 and 1999. It was not until the introduction of a quota system for women in 2000 that the extent of post-transition representation exceeded the 1973 historical high of 4.6 percent, with 6 percent securing legislative seats (Lee R., 2000). Even so, women's legislative representation remained well below international and Asian regional averages (14–15 percent) until the 17th Congress in 2004 (with women securing 13 percent of total seats) (see table 8.1). On Inter-Parliamentary Union (IPU) evaluations, Korea ranked only 91st out of 102 countries in 1997 and had shown little improvement by 2002 (102nd of 123), but improved sharply (65th of 125) following the 2004 breakthrough (IPU, 2005). Similarly, whereas Korea scored highly in terms of human capital development (31st out of 174 countries on the United Nations Development Programme's [(UNDP)] Human Development Index [HDI]) and 30th out of 174 countries on the Gender Development Index (GDI)), it ranked only 63rd out of 70 countries in 2002 on the Gender Empowerment Measure (GEM) index—a measure of women's representation in congressional, senior civil servant, and managerial positions (Kim W. et al., 2002: 13).[3]

How can we best explain Korean women's difficulties in securing formal political representation? Evidence from advanced democracies as well as Latin America and East Asia suggests that women are more likely to be elected in proportional representation (PR) systems, multi-member rather than single-member districts, closed candidate nomination systems, and, not surprisingly, when special quotas are allocated for women candidates (e.g., Christensen, 2000). Yet whereas PR systems are generally

Table 8.1   Women Korean National Assembly members

National Assembly	Number of women candidates	% of women candidates	Number of winning candidates	Winning candidates (% of total)	
				Total seats	District (non-PR) seats
1 (1948)	22	2.3	1	0.5	
2 (1950)	11	0.5	2	1.0	
3 (1954)	10	0.8	1	0.5	
4 (1958)	5	0.6	3	1.0	
5 (1960)	8	0.5	1	0.4	
6 (1963)	7	0.7	2	1.1	0.8
7 (1967)	8	1.0	3	1.7	0.8
8 (1971)	8	1.1	5	2.5	0
9 (1973)	10	2.4	10	4.6	1.4
10 (1978)	11	2.0	8	3.5	0.6
11 (1981)	25	2.9	8	2.9	0.5
12 (1985)	16	2.6	8	2.9	1.1
13 (1988)	27	2.2	6	2.0	0
14 (1992)	35	2.9	3	1.0	0
15 (1996)	41	2.6	9	3.0	0.9
16 (2000)	69	5.9	16	5.9	2.2
17 (2004)	136	10.4	39	13.0	4.1

Source: KWDI, 2004.

viewed as more broadly representative (e.g., Lijphart, 1984), in the Korean case the number of PR seats was scaled back in the mid-1990s, partly owing to concerns about cronyism (Diamond and Shin, 2000), and was not increased again until 2004 and even then not to 1988 levels (see chapter 5). Although military rulers had nominated women to national electorate seats to improve public relations, increasing party competition under democratic rule contributed to party leaders' reluctance to nominate women (Park K., 1999). The shift to single-member districts also reduced the electoral viability of women candidates. Because voters tend to have more negative attitudes toward female candidates, women are less likely to be successful in contests where voters only have a single choice than in electoral systems with several representatives per constituency (Darcy et al., 1994).

Finally, although campaign spending limits have been tightened considerably through a series of post-transitional electoral law reforms (EPIC, 2005), women remain disadvantaged vis-à-vis male candidates in terms of fundraising abilities, as well as community name recognition. Success in Korean public life is largely premised on the ability to call upon *yŏnjul* (close, personal) relationships involving school alumni or hometown fraternities, an area where women tend to be comparatively weaker due to their domestic sphere responsibilities and conventional single-sex socializing. In particular, political activist Cho Hyun-Ok stressed that the deposits required to run for political office have proved to be prohibitively high for many potential women candidates (2003 interview).

Mindful of the difficulties faced by women in formal politics, gender scholars argue that in order for governance to be more responsive to women's needs a critical mass of at least 30 percent of women is likely to be necessary (e.g., Rai, 2003). Korean women representatives are still far from achieving such a presence, which helps explain their limited impact within Congress. Legislator Han Myung-Sook, for example, noted:

> The hardest part about passing laws is low gender awareness among male law-makers. Although there are now more young professional law-makers, many have business backgrounds and are more easily swayed by employers' associations . . . To persuade lawmakers about the need for a gender-related reform, I focus not so much on the importance of women voters but women's human rights as enshrined in law and the need to stick to these legal principles. So if MPs are rational, they'll listen to this line of argument. (2000 interview)

The low percentage of congresswomen has also rendered their representation in important policy committees, such as Budget and Planning or Finance and Economy, either negligible or nonexistent until 2004. As (S)CCWA research officer Park Sook-ja pointed out:

> Women's strength in major policy areas is weak because of their low numbers. Not only is the budget for women-related issues always low but in times of economic turmoil these items are axed first. Male committee members always accord women's issues rock-bottom priority. (2000 interview)

These difficulties notwithstanding, the importance of support from gender-sensitive representatives for the passage of reforms was underscored in my discussions with activists and government officials alike. Former vice director of the KCTU Women's Bureau Lee Hye-Soon, for example, attributed the difference between the relative failure of the second revision of the EEA in 1995 and successful revisions in 1999 in large part to the presence of a handful of feminist congresswomen:

> The main problem in 1995 was that there were few sympathetic legislators. By 1999 we could draw on the support of Lee Mi-Kyoung and Han

> Myung-Sook. We succeeded because the Government wasn't really very active and women's groups were driving the reform process. (2002 interview)

Given the minimal ideological commitments of Korean parties, and relatively limited interest in policy development among many legislators (see chapter 5), strong interest in gender equity on the part of a few representatives with close linkages to civil society groups has proven to have a disproportionate influence in the Congress. Second-term legislator Lee Mi-Kyoung, for example, recognized her considerable influence within the Environment and Labor Affairs Committee in the case of the 1999 EEA revision regarding sexual harassment and indirect discrimination:

> The bill was passed as I did my utmost to persuade the Chairman, other committee members and also the Ministry of Labor . . . Many of them did not fully understand the bill's content, but said they would support the bill "as representative Lee Mi-Kyoung worked on it." Some even called the bill "Lee Mi-Kyoung's law." (2003 interview)

Cooperative linkages among women across party lines have also increased their relative influence. SCCWA research officer Park Sook-Ja emphasized that relationships between women have generally proved cooperative at least in part because their minority status has "compelled" them to work together (2000 interview).

2004 Breakthrough—The List of 100 Women

A combination of careful strategizing by proponents of gender equality and fortuitous political openings resulted in a dramatic increase in women's representation in the April 2004 congressional elections. Inspired by Emily's List, a well-known American NGO that has played a major role over the last 20 years in increasing American women's political representation, and also anxious to strip party officials of their conventional excuses about "the lack of appropriate women candidates," women's organizations developed a "List of 100 Women" candidates. After soliciting recommendations from diverse social groups, potential candidates ranging from lawyers and professors to activists and feminist media specialists were fully vetted, then listed alphabetically rather than ranked according to any particular set of criteria. The list was in turn presented to all political parties to serve as a database of viable women candidates and publicized by the newly established "Women for Clean Politics Network."

In addition to positive support from the mainstream media and an emphasis on the disjuncture between Korea's high level of development and educational achievement yet low women's political representation (Yoon, 2004 interview), the broader political milieu during the election season played an important role in this campaign's relative success. First, because the majority of the public dismissed the decision of the MDP and GNP to impeach President Noh in early 2004 as illegitimate (Min and Min, 2004), there was widespread public pressure for a change from traditional politics. Parties responded by drawing upon the List of 101 Women to develop their party lists and also by appointing women to high-profile party positions. Second, given that the civil-society–organized Blacklist Campaign in the 2000 election season (see chapter 5) had been broadly viewed as too negative, there was a general willingness to back positive methods of political reform such as the List (Yoon, 2004 interview).

Although falling short of the target of 100 female legislators, the victory of an unprecedented 39 women candidates (13 percent of total legislators) was nevertheless viewed as highly symbolic (see tables 8.2 and 8.3). As fresh(wo)man URI (Our Open Party) representative You Song Hye noted:

> Women were elected in order to represent issues of everyday reality, troubles and pains. Their election will mean a greater focus on disabled women, poor women, temporary workers, prostituted women, etc. (Quoted in Chang, 2004)

Table 8.2 Female candidates per party: 17th Congress 2004

	GNP	URI	DLP	MDP	ULD	Social democrats	Socialist party	Independents	Total
Number of women candidates	8	11	12	8	7	2	4	14	66
women as % of total candidates	3.6	4.5	9.7	4.3	5.6	7.1	66.6	6.3	5.6

Source: Data from National Election Commission (www.nec.go.kr).

Table 8.3 Female legislators per party: 17th Congress 2004 (number of female legislators and women as percent of total legislators)

	GNP	URI	DLP	MDP	Total
Local constituency seats	5 (5%)	5 (3.9%)	—	—	10 (3.0%)
Party list seats	11 (50%)	12 (55%)	4 (50%)	2 (50%)	29 (10%)
Total	16 (13%)	17 (11%)	4 (40%)	2 (22%)	39 (13%)

Source: Data from National Election Commission (www.nec.go.kr).

Table 8.4 Women's participation in standing committees: 17th Congress 2004

Women's Affairs	11	Unification	1	Health	5	Education	3	Defense	1	Finance	2	Environment	2
Science/ Tech	3	Culture	5	Legislation	1	Government Affairs	2	Policy	4	Commerce	1	Budget	2

Source: Data from the Korean National Assembly (www.assembly.go.kr).

Other observers, however, have pointed out important limitations to the List of 100 Women campaign. Although a number of former women's movement activists such as Lee Kyong-sook (KWAU), Kim Hee-sun (Korean Women's Hotline), and Son Bong-sook (Center for Korean Women and Politics) were elected, young feminists and gender scholars alike were quick to criticize the selection process for prioritizing numbers over commitment to gender equality (KWAU, 2004). Indeed, Korean WomenLink corepresentative Yoon Jung-sook admitted that the process had been hasty and that, unlike Emily's List, which is an explicitly partisan (pro-Democrat) organization, the List had not attempted to assess candidates' commitment to advancing gender equality (2004 interview). Although 31 congresswomen voted to end the *hojuje* and 36 voted for the Special Law on Trafficking, it is still too early to fully assess the impact of greater women's representation in the 17th Congress (Korean National Assembly, 2005). This is particularly the case given the gender composition of congressional committees. Although at least one woman sits on all standing committees, and women are well represented on Health, Culture, Women's Affairs, participation on several of the more powerful standing committees is still limited. For instance, as of 2005, there was only one women sitting on the Legislation and Judiciary Committee, which has jurisdiction over the introduction and direction of legislation to the broader Congress. (See table 8.4.)

Local Assemblies

Decentralization has been heralded as an important opportunity for women's political representation on the basis that community politics correspond more closely to women's interests and everyday needs (e.g., Atienza, 2000). Similar hopes of making "substantial inroads into politics" (Lee R., 2000: 51) were raised among Korean women activists with the reinstatement of local body elections in 1991 at the *kich'o* (county/city) level and the *kwangyŏk* (metropolitan/provincial) level in 1995. Although minor players in broader political life, Korean local governments hold responsibility for important areas of "everyday life politics," including managing culture, education, and welfare budgets (e.g., Seong, 2000). Such optimism proved unwarranted, however, as women accounted for less than two percent of total candidates and secured under one percent of total seats in the 1991 elections.

Activists were not overly discouraged, however, as the success rate among women who did stand for office was comparatively high, and women's organizations such as Korean WomenLink, the Korean Women's Political Research Center, and the KWAU established training programs for women candidates for the next round of elections as part of their "critical engagement" strategy (Sohn, 2000 interview). They also helped candidates organize and financially supported local government electoral campaigns (Yoon, 2000 interview). However, whereas in 1998, women's organizations supported women's candidacies irrespective of their party affiliation, successfully fielding 13 candidates, in 2002 a KWAU-led coalition took an ultimately unsuccessful gamble of backing independent candidates. This was in line with the decision by many civic groups to distance themselves from the ruling MDP for fear of tainting the civic movement with partisan colors. Because of the low probability of winning, only five women proved willing to run, resulting in just three victories. As a result, women were primarily elected via quota seats under the PR system (see table 8.5) and women's representation in both small- and large-unit local governments failed to break through the ten percent threshold.

A second argument in favor of women's involvement in local politics is that experience at the lower levels would serve as a "springboard" for their participation in national politics (e.g., Craske, 1999). However, this theory has not been borne out in Korea. Women's NGOs had hoped local politics would serve as a training ground for women to advance to the national level, but they have found that the same attitudinal, financial, and networking barriers faced nationally are mirrored or even exaggerated at local levels of government (Park K., 1999). As Lee Jae-Chun, one of only two women city councilors in Chonju City, laments, women legislators in smaller cities and rural areas often face more conservative colleagues than their national-level counterparts:

In North Cholla there are barely a handful of women and even when local councils agree to develop women's policies, there are few women bureaucrats to strongly push the implementation phase. Male bureaucrats agree to tackle women's projects to look good in the mayor's eyes but there is no genuine conviction . . . I am often completely outnumbered by tradition-bound "grandfathers." It's terribly difficult . . . sometimes I have to struggle against developing a defeatist attitude. (2000 interview)

Because of the difficulties involved in serving as a female legislator in such male-dominated arenas, the turnover rate among successful candidates has been relatively high, with several women deciding against standing for reelection (e.g., You, 2000 interview). Moreover, as local politics is primarily concerned with practical community concerns rather than macro-issues such as the economy and foreign affairs, the anticipated spillover effects from the local to the national have not been realized (e.g., Chin, 2000). Indeed, according to a 1998 survey of women's motivations for running for local assemblies, only 4.6 percent of female candidates selected advancement to national politics as their primary goal as compared with 82 percent for "community service" and 9 percent for the "promotion of an equal society" (Sohn, 1998).

Table 8.5 Women's local government representation

Women's participation in Small Unit local elections

Year	Candidates (% of total)	Winning Candidates (% of total)
1991	1	1
1995	2	1.5
1998	4	1.5
2002	6.5	2

Women's participation in Large Unit local elections

	Elected Seats		Proportional Representation Seats		Winning candidates (%) of total Large Unit assembly members
	Candidates (% of total)	Winning candidates (% of total)	Number of candidates	Number of winning candidates	
1991	2	1	n/a	n/a	1
1995	4.5	1.5 (of 875 seats)	77	42 (43% of 97 seats)	6
1998	6	2 (of 616 seats)	52	27 (36% of 74 seats)	6
2002	8	2 (of 609 seats)	116	49 (67% of 73 seats)	9

Source: KWDI, 2002b; Moon M., 2002.

Legislative Quotas

Quota systems have become an increasingly popular, albeit controversial, institutional measure to proactively redress the deficiencies of "gender-blind" political structures in both long-established and newly democratizing polities (e.g., Feijoo, 1998; Dahlerup, 1998). Advocates of quotas suggest they are the most effective means to ensure more equal gender representation in the policymaking process in the short term (Christensen, 2000). Quotas also have symbolic value, raising public awareness about the importance of gender equality and demonstrating the polity's commitment to inclusivity. Critics, however, range from the reactionary to the cautious. Some dismiss them as discriminatory toward men while stigmatizing beneficiaries, by insisting that qualified women will "naturally" advance in the political arena on the basis of their own merits (Htun and Jones, 2002). More thoughtful criticisms focus on the limitations of institutional rules and male political will. Whereas affirmative action measures are the most effective means of increasing women's formal political representation, the institutional rules governing quota systems as well as the relative willingness of male political elites to engage in good-faith compliance determine their ultimate efficacy (e.g., Huang, 2003).

In nascent democracies, legislative quotas took on increasing salience following the endorsement of "women's right to participate in decision-making" in the 1995 Beijing Platform for Action and its call to ensure "women's equal access to and full participation in power structures and decision-making" (Htun and Jones, 2002: 35). Across Latin America, for instance, quotas were widely embraced and by 2000, 12 countries in the region had established a minimum threshold of 20–40 percent for women's candidacies in national elections (32–33). In Korea, however, activists lacked a comparable level of regional commitment and networking. Although able to draw on the legitimacy of international conventions and best practices, movement groups were compelled to wage a drawn-out, piecemeal struggle, first for local elections and later for the National Assembly. Despite diverse lobbying and public education efforts, women activists repeatedly faced broken promises and/or half-hearted implementation efforts by political society before finally securing the 2000 Party Law reform.

A Decade of Struggle

In response to women candidates' poor showing in the 1988 congressional elections (only two women were elected to nonlist seats), various research centers were established to promote women's political participation, including a 10–20 percent quota system.[4] Arguing that the barriers to women's election in traditional single-member districts were insuperable, women's organizations and the women's bureaus of larger political parties began lobbying to introduce a PR system with a quota for women in the local government elections of 1991 (Kim K., 1998). Although presidential candidates and party leaders offered rhetorical support, there were few concrete advances at this stage (Kim W. et al., 2002).

In 1994, in the context of heightened public interest in women's political participation and with a view to the 1995 local government elections, the KWDI compiled a comparative report on quota systems for women, including a blueprint for governmental action (Kim S., 1995). The Institute also organized a meeting between the KWAU and the KNCW to promote more cooperative relations between the then still antagonistic camps (Yoon, 2002 interview).[5] As a result, a coalition of 14 major women's groups was formed, entitled "Women's Solidarity for the Introduction of a Women's Quota" (WSIWQ). This group held public forums and political education programs as part of a broader lobbying effort to introduce quotas for women in all areas of politics, including at least ten percent of local assembly PR seats (Sohn, 1998). They sought to frame their demands within a broader political discourse about women's role in contributing to a "clean election culture," and to this end participated in the 1995 campaign for electoral law reform organized by the Citizens' Coalition for Fair Elections.

The government's response, however, was lukewarm at best with officials agreeing to establish quotas only in larger-unit assemblies, and then just for PR seats (10 percent of total seats). Whereas the ruling party secretary general Kim Duk-Ryong promised to guarantee 50 percent of PR seats for women in recognition of the positive role women had played in promoting "clean candidates," interest groups including pharmacists and youth associations argued that the plan demonstrated "favoritism" toward a single segment of the electorate and as a result the 10 percent quota was divided between women and various professional interest groups (Kim W., 2003 interview).

These disappointments notwithstanding, provincial-level quotas introduced prior to the 1995 elections enabled women to net 43 percent of PR seats and 5.7 percent of total seats. Although unimpressive from a comparative perspective, the results were a clear improvement on the 1991 figure of less than 1 percent, and stood in marked contrast to the results of women candidates at the county level, which improved by only a half percent. Hopes were again raised in 1997 when intensive lobbying by the WSIWQ led to detailed pledges by presidential candidates to expand women's political representation and introduce quotas at the national and local levels (Kim W. et al., 2001a). Yet instead of securing significant advances, the June 1998 local elections coincided with two new challenges: a more conservative political climate following the 1997/98 economic crisis and intensified competition due to electoral law revisions, including a reduction in the total number of local assembly seats (Croissant, 2002a). In particular, although a larger pool of female candidates had been mobilized by women's organizations, many failed to be nominated by political parties.

To add insult to injury, pledges to nominate women for 50 percent of all PR seats were not fulfilled,[6] and a sizable percentage of the 236 women candidates (2.3 percent of the 10,020 total candidates) were nominated for unsafe seats (KWAU, 1998; Park K., 1999). As a result, women secured only marginal improvements vis-à-vis 1995 results. At the metropolitan city/provincial level, women's representation increased by just 0.2 percent, while women's share of party list seats actually declined from 43 to 36.5 percent (27 of 74 seats) (Kim R., 2000). Meanwhile, at the county level, despite a twofold increase in women candidates compared with the previous election cycle, success rates remained static at 1.6 percent. City council results were equally disillusioning: despite several successful candidacies in 1995 none of the eight women running for head of the city council was elected (KWAU, 1998).

The 2000 Party Law Reform
The successful passage of the 2000 Party Law reform depended on the emergence of a variety of new political opportunities, changing civic attitudes toward gender issues in the late 1990s, as well as cooperative interaction among activists, women legislators, and femocrats. Given the string of relatively ineffectual changes detailed above, both the women's movement community and women politicians seized upon discussions concerning broader political reform initiated in 1998 in the Special Congressional Committee on Reform of Political Legislation to demand more decisive measures to address women's underrepresentation (SCCWA, 2000). Female legislators, such as Shin Nak-Kyun, argued that establishing a quota system was essential to amend the current "distorted and unbalanced policy process," to "better reflect women's societal contribution," and "develop a democratic political arena and a gender equal society" (SCCWA, 2000: 190). Korea's embarrassingly low scores in the GEM index and the IPU rankings also meant that "the Government could no longer make excuses" for women's political

underrepresentation (Yoon, 2003 interview). Political elites' "wriggle room" was further reduced by Kim Dae-Jung's explicit electoral pledge to introduce a 30 percent quota for women, which he reiterated in his 2000 New Year's Address to the nation:

> Discussions on quotas were under way but not progressing quickly. However, after the President's annual message, the pace of this process accelerated rapidly. The President's interest was very important . . . because he emphasized the importance of women's political participation in his speech, Congress felt compelled to lend their support. (Kim W., 2003 interview)

The establishment of MOGE constituted a further important shift. As part of the Ministry's commitment to advancing women's political participation, Cho Sung-Hoon, director of the Women's Policy Division, secured for the first time a sizable budget from the Ministry of Planning and Budget specifically to expand women's political representation (ibid.). MOGE was therefore able to develop political education programs for women as well as increase the time allocated to promoting a quota system within the Cabinet and party affairs meetings. Although unable to directly lobby Congress for the introduction of a quota system bill—which would have violated the spirit of election law regulations—MOGE's persistent advocacy contributed to an atmosphere more receptive to women's organizations' demands (Kwon Y., 2003 interview).

Finally, despite a generally conservative political culture, by 2000, national survey data indicated that civic attitudes had become relatively open toward the idea of quotas for women. Some 54.3 percent of respondents agreed that quotas were important tools for increasing women's representation, compared with only 12.7 percent who were opposed (Kim Y. et al., 2000: 274).

The configuration of actors who took advantage of this expansion of opportunities included NGOs, the government-affiliated KWDI and MOGE, as well as feminist legislators. In civil society, the WSIWQ, now composed of 90 organizations, led the women's movement initiative in conjunction with the Korean Women's Political Solidarity, a new network established to encourage the political participation of women of the progressive *sam p'al yuk shidae* (386 generation).[7] The KWDI, building on its contribution to the theoretical dimensions of the quota debate in the mid-1990s, helped prepare a draft quota bill after consultations with women's party bureaus and NGOs, and presented it to the

SCCWA. In the Congress, former women's activists Lee Mi-Kyoung and Han Myung-Sook were the key supporters within the ruling MDP, and third-term legislator and founder of the Korean Women's Political Culture Research Center Kim Chung-Sook, and former KNCW president Lee Yon-Sook, championed the bill within the GNP (Cho H., 2003 interview). Given their respective activist backgrounds, there were few significant differences of opinion among congresswomen across party lines.

The women's quota campaign, however, provoked significant opposition among political elites. Whereas advocates emphasized Korea's poor GEM rankings and examples of quota systems from Europe in an effort to persuade male legislators, opponents argued that quotas would disadvantage men and "violate voters' freedom of choice" (Kim W., 2003 interview). Kim Dae-Jung's public endorsement, however, served to jump-start negotiations in the Government Administration and Home Affairs and the Legislation and Judiciary Committees, underscoring the importance of presidential commitment to overcome legislative inertia. Even so, although supporters had been quietly confident that a multiparty compromise involving a 30 percent rather than a 50 percent quota had been agreed following the presentation of the bill to Congress on January 15, activists were shocked to realize that their efforts had been undermined at the eleventh hour by the omission of the clause on women's quotas from the "final version" of the bill (Lee M., 2003 interview).

Fortunately, and in testament to the feminist community's growing familiarity with institutional rules of the legislature, congresswomen made creative use of parliamentary rules to attach an amendment to the bill. Insisting on a nonanonymous vote was also important to the bill's final passage:

> We asked the Chairman to do a standing vote and keep a record. Accordingly, even though we knew many men were opposed, when the vote was called, only one legislator stood up in opposition. Male congressmen did not want to be on record having resisted the women's quota bill! (Lee M., 2003 interview)

Thus on February 16, 2000, the Party Law reform was finally passed, marking a symbolic breakthrough that focused public attention on women's right to participate in the legislative process.

Successful passage, however, was not the end of the story. Debates with party officials concerning the placement of women candidates on party lists, as well as the open violation of the new law by both major opposition parties, the GNP and the United Liberal Democrats (ULD), highlighted the importance of good-faith compliance to ensure successful implementation of quotas.[8] Women's groups quickly realized that without a more specific legal mandate they would need to exert considerable pressure on parties to ensure that women candidates were allocated winnable seats rather than being slotted in at the bottom of party lists (Cho H., 2003 interview). By drawing on international examples and staging demonstrations outside the National Assembly, activists eventually secured such an agreement before the April 2000 elections. Even so, only the ruling MDP fully complied with the 30 percent requirement, whereas the GNP nominated just 22.2 percent and the ULD under 20 percent (Soh, 2000). The reluctance of political elites notwithstanding, the new quota law produced a substantial increase in the number of women elected to the National Assembly: 11 of the 36 candidates on the national party lists entered political office, resulting in women holding an unprecedented 6 percent of the 270 parliamentary seats (KWDI, 2000: 410).

In short, then, the Korean experience with quotas supports many of the conclusions drawn from other regions (e.g., Dahlerup, 1998; Huang, 2003). Although quotas can serve as a symbolic tool to raise public awareness about gender imbalances in the political arena, electoral system rules can significantly reduce the impact of seemingly generous quotas. In Korea, the equation of a 30 percent quota with the "critical mass" needed to push through new gender-equality policies was widely accepted in the media but little attention was drawn to the fact that PR seats constitute only 10–20 percent of total legislative seats. Moreover, without a specific agreement on list placement and a genuine commitment by political society to utilize quotas as an affirmative action tool, quotas can be reduced to "a relatively painless way to pay lip service to women's rights without suffering the consequences" (Htun and Jones, 2002: 51).

Only too aware of the half-hearted attitude of party officials, activists and law professors presented a subsequent reform bill to Congress in 2002, securing an amendment guaranteeing a 50 percent quota for women in the large-unit local PR seats as well as 30 percent of total candidate nominations for district seats (Kim S. H., 2005).[9] Importantly, this provincial quota system entails strong penalties: if one in two of the PR party list nominees is not a woman, the Election Administration Commission will not accept that party's application. Although change was slower than proponents had hoped, in 2004 a similar quota was introduced at the national level and played an important role in the

Table 8.6 Legislative quotas for women

	Year	Total seats	PR seats	PR seats (%)	Quota of PR seats promised by parties to women (%)	Successful women relative to total PR seats (%)
Local	1991	866	—	n/a	n/a	n/a
elections	1995	972	97	10.0	5	43.0
	1998	690	74	10.7	50+	36.5
	2002	682	73	10.7	30	67.1
National	2000	270	43	18.9	30	25.6
elections	2004	299	54	18.0	50	53.7

Source: Moon M., 2002; Republic of Korea National Assembly (www.assembly.go.kr).

more-than-twofold increase in women's representation in the 17th Congress. (See table 8.6.)

Civil Service Representation

Women's civil service representation has been relatively neglected in the gender and democracy literature, except to emphasize the bureaucracy's resistance to change (e.g., Craske, 1999). Yet, because of the key role that the civil service plays in policy formation and implementation and the fact that the balance of power between the legislature and bureaucracy tends to lie with the latter in nascent democracies, I argue that women's positioning in the bureaucracy constitutes a key indicator of progress in en*gender*ing democracy. In Korea, the importance of the bureaucracy as an institutional arena for policy formation is particularly salient, as laws tend to be passed quickly and with little deliberation. As a result, specific legal and policy details are decided by the relevant ministry's staff and formalized in a *shihaengnyŏng* (enforcement ordinance) (e.g., Kim K., 2000 interview).

Democratization has seen a gradual increase in the proportion of women civil servants, largely through the introduction of quotas, as well as in the appointment of women ministers. Whereas women accounted for just 8.5 percent of bureaucrats on the eve of the transition, the percentage of female public sector employees gradually increased following the Equal Opportunity Act of 1987, though primarily for support positions (grades 8 and 9) (Sohn, 1994: 260). Nevertheless, although women accounted for 34 percent of total national government officials by 2003, their representation at decisionmaking levels remained very low (only 5.2 percent

Table 8.7 Female bureaucrats in national (N) and local (L) government by civil service grade (%)

Year		*Total public officials*	*Women public officials*	*% of total bureaucrats*	*1st*	*2nd*	*3rd*	*4th*	*5th*	*6th*	*7th*	*8th*	*9th*
1989	N	86,593	7,394	8.5	1.6	0.3	0.3	0.1	0.7	1.8	5.6	10.6	10.9
	L	127,813	15,298	15.3	—	—	—	—	0.4	1.2	7.8	15.9	21.7
1993	N	99,014	11,358	11.5	0.0	0.8	1.9	1.7	1.7	4.7	13.3	15.9	24.7
	L	172,132	34,881	20.3	0.0	0.0	0.0	2.1	1.7	4.8	14.8	28.2	43.5
1997	N	91,697	12,224	13.3	—	0.9	1.1	1.3	2.8	6.2	12.1	22.9	26.2
	L	171,981	47,291	23.3	—	—	1.0	2.2	3.2	6.7	20.9	37.6	47.4
2003	N	891,949	302,830	34.0	1.3	0.7	1.5	3.2	5.2	10.8	28.8	40.6	48.2
	L	248,524	59,748	24.0			1.4	3.4	3.9	9.2	28.3	45.6	55.3

Source: Data from Ministry of Government and Home Affairs (www.mogaha.go.kr).

of grade 5, and a miniscule 1.3 percent of grade 1) (see table 8.7). The gendered patterning of representation was similar at local levels: whereas women occupying local government positions had increased from 15 percent overall in 1989 to 24 percent in 2003, fewer than 5 percent were to be found in decisionmaking roles.[10]

Improved representation among lower bureaucratic levels can be partly attributed to the removal of the 15 percent cap on women recruits that had been in place in the civil service until 1988 (Park W., 2000 interview), as well as the emergence of nonexamination public sector jobs as an attractive employment option for women. There has also been a notable rise in the number of women who entered at grade 7 based on their performance in the lower-tier civil service exam, which is seen as less time-consuming and competitive than the examination for entry at rank 5 (e.g., Kim J., 2001 interview).

Unsurprisingly, senior-level women bureaucrats are overrepresented in "caring"-related ministries, but remain poorly represented in finance-related, technology, and construction ministries. For instance, women with decisionmaking power in the MHSW make up 29.5 percent of total staff but are much rarer in the Ministry of Finance (1.2 percent), the Budget and Planning Office (2.2 percent), and Ministry of Government and Home Affairs (3.8 percent) (KWDI, 2000: 16–17).[11]

Numerical advances notwithstanding, however, only a minority of female civil servants could be described as, or would self-identify as, femocrats (i.e., explicitly committed to advancing gender equality in their work). As former officer in the PCWA policy division Na Yong-Hee noted:

Women from activist backgrounds strive to develop policy initiatives in response to issues from the field, but the career bureaucrats do not.

Sometimes they are very conservative, men and women both. (2000 interview)

In the case of cabinet posts, there have also been considerable advances post-transition, albeit from a low base. Since President Roh, the position of head of the state's women's affairs machinery (MPA2, PCWA, or MOGE) has been reserved for a woman, and subsequent administrations have appointed additional female cabinet members to demonstrate at least symbolic support for women's issues. For example, PCWA official Park Woo-Keon noted that Kim Young-sam

> appointed three women ministers because of their symbolic importance. In traditional Korean society women were never high bureaucrats . . . they could never be minister as this would mean the husband would be a lower rank . . . so by appointing women as ministers it pushed people to change their minds about women's capabilities. (2000 interview)

In keeping with bureaucratic representation more generally, women's ministerial posts have tended to be associated with "soft" ministries such as health, education, and social welfare. Indeed it was not until President Noh's appointment of Kang Kum-Sil as Minister of Justice in 2003 and Kim Sun-Uk as Minister of Legislation in 2005 that this tradition was broken (see table 8.8).

Coping with Conservative Political Society

My interviews with ministers and officials suggest that perceptions as to the extent to which gender attitudes hindered their work varied. Soh Myung Sohn, former MHSW Women's Policy Office Director, for example, believes that whereas senior-level civil servants have become more gender-sensitive over the past decade as a result of external pressure and the introduction of gender-awareness training programs, there remains a significant number of "very conservative" rank-and-file bureaucrats (2000 interview). Veteran civil servant Yang In-Sook, who entered the MHSW in 1968, has observed significant changes, however, in the overall level of gender-awareness in the bureaucracy:

> There was room for women as professionals (e.g., pharmacists and doctors) in the MHSW but there were very few opportunities for women in regular administration positions. Besides support staff, I was one of just three women. They also gave priority in promotions to men as they thought: "Men have large families but women are alone." (2000 interview)

Table 8.8 Women cabinet members in Korea 1987–2005

Presidency	Appt. date	Number of cabinet members	Number of women ministers	Women as % of total ministers
Roh	1988	24	1 (MPA2)	4.2
	1991			
Kim	1993	24	3 (Environment, Health/Welfare, MPA2)	12.5
Young-sam	1994		2 (Education and MPA2)	8.3
	1995	22	1 (MPA2)	4.5
	1997		1 (MPA2)	
Kim	1998	17	3 (Health/Welfare, Culture/Tourism, Environment)	17.6
Dae-jung	1999		2 (Health/Welfare and Tourism, Environment)	11.8
	2001	18	2 (Health/Welfare, MOGE)	11.1
Noh	2003	21	4 (Health/Welfare, MOGE, Environment, Justice)	19.0
	2004		4 (Health/Welfare, MOGE, Environment, Justice)	
	2005		2 (MOGE, Legislation)	9.5

Source: Data from the Ministry of Gender Equality (www.moge.go.kr) and the Korean Women's Development Institute (www2.kwdi.re.kr).

Moreover, whereas Yang had organized a support network for women across several ministries in the mid-1980s to counter their sense of isolation, she explained that this was no longer necessary and moreover there were now too many women to make their informal meeting structure feasible. She also noted a gradual shift in her ministry from viewing things solely from a male standpoint to an evaluation of issues from women's perspective:

> Because our society is so conservative we have sought to encourage policy development that gets men to consider things from women's perspective . . . The Beijing Conference slogan "Seeing the world through women's eyes" has been quite a turnaround in this regard. (Ibid.)

In the case of women ministers, Kim Chang-Suk, for example, looked back on her time (1994–96) as Minister of Political Affairs No.2 (MPA2) as "burdensome," largely because fulfilling her coordinating role among ministries was hindered by resistance from male colleagues (2000 interview). Her predecessor Kwon Young-Ja (1993–94) also acknowledged the "suspicions and criticisms" from men, but felt she was able to partially overcome this through the close ties she enjoyed with two other women ministers, as well as a cooperative relationship with the media (2000 interview).

By contrast, former minister Lee Yon-Suk (1997–98) suggested that the contradictory position of her male colleagues, who lacked gender sensitivity but wanted to be seen as providing opportunities for women, allowed her to push through important reforms such as the Basic Five-Year Development Plan for Women with surprisingly little resistance.

> I was very active in the Cabinet—I talked to every minister about what they were *not* doing for women. What is your plan for women? What proportion of women do you have in X division? They couldn't answer well and so they all tried to avoid me after a few months . . . That was my negotiating power . . . When I suggested something they just said "let it pass" . . . I was very much a headache for them. (2000 interview)

A possible explanation for these divergent attitudes among cabinet appointees is the differing levels of interest in and commitment to gender-equality issues. For women such as Kim Chang-Suk, whose involvement in the women's movement community was based on her standing as the head of the Women Chemists Association, her appointment as minister was daunting, as it involved decisionmaking in areas outside her direct expertise (2000 interview). However, for ministers such as Lee and Kwon, both of whom had extensive professional involvement in advancing women's strategic gender issues (Lee as KNCW president and Kwon in the KWDI and MPA2), their appointment was seen as an important opportunity to further their historic engagements.

Bureaucracy Quotas

Affirmative action measures to increase the percentage of women bureaucrats were first identified as a key policy goal by Kim Young-sam's *Segyehwa Hoeŭi* (Globalization Committee) in 1995. Whereas the low baseline of women in decisionmaking roles in public agencies (just one percent in 1995) created a structural need for concerted action, reforms were brought about by the proactive stance of women's organizations, the KWDI, and progressive officials in the Ministry of Government and Home Affairs (MOGAHA), and were facilitated by limited resistance from male civil servants (Hwang, 2000 interview). Unlike congressional quotas, which can directly threaten incumbents, introducing a quota system to the civil service entrance exam did not elicit significant internal protests as it concerned the fortunes of new recruits rather than senior civil servants (Kwon Y., 2003 interview). With the additional impetus of the Beijing Conference, the Public Officials Appointment

Act was revised in December 1995 to incorporate a time-bound 20 percent quota for women among successful civil service exam appointees at grades 9, 7, and 5 until 2002 and a 10 percent "gender equal target appointment system" for women in high decisionmaking ranks (grades 1–5) (Chang, 2001 interview). The policy was also included in the Women's Basic Development Act in December 1995, which provided for annual monitoring of all ministries' efforts to address the gender imbalance (PCWA, 2000a).

The fruits of this target system were not readily visible, however, in the first few years of implementation. Although the percentages appear significant, the number of actual women beneficiaries was limited, largely because of an affirmative action policy that awarded veterans 3–5 percent extra points in the civil service entrance exams.[12] In addition, the quota system itself proved inadequate to counter the general lack of gender sensitivity among civil servants and the discriminatory attitudes encountered by women civil servants (Korean Civil Service Commission, 2002). As long-term bureaucrat Yang In-Sook noted:

> Women officials are often not fully accepted by their male colleagues. They are very capable but usually have to work twice as hard just to fit in. I don't think quotas are the answer to these pervasive attitudes . . . quotas injure women's self-pride. They are usually viewed as favoritism. Although the percentage looks large on paper, in reality only a few women benefit. I think they should be a last resort only. (2000 interview)

Kim Dae-Jung's election, however, provided a window of opportunity to improve efforts to expand women's bureaucratic presence. As part of his electoral platform and in the name of "gender mainstreaming," the president pledged to accelerate improvements in women's standing in public agencies, including 30 percent representation in ministerial advisory committees and increasing the 20 percent quota to 30 percent by 2002. Yoon Hoo-Jung, the first PCWA Chair, in particular, capitalized on these promises to push ministers to take a more proactive approach toward women's promotion:

> In our ministries there are few women in high decision-making positions, but to be influential women need to be better represented in the high ranks. I emphasized that the 21st century will be a knowledge-based era and that it is the Government's responsibility to ensure women are equipped with the necessary resources and skills to adapt. (2001 interview)

The 1998 creation of a WFP in MOGAHA charged with improving women's status in central and local government also played an important role. Led by femocrat Hwang In-Ja, the WFP initiated a range of programs aimed at creating a more egalitarian civil service including compulsory gender-training sessions for bureaucrats, the establishment of a "women-only lounge" to facilitate women's networking and information exchanges, and a joint educational project with the PCWA to encourage female high school students to consider bureaucratic career paths (Hwang, 2000 interview). In preparation for the Beijing Plus Five Conference (2000), MOGAHA also launched the "Government Plan for Gender-based Human Resource Management in the Public Service Toward the 21st Century" in an attempt to increase the hiring of women at all ranks, strengthen their competitiveness, and create a more flexible and supportive work environment, particularly in terms of maternity and childcare leave (PCWA, 1999).

> Our aim is to change bureaucratic culture from a "gender-blind" to "gender-bright" policy development process. It is important to change the gender balance among employees—sometimes men are more effective, other times women. We need a dual strategy. (Hwang, 2000 interview)

The efficacy of these new policies has been mixed. In terms of women's representation on ministerial advisory committees, the Kim Dae-Jung administration was able to come close to fulfilling its campaign pledge of reaching an overall 30 percent target of female experts, largely because these quotas were relatively uncontroversial and appeared impressive without significantly altering the status quo (Kang K., 2000 interview) (see table 8.9). On the other hand, not only has women's representation in advisory committees been higher in caring-related ministries than in finance, foreign affairs, or defense ministries (Chon, 2000 interview), some analysts argue that feminist critiques of the

Table 8.9 Women's participation in governmental committees

Year	Percentage of women	Quota target
1984	2.2	
1988	5.5	
1994	7.2	
1998	12.4	20
2000	15.0	25
2002	25.2	30

Source: KWDI, 2004.

government have been muted on account of such participation (e.g., Chang, 2000 interview). As personal relationships are forged and external advisers learn more about the constraints facing bureaucrats, they become more hesitant about expressing strong criticisms (Yoon, 2003 interview).

In lower-level civil service positions, women's representation has also increased significantly, from approximately 11 and 19 percent, respectively, at the national and local government levels in 1989, to 44 and 50 percent, respectively, in 2003,[13] and even up to 80–90 percent within some local government departments (Lee H., 2003 interview). Ironically, however, male bureaucrats became sufficiently alarmed by this rate of increase that they approached MOGAHA to ask for measures to address this imbalance. Whereas women's minority status in all other government bodies has been addressed by only moderate policy responses, male "discomfort," especially in the context of lingering male sensitivity about the 1999 elimination of the veteran affirmative action system discussed above, prompted a marked change in the orientation of personnel quotas. With the advent of the Second Five-Year Basic Plan on Women's Development in 2002, there was a shift from "women's quotas" to "gender-equal quotas," whereby ministries are to strive to ensure that both sexes have at least 30 percent representation at all levels (Lee H., 2003 interview). As MOGE Women's Policy Division director Kwon Young-Hyung points out:

> [This move] is really quite different from our desired policy goal. I feel as if they [MOGAHA] have really distorted the spirit of the quota system. (2003 interview)

However, partly because MOGAHA was able to don the mantle of international legitimacy and justify its policy switch by referring to the Swedish model of gender equality (whereby equality is defined as a situation in which both sexes must be represented within a 40–60 percent range), MOGE officials felt constrained to oppose the change:

> The policy outcome was different from our original intentions. We were opposed in principle but . . . strategically [following MOGAHA's support of the abolition of the veteran affirmative action system] we decided that we couldn't resist it too stubbornly and so we reluctantly accepted it. (Kwon Y., 2003 interview)

Lastly and probably most importantly, however, improvements in women's representation in decisionmaking posts have proven frustratingly slow. Although affirmative action measures have resulted in a 30 percent increase in female recruits, given the hierarchical, highly competitive character of the Korean bureaucracy, it will take considerably longer for these women to be promoted through the ranks and become influential players in the decisionmaking process. For example, as late as 2005 no woman had ever been appointed a department head in eight central government bodies, including in the Ministry of National Defence and the Fair Trade Commission (Moon, 2005). In recognition of this lag and ongoing lobbying efforts by the women's movement, the Civil Service Commission initiated a new five-year plan in 2002, which included increasing the ratio of female civil servants in senior posts to 10 percent by 2006, the number of female public university professors to 20 percent, and the number of women employees in public enterprises to 30 percent.[14]

Party Representation

Korea's weak, nonprogrammatic party system has rendered political parties a considerably less significant arena for women's activism than anticipated by the literature in other nascent democracies (e.g., Jaquette, 1995). Although party membership rolls are split evenly between men and women, Chun (1996) cautions that it is premature to assume this reflects an "expansion of women's consciousness (or) political parties' realization of the importance of women's votes" (32). The clientelistic nature of Korean parties, especially in provincial areas, suggests that women's party membership is also motivated by the material perks (e.g., small gifts, free lunches, and community-level political favors) that candidates historically offer in order to entice voters (Lee S., 2000). Moreover, women's high membership rates have been unmatched in party governing bodies, where women still constitute tiny minorities.[15] In 1993, women constituted just 4–5 percent of party affairs committee members and less than 1 percent of district chairpersons in both ruling and opposition parties. In 2001, although the overall rate had improved, with women comprising around 15 percent of total party officials, their representation on party committees and district chairpersons ranged between only 5–8 percent and 1–3 percent respectively (Kim W. et al., 2001b). Moreover, those serving as party executives were predominantly concentrated in women-related committees.

Significantly, the record for nominating women candidates has been poor across the party spectrum. For example, in 2002 some 70 percent of women who sought nomination as municipal head and city councilor candidates within the MDP were rejected, and the GNP turned down 65 percent (Moon M., 2002). Likewise, at the National Assembly level, the proportion of female candidates rose from a mere 2.2 percent in 1988 to only 5.6 percent in 2000.[16] Only at the metropolitan/provincial assembly level has the rate shown any significant increase—from 2.2 percent in 1991, to 4.5 percent in 1995, to 6.1 percent in 1998, and to 12 percent in 2002 (Lee R., 2000; KWDI, 2004).

A major reason for this gender division of labor has been the persistence of male-dominant attitudes among party elite. MDP official Kim Young-Ae points out that most male party officials remain reluctant to promote a more egalitarian party culture:

> Men do not have much gender awareness or adhere to concepts such as "equal culture" or "partnership" . . . Some say: "Okay, if it's important for women [to be in decision-making roles] why don't you develop your ability and just fight with us one on one?" (2000 interview)

This belief system is further reflected in the kinds of seats for which women are typically nominated. Although studies have shown that there is a higher probability that women will win in large urban areas (Park K., 1999), Korean women candidates continue to be "over-represented" in

Table 8.10 Women in high-level political party positions

		Government party		First opposition party	
		Party Affairs Committee members	*District Party Chapter chairperson*	*Party Affairs Committee members*	*District Party Chapter chairperson*
1993	Total	47	237	65	222
	Female	2	2	3	1
	% Female	4.3	0.8	4.6	0.5
1997	Total	50	253	—	—
	Female	3	2	—	—
	% Female	6.1	0.8	0.8	—
2000	Total	41	225	55	225
	Female	6	6	3	5
	% Female	14.6	2.7	5.5	2.2
2001	Total	98	227	63	227
	Female	5	3	5	3
	% Female	5.1	1.3	7.9	1.3
2004	Total	76	n/a	51	n/a
	Female	16	—	10	—
	% Female	21.1	—	19.6	—

Source: KWDI, 2004: 433.

small cities where chances of success are low. Additionally, fewer women have been nominated in districts where their party enjoys a strong support base, and instead tend to be selected in the strongholds of rival parties (Kim W. et al., 2001b). Similarly, at the senior level, women who have held leadership positions have typically depended on the backing of supportive bosses. A case in point is former legislator Pak Yong-suk, who was encouraged to enter the political arena by then opposition leader Kim Dae-jung, and served as vice chair of Kim's Peace and Democracy Party between 1988 and 1992. Once Kim "retired" from politics following his 1992 presidential defeat, however, Pak was forced to resign from the executive committee (Soh C., 1994). Given this historical context, the appointment of women as leaders of the MDP (Choi Mi-Ae) and GNP (Park Geun-hye) in the run-up to the April 2004 National Legislative elections was more than symbolic, and reflected party officials' cognizance that the electorate was looking for a major change in "politics as usual." (See table 8.10.)

Accounting for Gradualism

Although there have been improvements in Korea's scorecard for women's formal political representation post-transition, particularly through the introduction of legislative and civil service quotas, the overall results are indisputably disappointing. How does my theoretical framework, focusing on the political opportunity structures of democratization, help account for this?

Institutional Rules

Formal institutional rule are clearly a contributing factor as hybrid electoral systems with only a small share of PR seats and single-member constituencies are less conducive to advancing women's representation (Huang, 2003). A catch-all, cadre-based party system, with relatively weak programmatic differences, has likewise provided few incentives for party elites to nominate women. Whereas left-wing parties in Scandinavia, for instance, actively recruited women on the basis of their ideological platform (Bystydzienski, 1995), Korean party officials' primary allegiance is to party bosses (e.g., Kwak, 2002). Similarly, the elitist, highly competitive civil service, which until 1999 implemented an affirmative action policy for veterans, has played a significant role in thwarting women's representation within the bureaucracy.

However, although such institutional mechanisms help explain women's rather limited gains in representation, more subjective dimensions appear to be of equal or greater importance. Gender discriminatory attitudes among political elites and to a lesser degree the general electorate, as well as an initial reluctance among women's organizations to actively engage with political institutions, have served as important constraints.

Political Society's Attitudes

Discriminatory attitudes among political elites constitute an important explanatory variable for understanding women's political underrepresentation. Research has pointed to a "male conspiracy" whereby women are selected for "unsafe" seats because of perceptions that they are electoral liabilities—less popular among voters, weak at fundraising, and poorly connected (Carroll, 1994). The Korean case is certainly no exception (e.g., Soh, 1993, 1994). Although pressure from domestic women's organizations and international conventions has helped political elites recognize the importance of at least token female appointments, skepticism as to women's political capabilities and suitability persists. For example, former SCCWA Chair Lee Yon-Sook notes dryly:

> Men in power feel it is important to "give opportunities to women." However, this is just thinking. In daily action, there are not many women—Korean politics is a very masculine society. Men easily forget. (2000 interview)

Other women politicians emphasized their differential treatment by male colleagues who still subscribe to traditional public/private gender scripts. Former minister Kwon Young-Ja, for example, explained:

> I think male ministers view their female counterparts through worried eyes—always questioning whether they will prove capable . . . But more than male cabinet members, party officials are the most critical—I'm confident that as a woman I am no less capable—but party people are very quick to blame any kind of problem on women. (2000 interview)

Although the introduction of gender-sensitivity programs has sought to address such attitudes, their overall impact has been limited. A national survey of local government officials, for example, found that whereas a majority of respondents concurred that "women's abilities must be developed" and their participation in economic, social, and political activities increased, 31 percent still agreed that "the small number of senior female public officials can be attributed to women's incompetence" and 53 percent thought "women have a weaker sense of professionalism than men" (Hahn, 2001a: 4–7). In the same vein, affirmative action measures to address the bureaucracy's gender imbalance are often dismissed as "reverse discrimination" (Moon, 2005). Equally problematically, a KWDI survey found that fewer than 9 percent of male officials had received gender-sensitivity training lasting for longer than a day, whereas four times as many women had. Moreover, the majority of male attendees were in nonmanagerial positions (KWDI and MOGE, 2005). In the judiciary, training programs have targeted the new generation of legal professionals, rather than those in positions of seniority. Similarly, civil service programs last for only a few hours, are not tested, and are often too generic to provide detail-oriented bureaucrats with practical guidelines.

Of further concern is the subtle structural discrimination that women face in the form of exclusion from politically influential "old boys' networks." Although not unique to Korea (e.g., Eisenstein, 1995), the dominant tendency toward single-sex socializing in Korean political culture renders this problem particularly salient. Soh (1993) argues that most Koreans juggle dual gender ideologies by "compartmentalizing the social arena not only into the public/private spheres but also into the formal/informal situations in each sphere," and alternating these ideologies appropriately based on *nunch'i* (sensitivity/tact) (2). A culturally specific phenomenon, *nunch'i* refers to an individual's assessment of a delicate behavioral situation and corresponding response (e.g., appropriate use of honorific language), and lies at the core of Korean social mores.

Possessing good *nunch'i* is particularly important for women in public life, as political decisionmaking is dominated by personal connections rather than the "intrinsic merit of an issue" (6). If women want to advance in their political careers they must engage in "active politicking"; however, this requires knowing how to behave appropriately when joining male socializing and avoiding being criticized for "immodest womanly behavior" or for being a "woman without *nunch'i*" (7). For example, whereas women can safely join men at a restaurant, they are likely to attract criticism for drinking afterward, particularly as such forays have often been associated with the sex industry (e.g., hostess bars). The challenge for women is to gain access to those informal political gatherings where many important decisions are made while avoiding transgressing unwritten social gender scripts. Legislator Han Myung-sook, for example, maintained that coping with the male drinking culture has been one of the major causes of stress during her congressional experience:

> The things congresswomen find most difficult to cope with are the influence peddling, struggles among political factions and of course the drinking. The latter is not our scene at all. But although I don't like it, I worry that if I don't go I'll remain in the dark about important issues. A few women can manage these situations well, but by and large we are weak at this—for me dealing with this kind of culture is the hardest aspect of politics. (2000 interview)

Exclusion from old boys' networks also has funding implications. Whereas men can appeal to businesses for support, obtaining the requisite financial backing is more difficult for women as companies remain skeptical about whether they will benefit from endorsing female candidates. Moreover, women are more inclined to run clean campaigns and shy away from "dirty money" (Manarin, 2000). Yet, rather than face up to these structural disadvantages, party leaders have tended to blame women's underrepresentation on their average later entry into politics and paint a picture of a limited pool of eligible women. This argument is clearly flawed, however, given that Korean women candidates have a higher average educational status than men, and that all female legislators have been professionals (e.g., Park K., 1999).

Civic Attitudes

Whereas one might expect that public prejudice would discourage women's political representation, survey data suggests that Korean civic attitudes toward women in formal politics have improved markedly over time. A 1988 survey showed that 91 percent of men and approximately 60 percent of women would support a male candidate over an equally qualified female, but by contrast a 1995 survey found that 31 percent of female voters and 24 percent of men cast ballots for women in the local election (Park K., 1999). Moreover, 70 percent of women candidates in the 1996 congressional elections perceived voters as having either more favorable attitudes toward women or the same attitudes as they do toward male candidates (Kim and Kim, 1998). By 2000, a KWDI survey found that a majority of respondents agreed that more women in power were needed at the National Assembly, ministerial and upper civil service levels. Although more men were indifferent to increasing the number of women decisionmakers, over 40 percent responded affirmatively in each category, and only a small minority (12–14 percent) were actively opposed. Women, on the other hand, were overwhelmingly in favor of addressing the gender imbalance (Kim Y. et al., 2000). Further, although the numbers were somewhat smaller, a majority (54 percent) believed that greater representation for women would result in positive change in the national and local assemblies.

Feminist Attitudes

The extent to which women's movement organizations should compromise with political society has been hotly debated post-transition in democratizing societies (e.g., Vargas, 2002). By participating in formal politics, social movements risk diluting their focus on new forms of nonhierarchical, people-centered politics or having leadership become distanced from the grassroots (e.g., Waylen, 1996a). Conversely, if activists insist on autonomy and concentrate on community and cultural politics, their sociopolitical influence will inevitably be circumscribed. Where women's organizations choose to position themselves on this debate depends largely on historical experiences of civil society–state interactions and whether the state is viewed as a provider of key resources or a source of potential co-optation and clientelism (e.g., Jaquette and Wolchik, 1998).

In Korea, generally low interest in entering the formal political arena among the *shimin undong* was reinforced by the absence of a KWAU member group that specifically dealt with women and politics issues (Yoon, 2003 interview). Although an emphasis on legislative reforms starting from the late 1980s necessitated a certain level of cooperation with political elites, this involvement was fluid and issue-specific, and was rarely expressed through an overt endorsement of a particular party. Activists focused on lobbying sympathetic individual party officials and congressional representatives, and were not generally bound by party loyalties. As KWAU policy officer Cho Young-Sook explains:

> We targeted the National Assembly, both on a party and an individual basis. There was a dilemma because of the shifting nature of the majority and opposition parties under Kim Young-sam: although the majority party was originally conservative and ex-military government, some activists with radical backgrounds joined as lawmakers in the name of change! . . . But these days we tend to ask both parties. (2000 interview)

The pool of women willing to stand for office, however, has been limited, despite political education and training efforts by both parties and women's groups. For example, although legislator Kim Jon-Chul established a political academy for women in 1999, very few of the 1,000 participants stood as candidates in the subsequent local elections (Kim W., 2003 interview). In this regard both the Women's Leadership training program launched at Ewha Womans University in 2003 and the 2004 List of 100 Women campaign constitute important steps forward. The Ewha initiative provides political education and leadership courses for women in political office as well as high-ranking public and private sector positions in order to improve women's general leadership capacities and increase levels of gender awareness among prominent women. In the case of the List of 100 Women, the challenge going forward will be to build upon the momentum of 2004 and to develop a databank not simply of women but of women committed to furthering gender equality *and* who are willing to stand for office.

Turning to the bureaucracy, Korean women's engagement was limited until the election of Kim Dae-jung. Given that the most urgent task facing women activists through the mid-1990s was the establishment of a legal framework that provided women with the rights to equal treatment and protection, monitoring and evaluating the implementation of new policies—the primary domain of bureaucrats—could not be women's groups' first priority. Only recently have women's groups begun to view the state as a site of ongoing negotiations, where with sufficient complementary pressure from without and within, advances in gender equality are possible (e.g., Lee R., 2000).

In order to take advantage of these opportunities in the future, it will be important for women's umbrella organizations to develop the capacity of their members to better understand the inner workings of the policy formation and implementation process (e.g., Lee O., 2000; Kwon, 2003 interviews), and to forge closer relationships with WFP staff in particular, but also bureaucrats in more traditional male-dominated ministries, especially the Ministries of Economy and Finance and Unification. My research suggests that bureaucrats are often unaware of the hidden gender biases embedded within policy approaches, but could potentially be persuaded if lobbied effectively. Lee Ok, former head of the Ministry of Justice WFP, for example, admitted that she had never considered creating legal literacy campaigns for women to help them understand their rights under newly reformed laws, but was open to the idea (2000 interview). Similarly, my experience working in the Korean Ministry of Foreign Affairs suggested that bureaucrats lack practical examples of how to implement gender analyses of the policies for which they are responsible and have little knowledge of where to turn for advice or information. In other words, bureaucrats are not necessarily opposed to creating new programs, but are often unaware of possible reforms and need to be persuaded (e.g., through examples of best practice) by the NGO community and femocrats.

CHAPTER 9

Conclusions: Assessing Cultural Change and Theoretical Lessons

Public awareness of gender issues has definitely changed, but we still have a long way to go. I recently talked to a group of highly educated professional men and the first question they asked was "are women really discriminated against in Korea?"! Because men take it for granted that women are much better off than in the past, it creates fuzziness about the reality so we need to show them the facts, the reality . . . .

Park Y., 2000 interview

This concluding chapter addresses three central questions:

- How has the political opportunity structure of democratization affected Korean gender relations?
- What lessons can we draw from Korea concerning women's efforts to participate in democratic politics more generally?
- In what ways does an analysis of post-transitional gender politics provide a window on to the dynamics of the Korean democratization process more broadly?

Before reflecting on these broader questions, however, the discussion begins with a brief analysis of the impact of political change on ordinary citizens' gendered attitudes and behavior.

Translating Institutional Reforms into Attitudinal Changes

The attitudes and perceptions that citizens hold concerning gender relations shape women's lived experiences in important ways, sanctioning some behaviors and discouraging others. As Friedman (2000) quoting Duverger (1995) notes:

> Purely political reforms are helpful in ameliorating gender discrimination but . . . "It is probably still more important to fight against the deeply-rooted belief in the natural inferiority of women." (292)

Accordingly, the practical impact of legislative/policy reforms will be circumscribed if the populace is either uninformed or strongly opposed to initiatives that disrupt existing gender dynamics. An activist minority may be willing to go against the tide, but shifts in public perceptions facilitate the average woman's ability to capitalize on those legal and institutional gains achieved by women's movement organizations and their state/civil society allies.

Although longitudinal data on the evolution of Korean attitudes concerning gender roles is limited, this section examines opinion surveys and ethnographic research to assess the extent to which gender-related changes at the formal politico-legal level have filtered down to average citizens' ways of thinking about family and workplace relationships, moral behavior, and bodily integrity.[1] Although it is difficult to differentiate between changes attributable to democratization and subsequent legislative reforms, and those that are part of broader modernization and globalization processes (Cho H., 2002), my research suggests that gender-related legal revisions and institutional reforms, as well as public awareness efforts initiated by women's organizations, have played an important role in accelerating the evolution of gender scripts in Korea. Available data paints a mixed picture: surprisingly progressive attitudes about gender relations and roles are held in tandem with deeply conservative viewpoints. As Kendall (2002) emphasizes:

> Over the last three decades, lives have been refashioned on the shifting ground of urbanization, industrialization, military authoritarianism, democratic reform and social liberalization. In this process, class and gender identities have been "construction sites" for new definitions of home and family, work and leisure, husband and wife. (1)

Family Relations

In the case of the family, recent opinion surveys suggest that rigid Confucian gender hierarchies, wherein men are viewed as "heaven" or "outside" and women as "earth" or "inside" (Yi, 1998: 170), have relaxed considerably over the past 20 years. Whereas a 1985 Gallup poll found that 83 percent of female respondents believed that "Women should have only a family-oriented life, devoted to bringing up the children and looking after the husband," over half of survey respondents in the 1990s thought that married women should pursue an independent career (Na and Cha, 2000: 308). Indeed, a 2001 poll suggested that 81 percent of unmarried men and 66 percent of married men wanted their wives to work (Jeon, 2002). Whereas this change is at least in part motivated by families' growing desire for a double income, it also suggests greater societal acceptance of women who pursue a career.

This shift in gender-role expectations, however, remains premised on an unequal division of labor in the household and especially in terms of childcare. Women's paid work is generally couched in terms of individual self-fulfillment rather than a contribution to family income as captured by the following excerpt from a 1998 ethnographic study on changing gender-role perceptions among middle-class families:

> It is not economic independence that motivates my wife to work. I have enough income to support the family . . . She wants to work to get a personal sense of self-achievement . . . Women's social activities such as studying, or having a job and her sense of personal achievement may be a consolation to the individual. But there are things that should be done when the wife is back in the family. Cooking, helping children with homework, cleaning the house, and so on." (Yi, 1998: 203–05)

Whereas men's share of housework responsibilities has gradually increased, especially if both partners are in the paid workforce, the primary burden continues to rest on women's shoulders. A 1991 survey found that 79 percent of husbands never helped with domestic chores, 19 percent did "a little," and a mere 2 percent did "a lot" (Kim Y. and Harrison, 1999: 26). Three years later, a 1994 National Survey on the Quality of Life indicated that although 33 percent of Korean males never engaged in household labor, those who did spent an average of 12.6 hours per week versus 50 hours for women, and in the case of dual-income families, still contributed less than 50 percent of the time women invested (Tsuya et al., 2000: 207). By 2001, attitudinal improvements were more pronounced. A Korean Federation of Housewives' Clubs survey showed that, contrary to the oft-cited adage that "if males go into the kitchen their hot pepper [genitals] will fall off," 91 percent of male respondents asserted that working in the kitchen "does not affect their pride," and 77 percent disagreed with the notion that domestic chores are only the wife's responsibility (*Korea Herald*, October 8, 2001).[2] Whereas we should expect male rhetoric to change faster than the amount of time actually spent pitching in, this itself would speak to positive cultural changes in the way household work is (de)valued by men. Childcare, however, is still largely perceived as a female duty, despite recent discursive shifts toward "parental leave" in politico-legal debates. A 2002 survey, for example, found that approximately 75 percent of men answered "yes" or "maybe" to the statement "child-raising and education is better left to the mother" (*JoongAng Daily*, November 10, 2002).

Traditional attitudes regarding family lineage and son preference have also proved resilient. Families continue to adhere to conservative gender scripts when performing the ancestor worship rituals that are practiced by a large majority of Koreans irrespective of religious affiliation. Traditional holidays are celebrated with the husband's family, thereby reinforcing the patrilineal order, with women responsible for preparing elaborate food offerings for rituals that only men are entitled to perform. To raise public awareness about the need to reform these traditional practices, Korean WomenLink and the MOGE have organized annual "egalitarian holiday custom campaigns" since 1999. Perhaps not surprisingly, change has been gradual at best owing to the continued cultural importance of filial piety and deference to elders.

More disturbingly, the cultural preference for male offspring has shown limited improvement, with the sex ratio imbalance actually worsening between 1980 and the mid-1990s (from 104 male births to every 100 females in 1980 to 116 males per 100 in 1995). The ratio improved to 105 by 2003 following concerted awareness campaigns by activists and local governments, but the rate of selection remains especially high for the third and fourth child in a family, suggesting that many parents still go to considerable lengths to realize their preference for a son (KWDI, 2004). Although the practice has historically been justified by the need for support in old age or the provision of family labor, the primary issues today concern family lineage and prestige (Yoon, 2002 interview). For example, in a recent survey on male attitudes toward "women's worth," one respondent noted that her husband ridiculed her when she criticized his extravagant spending: "Don't say that I have to save money. We don't have a son who can inherit our money" (Ko, 2002).

Finally, support for the cornerstone of Confucian traditions, the family headship system, was slow to erode. As late as 2001, KWDI research found that only 19 percent of men and 30 percent of women supported ending the family headship system (Kim Y. et al., 2001: 6).

However, as discussed in chapter 6, by 2003, following a large national cross-movement campaign, survey results showed that 70 percent of respondents (82 percent women and 50 percent men) favored repealing the law. There was, however, a stark generation gap: 83 percent of respondents in their thirties favored reform in contrast to only 54 percent of those in their thirties and 38 percent in their sixties. Similarly, 65 percent of men and 81 percent of women thought the child's name should be registered with the caregiver's family postdivorce rather than automatically remain with the father's registry (ibid.).

Workplace Relations

Recent public opinion studies suggest that women's recently won employment-related rights remain far from internalized. Although not surprising given that the language of discrimination and sexual harassment has only recently been introduced into the Korean lexicon, it is noteworthy that both men and women recognize that women are disadvantaged in the workforce. A majority of mixed-sex respondents in a 2001 survey concurred that male employees are favored in terms of postings (54 percent), assignments (51 percent), and promotions (53 percent); likewise, some 61 percent of male employers thought that men should be appointed first to CEO-level positions, and 45 percent had no qualms about promoting men ahead of women and agreed that women should be laid off before their male colleagues (Hahn, 2001b). Moreover, a 2002 survey found that almost 30 percent of men in their twenties agreed with the statement that "women are better for simple and easy jobs," while over one-third expressed disliking working under female supervisors or complained that "working women are too aggressive" (*JoongAng Daily*, October 28, 2002).

In terms of recruitment, most respondents in a 2001 employee survey agreed that practices such as compulsory retirement upon marriage had all but disappeared (83 percent), and that expecting women staff to serve tea or do office cleaning by virtue of their sex was unacceptable (53 percent) (WomenLink, 2001). However, a study on employment recruitment and interview processes in 2000 found that biases against women job candidates persist (Seo, 2000). Despite the 1995 ban on appearance requirements, for instance, many employers still request a photo and height/weight details on application forms, and questions commonly asked of female graduates reveal employers' assumptions that women will be less committed professionally on account of family responsibilities and are better hired as "flowers of the office" (2).

Studies also suggest that the glass ceiling in Korea is particularly hard to crack, with women holding very few senior positions within the workforce. Between 1985 and 1999, the percentage of women in professional/technical and administrative/managerial positions only improved from 5.4 to 13 percent, despite an increase of 40 percentage points in the number of women with some college education (NSO, 2002). Among women interviewed in prominent positions in the fields of politics, law, and business, 80 percent believed their success was premised on a greater investment of time when compared with their male counterparts, whereas only 10 percent believed their career paths had been unimpeded by discriminatory attitudes.[3] As one female senior manager recalled:

> Male employees in general were promoted to assistant managers within the first 2 or 3 years of working for the company. But I was still a regular employee even after those who started working after me got promoted. (*JoongAng Daily*, October 21, 2002)

Morality and Bodily Integrity

The erosion of strict Confucian codes over the past two decades has led to dramatic shifts in public perceptions of appropriate moral behavior for men and women, particularly among younger generations. For instance, Na and Cha (2000) found that whereas 88 percent of respondents in 1979 believed chastity was necessary prior to marriage, by 1998 this proportion had fallen to 71 percent and among people in their twenties the rate was as low as 55 percent (305–07). As social critic Lee S. (2002) notes:

> There can be no return to a sexually inarticulate past . . . We will find Korean women's sexual subjectivity in that particular borderland of the global village between Korea's Confucian cultural heritage and Western views of sexual pleasure and desire. (160)

Whereas open discussions about sexuality were largely taboo until the mid-1990s, attitudinal changes have become increasingly rapid, thanks in part to international influences, a sudden flourishing of popular novels and TV dramas addressing sexuality issues, and a popular TV sex education program launched in 1998 (Park S., 2002). University student union Internet pages now provide comprehensive sex education information, condoms are distributed on campuses, and even the Ministry of Education has introduced compulsory sex education modules in schools.

Although women in particular remain reluctant to talk openly about their personal experiences, a 2002 report estimated that between 33 and 50 percent of female college students were sexually active (e.g., Park S., 2002), and a 2004 survey found that 71 percent of women in their twenties and thirties would consider having premarital sex if they were in love or engaged and only 20 percent thought it necessary to wait until marriage (*Seoul Newspaper*, December 28, 2004).

Ideas about marriage have also been revolutionized. Far from the sacrosanct position of Korean tradition, marriage itself is increasingly seen as optional, and divorce rates have skyrocketed. Not only do one-third of women (compared with 20 percent of men) intend not to marry (*Seoul Newspaper*, June 20, 2004), but Korea now has one of the world's highest rates of divorce: 2.8 per 1,000 couples (Hayes, 2003). Acceptance of divorce has risen correspondingly: only 28 percent of respondents in a 1985 Gallup poll agreed that "if and when one cannot find happiness and satisfaction with one's partner, it is better to get divorced" (Kim B., 1994: 244); yet in 2001, 80 percent of respondents were willing to condone divorce depending on the circumstances and 70 percent believed divorce was acceptable even in the case of couples with children (Han, 2001).

There has also been a significant shift away from traditional conceptions of women's bodies as familial and societal property, as well as a greater (albeit still partial) acceptance of women as citizens with individual rights over their own sexuality.[4] Although the chastity ethos lingers, speaking of sexual crimes as a violation of family honor is no longer socially acceptable (Shim, 2002). Rape and sexual assault are increasingly seen as crimes against individuals, as suggested by rising numbers of women prepared to report attacks and avail themselves of counseling services (Lee M., 2002 interview). Although there is a dearth of consistent longitudinal data, the number of women seeking sexual violence counseling after the passage of the Sexual Violence Prevention and Relief Act increased rapidly from 3,245 in 1995 to 12,358 in 1997 to 24,788 in 1998 (KWDI, 2004: 468). Comparable data is unfortunately unavailable for later years, but increasing usage of the Government's Women's Hotline "1366" for sexual or family violence suggests a similar trend (4,248 women in 1999 but 7,129 in 2004).[5]

Likewise, there has been a growing realization that family violence must be publicly exposed and addressed through governmental intervention. Although estimates of the prevalence of domestic violence tend to be more meaningful in a political rather than academic context,[6] increased reporting rates and participation in counseling programs over

Table 9.1 Frequency of domestic violence trials

Period	*Number of domestic violence trials*
1998 July–December	1,455
1999 January–December	9,210
2000 January–November	11,999
2001 January–December	14,583
2002 January–December	15,151
2003 January–December	16,408

Source: Data from the Korean National Police Agency (http://www. police.go.kr).

Table 9.2 Level of public awareness of major gender-related legislation in 2000

1995	Women's Basic Development Act	21.8%
1999	Gender Discrimination Prevention and Relief Act	72.6%
1997	Special Law on Punishment of the Crime of Domestic Violence and the Law on the Protection of Domestic Violence Victims	90.4%
1987	Equal Employment Act (EEA)	74.6%
1999	Workplace Sexual Harassment prohibition provision (EEA third reform)	93.9%
1998	PCWA establishment	49.0%

Source: Kim Y. et al., 2001.

time indicate that women are increasingly aware that they have legal alternatives to tolerating abuse. Moreover, high levels of public awareness about the existence of the 1997 Special Law on Punishment of the Crime of Domestic Violence and the Law on the Protection of Domestic Violence Victims (90 percent in 2001) suggest that at the very least citizens recognize that violence against women constitutes a crime (Kim Y. et al., 2001) (see table 9.1).

Legal Literacy

Significant post-transitional attitudinal changes notwithstanding, much remains to be done before de jure gender rights become embedded in the Korean civic consciousness. Although a surprisingly high proportion of the populace is aware of the existence of major gender-related laws, they lack the legal literacy skills necessary to take advantage of such legislation (see table 9.2). Legal scholar and MDP gender expert Kim Young-Hee explains the problem as follows:

> People often say that low awareness is one aspect of poor implementation
> [of gender-related legislation] . . . But actually I think people are more
> aware of women's laws than of other types. The problem is that when there
> is a [gender-related] complaint or dispute then ordinary people don't
> know what steps to take to secure legal protection. (2000 interview)

In order to address this lacuna, it is important for activists and
policymakers to understand exactly where public biases lie and to inform
citizens about the realities of gender inequality. KWDI analyst Park
Young-Ran uses the following example to highlight this urgency:

> Public awareness of gender issues has definitely changed, but we still have a
> long way to go. I recently talked to a group of highly educated professional
> men who asked "are women really discriminated against in Korea?"! I tried
> to analyze why they asked this question and concluded that men feel that in
> their private lives they are pretty much equal or in some cases give more
> power to their wives for the sake of a peaceful family life.[7] They carry that
> mentality into the workplace and cannot see the discrimination. Because
> they take it for granted that women are much better off than in the past, it
> creates fuzziness about the reality so we need to show them the
> facts . . . One class participant told me how he was shocked by a documen-
> tary on rape and how he had come to realize that women are truly discrim-
> inated against! So a lot of education needs to be done . . . . (2000 interview)

Whereas the women's movement and, increasingly, WPMs have the
legal tools necessary to challenge direct and indirect forms of discrimination, effective implementation will require more systematic efforts to
break down traditional gender scripts and educate citizens about how to
exercise their legal rights. Such programs are particularly necessary, given
Korea's short democratic history and a general dearth of familiarity with
the legal system, on the one hand, and the far-reaching gender-related
legislative changes over the last decade-and-a-half, on the other.
Although MOGE has a Gender Complaints Unit to handle violations
covered by the 1999 Gender Discrimination Prevention and Relief Act
(primarily relating to sexual harassment cases) and a national hotline,
"1366," to cover domestic violence cases, these services suffer from a
number of shortcomings. Besides limited funding and geographical coverage (face-to-face services are only available in Seoul), their mandate
does not extend to legal advice and counseling services for family-related
issues such as divorce, child custody, and child maintenance payments.

In this regard, the Chilean model of women's legal advisory services or
Centers for Information on Women's Rights (CIWR) could offer

valuable lessons. Staffed by lawyers and social workers, the CIWR were established by the government in all provinces in 1990 to provide counseling on a comprehensive array of gender- and family-related issues including divorce, child custody, recognition of illegitimate children, and gender violence (Waylen, 1996b). They not only help women in immediate need of legal advice but also enable average citizens to become better informed about their legal rights and responsibilities following post-authoritarian legal changes. The CIWR also help to inform the policy development process: that is, they provide the SERNAM, the national WPM, with an invaluable data source regarding the needs and interests of average women (Valenzuela, 1998).

Additional measures to encourage women to act on such information and seek legal redress are also necessary. Data from the Korean Sexual Violence Relief Center, for example, suggests that only a tiny minority of women who call to report sexual violence crimes are willing to press charges, in part because they perceive the judicial system to be gender discriminatory (Lee M., 2003 interview). Here again an example of good practice from Latin America, the paralegal bridging program pioneered by the Brazilian NGO Themis, could be instructive. Established in 1993 and now backed by Ministry of Judiciary funding, Themis trains low-income community women as paralegals to serve as a bridge between grassroots citizens and the court system (Macaulay, 2002). Over the course of an intensive training program, encompassing the basic precepts of the law, the Brazilian judicial system as well as more specific information on women's constitutional, human, and workplace rights, relationships with legal professionals are established, upon which trainees can subsequently draw as court assistants or when accompanying women to police stations to file charges. Macaulay concludes:

> Themis' experience in running a legal literacy programme highlights the dynamic relationship . . . between women's increased knowledge of their rights and of the mechanisms of the law, and eventual campaigns to change both the law and the institutions of the justice system. (96)

In short, although Korea has made impressive strides in legislating for gender equality, transforming formal gender rights into fundamental improvements in women's lived experience will necessitate concerted efforts to teach ordinary citizens to value egalitarian gender relations and inform women about their options for legal recourse should their rights be violated. In this regard, Korean femocrats and women activists could gain important insights from the best practices of other nascent democracies, especially the pioneering work of Southern Cone feminists outlined above.

Democratization and Gender Equality: Korean Exceptionalism or Transferable Lessons?

One of this book's central hypotheses (see chapter 1) was that the Korean case would serve as a useful litmus test for the transformatory potential of nascent democracies. Although characterized by a conservative gendered political culture, the former Hermit Kingdom has been hailed as one of the success stories of Third Wave democratization, facilitated by robust economic growth in the immediate post-transition decade. Even so, the gender and democracy literature suggested we should at best expect mixed improvements in women's status. Whereas growing international attention to women-related concerns and transnational networking might enhance women's legitimacy and collective strength, examples from Latin America and Eastern Europe highlighted a range of potential impediments to securing greater rights and opportunities: waning social movement cohesiveness and relative marginalization from mainstream politics; difficulties in influencing the agenda of political parties now occupying center stage; vocal and politically influential conservative opponents; as well as the relative inertia of political institutions. As this book has argued, however, Korea's surprising advances in gender equality raise questions about important elements of extant explanatory frameworks.

Actors' Relative Strength and Gendered Interests

Although voluntarism does not usually make for satisfying social science, the book's process-tracing methodological approach has underscored the central importance of the Korean women's movement's organizational and lobbying strategies in pushing through policy reforms and challenging traditional gender norms. It suggests that greater gender equality is not a simple by-product of democracy and a general expansion of citizenship rights (e.g., Shafir, 1998), but rather results from deliberate, strategic efforts by women's movements and their civil society and state allies to equalize gender relations. The Korean women's movement has effectively negotiated contingent and evolving "access points to state policy arenas" (Alvarez, 1990: 272) to push through gender-related reforms, while simultaneously maintaining a sufficient degree of autonomy and cohesiveness to stave off the dangers that have frequently plagued movements in other regions: movement fatigue, isolation, "decapitation" (as leaders flock to more stable and lucrative bureaucratic positions), co-optation or splintering (particularly due to conflicting party loyalties). Although much remains to be done in order to expand and deepen recent gains (especially in terms of improving the women's movement's grassroots reach), Korea represents a relatively successful example of movement-led initiatives and, more recently, movement–WPM partnerships that have taken advantage of the new political opportunity structures to reduce gender discrimination. But to what extent can the Korean "model" of feminist activism be applied to other nascent democracies? More specifically, to what degree was the internal organizational strength and cohesiveness of Korean women's movements facilitated by broader structural or institutional variables that are largely outside the control of women's groups versus what we might term "strategic choices" or agency?

My conclusions are mixed. Structural factors, particularly economic growth (pre- and post-transition) and the relative absence of crosscutting cleavages such as race/ethnicity or class, clearly facilitated the organizational strength of the Korean women's movement in the 1990s. Likewise, a weak, nonprogrammatic party system provided greater political space for social movements to influence public policy. However, the organizational model adopted by women's groups, as well as their approach vis-à-vis parties and other political actors, was also the result of strategic choices and a considerable investment of movement resources and energy.

Because women find themselves divided both in terms of their ideological approach to advancing women's status as well as their social positioning (e.g., class or ethnicity), they cannot be assumed to constitute a unified interest group (e.g., Radcliffe and Westwood, 1993; Friedman, 2000). A case in point is the so-called nanny problem where middle-class feminists find themselves socially positioned with opposing economic interests to those of their domestic helpers. Although the relatively muted expression of such cleavages in the Korean context clearly simplifies the task of forging and sustaining alliances among women, the presence of such divisions need not be insurmountable. For instance, despite divergent ideological underpinnings and class composition, the progressive KWAU and the more mainstream KNCW adopted an effective mode of cooperation to push for the criminalization of family and sexual violence, the introduction of political quotas, and the revision of the EEA following the 1997/98 economic crisis.

In short, although structural factors "facilitated" women's organizational cohesion and influence in Korea, they constituted neither necessary nor sufficient variables. This conclusion is further supported by even a cursory glance at other Asian cases. For example, although Japanese women have also benefited from rapid economic development and relative social homogeneity, analysts and activists alike concur that the Japanese women's movement has been significantly less cohesive and influential than its Korean counterpart (e.g., Byun W., 2000 interview). By contrast, the Philippines, which has suffered from persistent economic crises throughout the 1990s, and is characterized by marked ethnic and class diversity, boasts a vocal and politically influential women's movement that is often regarded as a model in the Asian region (Sobritchea, 2005).

More compelling explanatory variables underpinning Korean women's success, which may offer broader transferable lessons, involve three key strategic choices: fostering and working through movement umbrella organizations, developing intra- and cross-movement conjunctural coalitions, and regular movement introspection and flexibility. First, given gender scholars' emphasis on the need for feminists to pursue a dual political strategy both within and outside the state (e.g., Alvarez, 1990; Pringle and Watson, 1992), the Korean case could be viewed as a "best practice" of movement coordination. A nonpartisan movement umbrella organization that is respected (although certainly not free from criticism) by organizations with diverse gender-related interests is more effective at representing women's voices when engaging with state actors than if individual movement organizations were to pursue a decentralized political model. Whereas proponents of new social movement theory argue that movement organizations focusing on community activism, cultural/discursive politics and consciousness-raising, can play an important role in effecting cultural change and should be read as a sign of evolving, maturing movements (e.g., Frohmann and Valdes, 1995; Alvarez et al., 1998), we cannot shy away from exploring organizational formats that best facilitate legislative and political institutional reforms, especially in light of women's general status as second-class citizens at the point of transition. As Tarrow has observed:

> While encouraging base autonomy and allowing activists free spaces of democracy and participation, [loose mobilizing structures] permit—and indeed encourage—a lack of coordination and discontinuity." (1994: 149)

Clearly the case should not be overstated. A strong movement umbrella organization cannot be viewed as an alternative to women's involvement in party politics or to femocrats within the state, but the presence of a unified civic interlocutor with political expertise and networking skills is likely to enhance the representation of feminist demands on the political stage. In contrast to the Chilean case, for instance, where the absence of a strong coordinating body contributed to the splintering of the women's movement and the emergence of the national WPM, SERNAM, as the main interlocutor for gender equality on the political stage (Waylen, 1996b), the KWAU has maintained its independence as the representative of progressive women's organizations, and simultaneously worked *alongside* MOGE to promote reforms.

The organizational strength built up by the Korean movement also owes much to carefully thought-out, multipronged discursive and networking strategies with civil society and state actors. The energy and resources invested by women's organizations in forging and maintaining intra- and inter-movement solidarity around broad political and social justice concerns, rather than a narrower concern with specific gender issues, per se, has reaped considerable dividends. Moreover, although the movement has at times relied on temporary conjunctural coalitions to ensure the success of individual reform campaigns,[8] such pragmatism has not precluded efforts to sustain more lasting cross-movement bonds and promote a broader progressive civil society community.

Equally importantly, the Korean movement has forged a path of cooperative but critical partnership with state agencies and political parties. Recognizing that the state is neither a monolithic adversary nor a proponent of gender equality, but can rather afford important sites of engagement and resistance for women's groups, activists have moved beyond concerns with retaining movement purity toward engagement with the state. For instance, in formulating and implementing reform policies, women's groups have been willing to accept state funding for gender-equality initiatives and to work more closely with WPMs.

The third proactive measure that has contributed to the Korean movement's efficacy has been the ongoing organization of discussion forums and workshops to reflect on the movement's progress and future directions. Both individual movement organizations and the larger KWAU engage in annual evaluations of their activities, staff dynamics, and movement philosophy in order to facilitate communication and avoid complacency (e.g., Lee M., 2000 interview). A case in point was women activists' questioning in 2004 of their "overly close" relationship with the government, despite having secured the largest increase in women's political representation since the transition and enjoying considerable influence within the Noh administration that resulted in the successful passage of highly contentious reforms on family law and prostitution (Yoon, 2004 interview).

Gender Blocs

The balance of power among progressive and conservative actors with gendered interests also emerged as a key explanatory variable for policy change. Despite a deeply conservative Confucian culture, a fortuitous combination of a strong, progressive civil society community and fragmented and weakly institutionalized conservative groups has played a major role in facilitating the rapid passage of gender-equality legislation in Korea. Progressive civic groups (*shimin undong*), bound together by close personal networks, a shared history, and a common paradigm, have forged loosely organized but sustainable alliances in order to cooperate across a range of sociopolitical concerns. Although inter-movement tensions, particularly regarding traditional notions of the gender division of labor, continue to affect social reform priorities, overarching civil society solidarity has lent the demands of Korean women's groups a source of public legitimacy and lobbying strength unmatched in other regions.[9]

The composition and dynamics of Korean conservative groups contrasts sharply with those of their progressive rivals. Although historical constraints, especially the division of the Peninsula, truncation of the Left, and revival of Confucianism as a nation-building tool in the postliberation period, contributed to a conservative political culture that continues to impinge upon current reform initiatives, the Korean case highlights the way in which the political impact of conservative values largely depends on their institutional expression. The disjuncture between the broad cultural resonance of Confucian values and relatively weak institutional capacity of Confucian groups suggests that any assessment of the balance of power among progressive and conservative gender coalitions must consider the mechanism through which conservative ideas are articulated and the relative political strength of the institutional carrier thereof. References to general cultural traditions may explain difficulties in reshaping attitudes and barriers to the successful implementation of reform policies, but do not offer adequate explanatory purchase on the contestation of gender policies and women's representation.

Finally, on the basis of my reading of the women's history literature, I questioned the gender and democracy literature's tendency to overlook the importance of state actors' independent gendered interests. The post-authoritarian Korean state clearly has its own gender-related agenda—improving political legitimacy both domestically and internationally, maximizing human resources, reproducing the workforce, and minimizing welfare expenditures—but until the late 1990s its approach to gender relations was largely piecemeal, often inconsistent and reactive. In particular, the operating paradigms of WPMs have often diverged significantly from officials in more conservative mainstream ministries such as Budget and Planning, Justice and Labor. Such internal differences, combined with Korean officialdom's broader desire to "catch up" with peers in the OECD, have opened up multiple micro-sites of opportunity for nongovernmental groups, while simultaneously reducing the capacity of state actors to actively mold gender relations relative to that of their authoritarian predecessors.

Political Institutional Matrix

The book's detailed analysis of institutional access opportunities and veto points shows that the political spaces available to the Korean women's and other social movements are significantly different from both the political terrain under authoritarianism and that of the initial post-transition period. Gender-equality advocates have developed flexible, multipronged strategies to negotiate a policymaking context comprising the following:

- A legislative system that minimizes public debate, skimps on policy expertise, but facilitates the rapid passage of legislative reforms;
- a dominant but no longer omnipotent executive wherein individual presidents' personal ideological commitments still carry notable weight;
- a highly competitive, hierarchical bureaucracy, with a growing role in social policy formation;
- an increasingly independent judicial system, particularly an activist Constitutional Court; and a
- noninstitutionalized, personalistic, regionally based party system.

Although cross-regional comparisons are difficult, given few comparable fine-grained analyses of the political institutional matrix in democratizing polities, existing research suggests that the Korean political party system and judiciary stand out as the most important source of variance.

Political Parties

My research suggests that parties matter, but not necessarily in the ways predicted by the literature. Korean women have been able to escape some of the problems faced, for instance, by movements in Chile and Brazil, by operating within a political arena that is dominated by regional rather than ideological cleavages. In particular, they have avoided movement fragmentation along party lines, subordination of movement goals to party politics, as well as partisan rivalries within WPMs. Moreover, in the context of nonprogrammatic catch-all parties, targeted lobbying of sympathetic legislators has had a disproportionate influence on policy outcomes, as parties seek to avoid politicizing gender issues and strive instead to match the promises of rival parties. Accordingly, we have seen the passage of significantly more progressive legislative reforms than the conservative leanings of Korean political parties would have led us to expect.

The absence of an institutionalized, politically savvy conservative opposition has been a decisive factor. For a variety of historic and socio-economic reasons, Korea's economic elites have been unable to found or control their own party. Had they been able to do so, they, like their Latin American counterparts, would have needed to attract electoral support via clientelistic networks and very likely appeal to conservative sociocultural values and institutions. The argument here is a strong one: conservative social values are not "natural" political cleavages but are, rather, manufactured and sustained by political parties over time (Lienesch, 1993). Parties need to create a mass base of support and often attempt to cultivate, expand, and promote the institutionalization of existing cleavages by relying on gender as an important tool. By advocating culturally reactionary policies involving the family, sexuality, or welfare provision—areas that inspire impassioned responses because they challenge people's core definitions of self, morality, and community—fiscally conservative parties have often been able to entice those with divergent economic interests into a coherent voting bloc (e.g., Stacey, 1999). In Chile, for example, the manufacturing of divisions around morality politics has been especially important post-transition, as traditional economic debates have been largely kept off the political agenda for fear of reigniting historical antagonisms (Blofield, 1998). In Korea, however, the peculiarities of party history have precluded the need to mobilize on the basis of such value cleavages. Parties have served as the personal vehicles of the "three Kims"—each of whom tried to appeal to the broad middle class while simultaneously relying on strong support from their home regions.

The *shimin undong* community has enabled progressive women's groups to compensate to a considerable degree for the absence of a strong ideologically left-wing party. Nonetheless, existing evidence on the relationship between left-wing parties and advances in gender equality suggest that the Korean alternative is likely to be only a second-best option (O'Connor et al., 1999). The formidable progress made in reducing gender inequalities in Scandinavia, Western Europe, and Australasia all occurred during left-wing administrations, which actively championed gender equality.

It is, however, open to debate as to whether a comparable model of strong programmatic parties would be in the best interests of Korean women. If we consider the counterfactual scenario and imagine a well-institutionalized programmatic Korean party system, is it likely that Korean proponents of gender equality would have been as influential? Although any answer must remain speculative, my concern is that the open politicization of gender issues would encourage the mobilizational and organizational efforts of those resistant to change. Most basically, public opinion surveys and analyses of post-transitional political culture attest to the general conservatism of the Korean polity (e.g., Shin D., 2003). Moreover, the recent rapid rise in visibility of conservative movement groups following the election of progressive presidential candidate Noh Moo Hyun in 2003 suggests that conservative forces might be able to mobilize effectively to counter the emergence of a genuinely programmatic left-wing party. Whereas neoconservatives have been primarily motivated by national security concerns and not gender and morality issues (Shin, 2004 interview), they are clearly concerned about two successive progressive administrations and actively rethinking their organizational strategies following their 2002 and 2004 defeats (Kim S., 2003 interview).

To what extent are these findings about gender politics and weak party systems likely to be transferable to other nascent democracies? Peru, Bolivia, Brazil, and Ecuador in the Latin American context all share inchoate rather than institutionalized party systems (Mainwaring and Scully, 1995), as do Indonesia, Thailand, Cambodia, and the Philippines in the Asian region (Croissant, 2002b), suggesting that the Korean women's movement strategy of prioritizing movement autonomy and conjunctural coalitions over party linkages might have considerable cross-regional relevance. However, for polities with institutionalized, programmatic systems, we may need to be content with viewing the Korean case as a lesson in highlighting the challenges facing advocates of gender equality. Even with dependable progressive allies, the absence of a strong institutionalized right, and relatively greater political space afforded by weak political parties, Korean women's work toward securing equal civic, political, human, and socioeconomic rights has been far from easy.

Judiciary

Although Korean courts post-transition have not consistently upheld individual rights in the face of political pressure, most observers concur that the justice system is gradually becoming more autonomous and accessible to the citizenry (e.g., Lee C., 1998). In contrast to Latin America where the weakness of the judiciary has not only limited the implementation of social reforms but given rise to the term "disjunctive democracy"—denoting the contradictory tendency whereby the routinization of formal democratic procedures is simultaneously accompanied by increased civilian and state violence (Jelin and Hershberg, 1996; Holston and Caldiera, 1998)—the Korean Constitutional Court has taken a surprisingly activist role and has reached progressive verdicts regarding a number of important gender issues. Moreover, citizens' ability to directly petition the Court constitutes a particularly important avenue of redress of which women's movement organizations have made skilful use to date.

Legislature

Neither the legislature's relative weakness vis-à-vis the executive and its limited policy deliberation capacities, nor the frequent scandals and standoffs that disrupt legislative proceedings, set Korea apart from other Third Wave democracies (e.g., Shin D., 1999). However, the rapid pace of the legislative process and a political culture that is not conducive to deliberation and debate have facilitated Korean women's ability to secure a wide array of reforms in a short period of time, and to seek successive revisions of legislation that did not initially meet their demands. Even if such swift passage has tended to come at the price of legislative specificity and strong enforcement mechanisms, it can be juxtaposed with Latin American cases such as Brazil, Chile, and Mexico, where gender-related bills have often languished in the Congress for years (e.g., Haas, 2000; Stevenson, 2000). Yet, although limiting the expression of the conservative Right and capitalizing on National Assembly ignorance or indifference may facilitate the passage of more contentious gender-related reforms, the negative corollary is likely to be weakened spillover effects. Not only are ordinary citizens less likely to recognize and act upon violations of the new legislation, but the judicial personnel who are responsible for its interpretation may be less inclined to devote sufficient attention to understanding the content and implications of often new, relatively abstract, but potentially transformative concepts such as "indirect discrimination" or "sexual harassment."

Presidency

Although observers of most nascent democracies emphasize the dominance of the presidency, the typical *yŏso yadae* (ruling minority, opposition majority) pattern in the Korean Congress has frequently left presidents with less capacity to influence the policy process than might be expected. Moreover, while the president may resort to executive decrees or various extralegal means to secure policy decisions in areas of major national concern, such as the economy or national security (e.g., Kang, 2003), Korean presidents have not employed and are unlikely to employ such tactics in the name of gender-related reforms. Nevertheless, presidential support is important in three key ways. First, because presidents have the power to establish WPMs, determine their institutional positioning and to some degree their resource base, as well as appoint gender-sensitive ministers, they can exercise considerable influence over the direction of state machineries charged with addressing gender inequalities. Second, presidential backing can also be an important factor in ensuring that a particular issue is placed on the policy agenda and deliberated upon in a timely fashion. Implementation, however, is likely to depend on the political will of public service officials and the courts, as even rhetorically supportive executives are unlikely to devote sufficient energy and resources to overseeing the implementation process. Last, as demonstrated clearly in the growing willingness of the Korean women's movement to engage with the state over the course of successive democratic presidents, executive endorsement of gender-equality initiatives encourages civil society–state partnerships in tackling gendered injustice.

Bureaucracy

The level of accessibility the bureaucracy affords women to join the civil service in decisionmaking roles, as well as to participate as external experts in the policy formulation and implementation stages, is an important determinant of gender-policy success. The centuries-old elitist bureaucratic tradition in Korea arguably renders the civil service less hospitable to women and their demands than its cross-regional equivalents. Such rigidity has been alleviated to some degree, however, by the establishment of a hub–spokes WPM network that is gradually increasing in political influence and expanding the level of access provided to nongovernmental women's organizations. Moreover, although WPMs in some country contexts have contributed to the marginalization of women's movement groups from the political stage (e.g., Alvarez, 1990; Valenzuela, 1998), over the past five years Korean WPMs have become increasingly effective, partly thanks to their ability to forge civil society–state partnerships with the women's activist community. The introduction of quotas for women in the civil service recruitment exams, as well as in ministerial advisory committees, have further opened up new, albeit still limited, spaces for women.

Evaluating Post-Transitional Change

Although much remains to be done to close the still significant gaps between women's de jure and de facto rights, the breadth of gender-policy changes passed after Korea's 1987 transition is impressive. From a very low baseline, Korean women now enjoy a wide range of formal civic, political, human, and socioeconomic rights. Increasingly professional lobbying strategies; conjunctural coalitions with progressive civic groups, WPMs, and sympathetic legislators; as well as the skilful use of international norms and best practices, have contributed to securing these achievements. However, in determining the dynamics of the policy negotiation process in different issue areas, the nature of the opposition contesting a particular policy emerged as the most salient explanatory variable. In the case of violence against women, the absence of a specific institutional carrier of conservative values allowed women to successfully push through legislation that criminalized domestic and sexual abuse, and provided for state provision of legal, counseling, and medical services. In contrast, owing to the presence of well-coordinated employers' federations, women had to significantly compromise on their demands for equal employment rights and were compelled to pursue multistaged, piecemeal revisions. Nevertheless, while employers' opposition to gender reforms has been tempered by international influences over time, Confucian opponents of family law reforms, who draw on traditionalist and nationalist discourses, remained unchecked either by international pressures or by state imperatives until 2005.

The Korean state apparatus has significantly evolved over the past decade, allowing for powerful feedback mechanisms between efforts by women's movements to create and strengthen women's political machineries and policy changes across a variety of issue areas. Korea now boasts a hub–spokes WPM infrastructure spanning the Standing Congressional Committee on Women's Affairs, the Ministry of Gender Equality, women's policy units in all government ministries, the Korean Women's Development Institute, and gender expert positions within the major political parties. Although the institutional positioning of these WPM units remains comparatively marginalized, the establishment of a full-fledged Ministry of Gender Equality in 2001 secured for femocrats the ability to propose their own legislation and participate fully in Cabinet meetings. Moreover, from the Kim Dae-jung administration onward, these machineries have become increasingly accessible to women's organizations and solicitous of their input in policy development.

In order to make gender mainstreaming a reality, however, political society will need to go beyond the mere letter of the law and provide adequate staff and funding to carry out the far-reaching commitments embodied in the 1995 Women's Basic Development Act and the 1999 Gender Discrimination and Prevention Act. Moreover, whereas the systematic eradication of authoritarian institutional practices clearly plays a major role in enhancing the overall quality of democratic governance, the Korean case suggests that an equally pressing change is the institutionalization and monitoring of gender-sensitivity programs for officials. A fundamental shift is required in political society's treatment of female colleagues as well as attitudes vis-à-vis gender-equality initiatives.

To facilitate these changes, MOGE's oversight functions need to be strengthened to ensure that individual WPM units regularly cooperate and coordinate with affiliated machineries. Whereas MOGE's efforts to secure specific policy implementation policies, for example, violence against women and childcare services, are important in terms of practical budget, resource, and institutional status concerns, it is imperative that these issues do not become the ministry's major focus if its *raison d'être* as a coordinating body is to be taken seriously. Formal and informal channels among respective machineries need to be established and/or strengthened, and viable overarching strategies developed to ensure optimal synergy effects, in terms of policy development and implementation, as well as personal networking/support.

Moreover, now that women's organizations have successfully secured the policy hardware within the state for which they have been campaigning for nearly 20 years, the challenge will be to reorient their focus to more micro-level monitoring of the policy goals and program content of individual WPM divisions. Although it will be tempting for the movement community to retain its broad-brushstroke critiques of state machineries, only through careful, systematic analyses of WPM policy and budget expenditures, along with the provision of concrete, politically viable alternatives, will activists be able to ensure that WPMs are responsive to their demands for substantive gender equality. In particular, effective monitoring of legislative reforms will require femocrats and women's groups to more systematically assess the production of statistical information by the Korean National Statistics Office (NSO), which continues to collect data of only marginal utility to the policy development process. The NSO publishes, for instance, statistics on "the level of satisfaction with regional cultural programs by sex" or the rate of "video watching by sex and age" (NSO, 2002), but lacks data on issues such as government expenditure on gender policies over time, the rate of prosecution and sentencing of gender-violence offenders, the gendered composition of line ministries at all levels, gender differences among voters with regard to specific issues, or voting records in the legislature among congressional representatives by sex.

Advances in women's formal political representation, both in elected positions and decisionmaking ranks of the civil service, have been considerably slower, with women not breaking the 10 percent threshold until 2004. This disappointing progress can be largely attributed to the lack of effective institutional response (e.g., quotas) to a deeply conservative political society, as well as women's general reluctance to launch political careers and/or support the political ambitions of female colleagues (especially through the mid-1990s). At the institutional level, the electoral system, particularly the relatively small number of PR seats and single-member districts, has reinforced such cultural biases. Although quotas for women in the bureaucracy and legislature (PR seats only) have begun to mitigate these shortcomings, such policies will remain tokenistic until affirmative action measures are expanded at the bureaucratic decisionmaking levels and cover a more meaningful percentage of total congressional seats. Nevertheless, the significant improvement in women's representation from 2004 does offer room for cautious optimism. It was no coincidence, for instance, that the repeal of the Family Law (2005) followed closely on the heels of the sharp increase in the number of women legislators. With time, improved representation for women (especially advocates of gender equality) could help moderate some of the more problematic legacies of the Korean legislative process: hasty and immature deliberation procedures, often weak enforcement mechanisms, and state actors' limited political will.

Lessons for Korean Democratization

In addition to understanding the dynamics of post-transitional gender-policy change in Korea and teasing out potentially transferable lessons, I also argued in chapter 1 that an analysis of the democratic consolidation process through the lens of struggles to advance gender equality would provide valuable insights into the broader Korean democratization process. This final section discusses these findings in terms of movement strategy, actor constellations, and institutional spaces.

Movement Strategy

The relative success of the Korean women's movement suggests that to be effective in the new democratic milieu, movement organizations are most effective when they employ creative multipronged strategies of critical engagement with the state rather than rely on authoritarian-era antagonistic modes of activism. Although the Korean labor movement, for instance, is famed for its highly visible politics of resistance, its overall post-transitional success has been limited, not least because its more contentious approach has failed to win the support of the public, government officials, and legislators (e.g., Koo, 2001).

Cross-movement cooperation is equally important. One of the key ingredients of Korean feminists' success has been their investment in the broader progressive movement community and the framing of gender rights in terms of broader notions of social justice. In this regard, environmental and immigrants' rights organizations, for example, would be well served by aligning themselves with broader political and economic reform initiatives and striving to cast their specific reform goals in the language of "democratic deepening" or "citizenship rights" in order to secure political legitimacy and leverage.

Discursive sensitivity would also seem to require a careful balance between appealing to international norms and best practices, and ensuring that cultural or national specificities are taken into account. For example, Korean advocates of gender equality have trodden a delicate line of pushing to expand women's individual rights while seeking to respect and strengthen the positive elements of culturally-specific family dynamics. By contrast, the Korean labor movement has been less successful in modernizing its hard-line image or in broadening the movement composition and political agenda to go beyond employment issues and incorporate the broader interests of the progressive political community.

The importance of these insights notwithstanding, I would neverthe-less venture that they are not able to fully account for the relative success of the women's movement vis-à-vis other Korean progressive civic orga-nizations, particularly groups such as the PSPD. As the largest progres-sive civic group, the PSPD has enjoyed strong leadership and drawn extensively on international best practices, is considerably better funded than its feminist counterparts, well-networked with government, legisla-tive, and party officials and has drafted and presented multiple reform bills to the National Assembly (Shin, 2004: 10). Yet many of its demands for political and economic reform have remained unfulfilled. How are we to explain this? In part, gains by women's groups appear relatively more impressive because gender inequalities were so pronounced in the late 1980s. Moreover, as many policy reforms secured by women activists involved changes in legal identities and rights rather than (necessarily) large outlays of funds, politicians have tended to dismiss some of the demands of women's groups as insignificant political issues or were sim-ply unaware of the scope of the changes they were signing into law. Finally, even where opposition to reforms was vocal and entrenched, women's groups could still realize policy gains where implementation was likely to be partial or postponed (for instance, employers groups acquiesced to the extension of paid maternity leave when they realized the costs of noncompliance would be limited).

Actor Constellations

The literature on Korean civil society has focused predominantly on the internal dynamics of the *minjung* and *shimin* movements and the impor-tance of the political space afforded by weak, non-ideological political parties. However, by placing the Korean case in comparative perspective, this book has underscored the importance of the balance of power between progressive and conservative civil society camps. A key factor in the growing political influence of progressive civil society, and the grad-ual expansion of civic and socioeconomic rights for women, has been the inability of economic and cultural conservatives to form lasting coali-tions or to work closely with political parties. However, as demonstrated by the sudden and unprecedented mobilization of a broader array of conservative groups in response to the election of Noh Moo Hyun in December 2003, the past 15 years may have represented a fortuitous political opening for advocates of social change and should not be assumed to be a permanent feature of Korean democracy. Given the powerful obstructionist tactics of the conservative alliance in Latin

America and Eastern Europe (consisting of right-wing parties, business groups, and religio-cultural conservatives), Korean activists will need to pay particular attention to their framing of new reform measures to ensure that they do not unnecessarily antagonize or inflame the mobilization of conservatives. In this regard, it will be important to carefully deconstruct the reasons for the emergence of Korea's fledgling conservative alliances in order to better understand the shifting political landscape and the threat these changes potentially pose to the full extension of citizenship rights to women.

Institutional Spaces

Although a macro-level snapshot may suggest that institutions are resilient to change, my analysis of Korean political institutions identified multiple sites of resistance within the democratic state that are likely to be important to a broad array of reform initiatives. Two examples will serve to illustrate this point. First, whereas *shimin* groups have primarily focused on the legislative arena, the women's movement's relatively successful efforts at state transformation have led to the establishment of a multilayered network of units embedded in the state mandated to exclusively address gender-related concerns. Although this model is clearly not transferable to all issue areas, given the comparative strength of the Korean bureaucracy vis-à-vis other branches of government and the relative importance of the bureaucratic implementation ordinances, it does suggest that other civic groups would be well advised to lobby for more permanent channels of access to the state.

Second, the broader movement community has paid insufficient attention to the judiciary and the court system given the encouraging progress achieved in (parts of) the Korean court system over the past decade in terms of political neutrality and transparency. It may be advisable for *shimin* groups to become more involved in preparing lawsuits that test the boundaries of extant legislation, as well as monitoring trends in the outcome of litigation. Lobbying efforts are also needed to influence the training and educational programs of both incoming and incumbent judicial personnel to ensure that they are aware of new legislative developments, at both the national and international levels.

Finally, although political analysts and movement activists may be sufficiently immersed in the institutional arena to appreciate the dynamism of political opportunity structures, public education programs are needed to raise citizens' awareness about available channels to voice concerns and seek redress through the state. As my analysis has emphasized, heightened political and legal literacy will be necessary for citizens to take advantage of new opportunities to influence and check state power. Accordingly, civic education curricula should be revised and monitored, with nationwide citizens' information centers or hotlines established to ensure that citizens have access to the requisite knowledge to participate in the democratic process in a more meaningful way.

Appendix: Interviews with Key Informants

Name	Institutional affiliation	Date
Byun Wha-Soon	KWDI Senior Researcher	2000
Chang Kyung Sup	Seoul National University, Professor of Sociology	1998
Chang Pilwha	Ewha Womans University, Asian Center for Women's Studies, Head	2000
Chang Song-Ja	Gender Discrimination Prevention Office, Head	2001
Chin Mi-Kyung	Ajou University, Professor of Political Science	2000
Cho Hee-Jin	Ministry of Justice, WFP, Head	2000
Cho Hyo-Je	Anglican University, Professor of Social Movement Studies	2002
Cho Hyun-ok	Korean Women's Political Solidarity	2003
Cho Soon-Kyung	Ewha Womans University, Professor of Sociology	2002
Cho Young-Sook	KWAU Policy Officer	2000, 2003
Cho Yunye	MOGE, International Cooperation Division	2002 personal correspondence
Choi Myung-Sook	Korean WomenLink, Women's Labor Center, Head	2000, 2001
Choi Song-Soo	Federation of Korean Industries, Social Policy Division	2002
Chon Hyun-Baek	Sookmyung Women's University, Professor of Political Science	2000
Chong KangJa	Co-director of Korean WomenLink, Women's Labor Center, Head	2000, 2002
Chung Hyun-Back	Sungkyunkwan University, Professor of History, Women Making Peace, Head	2000
Chung Jung-Ae	Chunbuk Government, Women's Policy Unit, Head	2001
Gwak Bae-Hi	Korean Legal Aid Center for Family Relations, Head	1998
Ha Young-Sook	PCWA, International Cooperation Division	2000
Han Myung-Sook	MDP, Legislator	2000, 2002
Hwang In-Ja	Ministry of Government and Home Affairs WFP, Head	2000
Ji Uhn-Hee	MOGE	2003
Joshua Pilzer	University of Chicago, Fulbright Researcher	2003
Kang Hyun-Hee	GNP, Gender Expert	2000
Kang Ki-Won	PCWA Chairperson	2000
Kang Nam-Shik	KWAU Research Center	2001

Continued

Appendix Continued

Name	Institutional affiliation	Date
Kang Sung-Hye	International Cooperation Division, Head	2004 personal correspondence
Kim Chang-Suk	MPA2 Minister	2000
Kim Eunshil	Ewha Womans University, Professor of Women's Studies	2003
Kim Gi Bong	*Women's News*, Journalist	2005 personal correspondence
Kim Hyun-Mee	Yonsei University, Professor of Sociology	2000
Kim Jeong-Ja	MOGE International Cooperation Division	2001–02 personal correspondence
Kim Ji-Hyun	Korean Women's Trade Union	2000
Kim Jung-Rye	MPA2, Minister	1999
Kim Kyung-Hee	KWDI, Researcher	2000
Kim Myung-Jin	Korea Feminist Art Collective	2002 personal correspondence
Kim Sok-Joon	Ewha Womans University, Professor of Public Administration	2003
Kim Sung-Kwon	Korea Institute of Health and Social Affairs (KIHASA), Senior Researcher	2000
Kim Sun-uk	Ewha Womans University, Professor of Feminist Jurisprudence	2002, 2003
Kim Won-Hong	KWDI, Senior Researcher	2000, 2003
Kim Young-Ae	PCWA, General Secretary	2000, 2001
Kim Young-Ae	MDP, Women's Bureau	2000
Kim Young-Hee	MDP, Gender Expert	2000
Kim Yung-Chung	MPA2, Minister	2000
Kwon Huck-ju	Sungkyunkwan University, Professor of Public Administration	2000
Kwon Hyang-Yop	MDP, Women's Bureau	2000
Kwon Young-Hyung	Women's Policy Division	2003
Kwon Young-Ja	MPA2, Minister	2000
Lee Ho-Sung	KEF, Social Affairs Division	2000
Lee Hwa-Young	ULD, Gender Expert	2000
Lee Hyeo-kyeong	MOGE International Cooperation Division	2003 personal correspondence
Lee Hye-Soon	Korean Confederation of Trade Unions, Women's Policy Division	2002
Lee Hyun-jin	Ewha Womans University, Department of Korean Linguistics	2001 personal correspondence
Lee Hyun-Kyung	Korean WomenLink, Women's Labor Center	2001
Lee Jae-Chun	Chonju City, Legislator	2000
Lee Jun-Ho	League of Women Voters, Head	2001
Lee Kisoon	Gender Discrimination Prevention Division, Head	2002, personal correspondence

Continued

Appendix Continued

Name	Institutional affiliation	Date
Lee Ki-Soon	Blue House, Secretary for Women's Affairs	2004 personal correspondence
Lee Mikyong	Korean Sexual Violence Relief Center, Head	2000, 2002, 2004
Lee Mi-Kyoung	MDP, Legislator	2003
Lee Ok	Ministry of Justice, WFP, Head	2000
Lee Sung-Hee	Blue House, Secretary for Women's Affairs	2000
Lee Sunny	Korean Employers Federation, International Affairs Division	2002
Lee Yon-Sook	GNP, Legislator, KNCW, former Head	2000
Lori Crocker	Korean Church Women United	2000
Myung Jin-Sook	Korean WomenLink, Women's Environment Center, Head	2000, 2002
Na Yong-Hee	PCWA, Policy Division	2000
Nam In-Soon	KWAU, General Secretary	2000
Nam Sung-Hee	Ministry of Education, WFP, Head	2000
Noh Mi-Hye	Seoul Metropolitan City Government, Women's Policy Unit, Head	2000
Oh Han Sook-Ki	Feminist author and activist	2002 personal correspondence
Oh Hye-Ran	KNCW, General Secretary	2000
Park Chang Kuin	MOGE Policy Coordination Division	2005 personal correspondence
Park Song-Ja	Ministry of Agriculture and Forestry, WFP, Head	2001
Park Sook-Ja	SCCWA, Research Expert	2000
Park Sung-Tae	Ministry of Labor, WFP, Head	2002
Park Woo-Keon	PCWA Cooperation and Liaison Division, Head	2000
Park Young-Ran	KWDI, Senior Researcher	2000
Rev Lee Mun-Sook	Korean National Council of Church Women	2001
Shim Younghee	Hanyang University, Professor of Sociology	2000
Shin Heisoo	Korean Women's Hotline, Head	2000
Shin Kwang-Yeong	Chung Ang University, Professor of Sociology	2004 personal correspondence
Shin Myung	Ministry of Labor, Equal Employment Policy Bureau, Head	2002
Shin Solee	Sullajabki/ Feminist Gathering of the College of Humanities, Ewha Womans University	2003
Soh Myung-Son	Ministry of Health and Social Welfare, WFP, Head/ MOGE Cooperation and Liaison Division, Head	2000/2002
Sohn Bong-Sook	Center for Women and Politics, Head	2000
Wang In-Soon	Korean Women Workers' Association United	2000
Yang Hae-Kyung	Korean WomenLink, Family and Sexual Counselling Center, Head	2001
Yang In-Suk	Ministry of Health and Social Welfare, Women's Welfare Division, Former Head	2000

Continued

Appendix Continued

Name	Institutional affiliation	Date
Yoon Hoo-Jung	PCWA, Chairperson	2001
Yoon Jung-Sook	Korean WomenLink, Co-director	1998, 2000, 2002, 2003, 2004 interviews/personal correspondence
You Song-Hee	MDP Women's Bureau, Head	2000

Notes

Chapter 1   Modeling the Gendered Political Opportunity Structures of Democratization

1. The Third Wave refers to the series of democratic transitions starting with Portugal and Spain in the 1970s, followed by Latin America in the 1980s, and Asia, Eastern Europe, and Africa in the late 1980s–1990s.
2. "Femocrats" refers to bureaucrats with a feminist standpoint, generally with links to organized women's movements.
3. Mainstream political analysts grappling with the idiosyncrasies of Korean democratic consolidation have paid scant attention to gender relations (e.g., Hahm and Plein, 1997; Diamond and Plattner, 1998; Diamond and Shin, 2000; Helgesen, 1997; Shin, 1999; Samuel Kim, 2000 and 2003).
4. Htun (2003) is a partial exception here.
5. In contrast to a significant body of research focusing on women and democratization in Latin America and Eastern Europe, scholarly attention to the Asian region has been relatively limited (e.g., Lee and Clark, 2000; Moon S., 2002, 2003).
6. Cross-regional differences are further accentuated by the differential relative strength of Korea's progressive civic groups. As discussed in chapter 4, whereas the reemergence of political parties to center stage contributed to the post-authoritarian splintering of many Third Wave pro-democracy movements, Korean progressives have been able to capitalize on the greater political space afforded by a weak, nonideological party system as well as a powerful movement frame involving a commitment to democratic deepening to emerge as influential and respected political players.
7. In line with the concept of movement cycles, social movement theorists (e.g., Tarrow, 1994) have argued that movements tend to ebb and flow in response to shifting political opportunities and the availability of organizational resources. In particular, "mobilizational fatigue" can contribute to the retreat of activists from the public arena following the realization of the immediate goal of toppling the dictatorship (e.g., Frohmann and Valdes, 1995).
8. Although the identity of "political motherhood" proved effective during the authoritarian era, the emphasis on moral superiority and a distancing from political corruption has, ironically, limited women's citizenship claims and participation possibilities in democratizing polities (e.g., Craske, 1999).

9. Caldiera (1998) argues that widespread violence and human rights abuses exacerbates a general lack of confidence in the justice system and indicates that procedural democracy is too often accompanied by a simultaneous devaluation of individual and civil rights. This disjunctive democracy tends to have a strongly gendered dimension: whereas demands for collective social rights (e.g., health and education services for women and children) have historically been considered a legitimate aspect of Latin American citizenship, calls for women's reproductive rights and protection from violence have met with greater cultural resistance because they threaten traditional gendered hierarchies.

10. Although the economic environment is not typically included in the POS, the domestic and international economic climate can profoundly affect the ability of actors to take advantage of new political windows (see chapters 2, 3, and 6).

11. Partial exceptions include recent studies on a single institutional aspect—e.g., congressional–executive balance, party systems, or centralized versus decentralized bureaucracies—and gender-policy reform (e.g., Stevenson, 2000; Macaulay, 2002).

12. The term "Beijing effect" refers to the broader set of initiatives and discursive shifts (especially the concept of "gender mainstreaming") surrounding the 1995 Beijing Conference.

13. For example, have women been able to maintain a coherent movement frame and public visibility?

14. Such measures, though clearly worthy of study and important indicators of women's socioeconomic status, are beyond the scope of this book.

15. *Servicio Nacional de la Mujer* is a WPM directly responsible to the Chilean president.

16. For a more complete list of the Korean language sources that influenced the thinking behind this book, see Jones (2003).

17. A number of informants were interviewed more than once.

Chapter 2   Historical Constraints

1. Korea's GINI coefficient was low at 0.344 in 1965 and 0.332 in 1970. Although inequality rose in the 1970s, with the GINI coefficient peaking at 0.391 in 1976, the 1980s saw trends reverse toward more equal distribution to 0.337 in 1988 on the eve of the transition (Choo, 1985; Adelman, n.d.).

2. See chapter 10 on problems of son preference and rising selective abortion rates as family size shrinks.

3. According to Confucian traditions, occupations are ranked in terms of cultural desirability, summed up by the Chinese characters "Sa-Nong-Kong-Sang" referring to scholar/officials, farmers, artisans, and merchants in descending order. This well-ingrained cultural ethos partially accounts for the prioritization of education in postliberation Korea.

4. The age distribution of Korean women's labor-force participation is M-shaped: high from age 20 to 24, dropping when women temporarily leave the labor force between 25 and 34 years, and rising again when they are in their late thirties/early forties (Kim K., 1998: 58–59).

5. In fact, the number of female factory workers increased faster than that of men during the 1960s–1970s, reversing only after the mid-1980s (Koo, 2001).

6. A combination of high levels of biosocial homogeneity and the eradication of the *yangban* (landed elite) through Japanese occupation and the Korean Civil War, meant the state had to play an active role in fostering economic classes when it embarked on a full-scale industrialization program in the 1960s (e.g., Chang, 1995; Koo, 2001).

7. Military spending accounted for 20 percent of the total national budget in Korea for most of the 1990s; although priorities began to shift from 1998 with the election of Kim Dae-jung, as well as the 1997–98 financial crises, defense spending still accounted for 16.6 percent in 2000 (US-DoD, 2000). By comparison, Korean WomenLink estimates that the entire social security budget was equivalent to just 15 percent of the government's annual budget in 2000 (www.womenlink.org.kr).

8. The narrow loss of Grand National Party presidential candidate Lee Hoi-chang in 1997 and 2002, was partly attributed to his sons' evasion of military service.

9. By the 1970s, female-dominated light manufacturing accounted for 70 percent of total exports, with the number of women industrial workers tripling between 1970 and 1978 (Kim H., 1999).

10. The following discussion draws heavily on Kim S. H. (2000).

11. Although democracy advocates were regularly subject to surveillance, torture, and imprisonment under the far-reaching Anti-Communist Laws (e.g., Cumings, 1997), a mid-1990s national opinion survey suggested that just three percent of Koreans had experienced or remembered abuses suffered by relatives or friends (Shin D., 1999: 248). Official death statistics number in the hundreds, with activists claiming up to 2,000 during the Kwangju massacre; by comparison, over 10,000 Argentines were "disappeared" by the military junta between 1976 and 1982. Differential levels of state violence can be partly explained by lower levels of prior civic mobilization and the absence of guerilla warfare experienced in Latin America.

12. As the labor force grew from 1.3 million in 1960 to 8 million by the mid-1980s, the unionization rate also mushroomed (from 914 unions in 1960 to 4,068 by 1987) (Koo, 2001).

Chapter 3 *Minjung* Feminism to Gender Mainstreaming

1. To counter claims that women's rights struggles are a Western import, Korean feminists emphasize their historical roots in the independence struggles of the early twentieth century (e.g., Choi, 1985).

2. As Koo (2001) emphasizes: "The absolute majority of labor disputes involving unionization struggles in the 1970s were led by female workers in . . . female-dominated export industries. Even where the independent union movement was led by male workers, female workers were the main participants in the struggle, demonstrating stronger resistance, determination, solidarity, and resilience than male workers" (92).

3. Under authoritarian rule, foreign travel for the average citizen was largely proscribed, whereas state engagement with international governmental or intergovernmental organizations was limited. However, encouraged by the success of the Seoul 1988 Olympics, Korea's desire to engage the international community accelerated post-transition (Kim, 2000).

4. Whereas the KNCW's ideological underpinnings can be loosely described as "liberal feminism," the KWAU combines "socialist", "radical," and "liberal" feminisms (Cho S., 1994; Lee Y., 2000 interview). However, none of these Western-derived frameworks fully encapsulates the Korean women's movement, whose more progressive wing conceptualizes the struggle for gender equality as intertwined with the need to achieve reunification with the North and independence from U.S. imperialism, as well as greater democratic deepening and political transparency (Cho H. J., 1994).

5. Groups such as Korean WomenLink, Korea Women's Hotline and the League of Women Voters now have provincial branches and strive to incorporate local issues into their reform agendas (e.g., Lee J., 2001 interview).

6. Because remuneration of junior activists is near subsistence levels, support from family members is required to pursue a longer-term activist career (e.g., Lee M., 2002 interview).

7. The KWAU's Seoul headquarters has 10 full-time staff, with branch offices in all 16 provinces/metropolitan areas.

8. This characterization of the movement does not encapsulate all groups. The so-called third group, including the YWCA, the League of Women Voters, the Korean Institute for Women and Politics, and the Center for Korean Women and Politics, focuses primarily on political representation. Although women's religiously affiliated organizations were also active in social change efforts during the 1980s, post-transition they have primarily focused on addressing internal gender discrimination and abuse (e.g., Crocker, 2000 interview).

9. Newspapers include The *Women's News* (http://www.womennews.co.kr), a weekly magazine with a readership of 240,000, *the Woman Times* (www.iwomantimes.com), and *Feminist Journal* **If**.

10. See Chang (1999) for a discussion of women's cyber activism.

11. Likewise, political motherhood, which served as a powerful organizational referent in other nondemocratic contexts (e.g., Jaquette, 1994), did not emerge as an important framing tool or significant organizational referent in Korea due to lower levels of state repression. The 1987 "Campaign against

the Use of Tear Gas" in which Korean women mobilized to end police brutality against their children was an exception (Kim K., 1998).

Chapter 4   Competing "Gender Coalitions"

1. Examples of *minjung* organizations include Students' Action and Solidarity, Working-Class Power, and the Korean Peasants' League.
2. For instance, in 2000, women's organizations and *shimin undong* groups jointly launched the Citizens for Abolition of the Family Headship System (CAFH) and presented the National Assembly with a 30,000-signature-strong petition to abolish the *hojuje*. The Coalition also jointly appealed to the Constitutional Court to review the matter.
3. The *Chongshindae* (Comfort Women) issue has, however, been framed as a nationalist rather than a gender rights issue: "It's not that the comfort women are [supported because they were abused as] 'women' and 'people,' but they are the 'motherland' and when they were raped it was the same thing as the colonial rape of Chosun" (Pilzer, 2003 interview).
4. Union membership declined from 1.9 million members in 1989 to 1.5 million in 2002, whereas unionization rates fell from 18.6 percent in 1989 to 12 percent in 2002 (Mah, 2002: 244).
5. The Blue House is equivalent to the American White House.
6. Women's trade unions, including the Korean Women's Trade Union and the Seoul Women's Trade Union, were launched in the late 1990s in response to the gendered biases of economic crisis.
7. The Christian Party was established by the Korean Christian Council, a conservative organization of 44,000 churches nationwide, just prior to the April 2004 National Assembly elections, but gained just 1 percent of the vote (www.christiantoday.com).
8. Examples include YMCA, Buddhist Commission for Human Rights, and Korean Christian Action Organization.
9. Although Christian groups petitioned Congress against the provision for late abortions in the case of rape during the 1998 Sexual Violence Prevention Law revision, the matter was debated no further after the Special Congressional Committee on Women's Affairs (SCCWA) wrote a counter-opinion paper (Lee M., 2002 interview). Public attitudes toward access to abortion are also very accepting: a 2004 survey found that 77 percent, 62 percent, and 63 percent of respondents agreed with abortion in the case of an unwanted pregnancy, economic hardship, and genetic abnormalities, respectively (*Seoul Shinmum*, November 10, 2004).
10. The FKI (1961–) represents 475 large enterprises, while the KEF (1970–) is composed of 13 regional employers' associations, 20 economic and trade associations, and 4,000 manufacturing enterprises.

11. Employers are responsible for the costs of the first 60 days, and are also the principle contributors to the employment insurance, which covers the additional 30 days.

Chapter 5   The Political Institutional Matrix

1. This evolution was clearly not "inevitable" and could have been reversed by the election of conservative Lee Hoi-Chang in either 1997 or 2002 (e.g., Lee M., 2003 interview).
2. Even though frequent party name changes conceal continuity associated with major party leaders, longevity has been a function of a regional strongman rather than party institutions.
3. If we consider parties headed by the "three Kims," a greater degree of continuity emerges, with the share of seats held by significant parties declining only 18 percentage points (from 93 percent in 1988 to 75 percent in 2000).
4. Survey data shows that civic trust in political institutions has fallen dramatically between 1996 and 2003, and parties are no exception with confidence levels falling from 39.5 to 14.9 percent. This lack of public confidence can be attributed to the growing polarization of the electorate—whereas progressives want institutions to actualize more and deeper reforms, conservatives regard the reforms pursued by Kim Dae-jung and especially Noh as radical and impetuous (Kim S. H., forthcoming).
5. Parties associated with Kim Dae-jung have been more supportive of social movements in general, while the KNCW has been more closely aligned with the Center–Right GNP (e.g., Lee R., 2000).
6. Women were granted suffrage under the 1948 Constitution, but as it did not result from organized struggle, the immediate impact was limited, with considerably lower female than male voting rates during authoritarianism (Moon S., 2002).
7. The ruling party created a "gender expert" position in 1998 to offer expert advice to the party's policy committee.
8. Between 1989 and 2000, the Constitutional Court adjudicated 4,500 cases, declaring approximately 200 unconstitutional. Between 2000 and 2004, an even larger volume, 5,411 cases, was reviewed, and 126 were declared unconstitutional (www.ccourt.go.kr/english/emain.html).
9. Although only a small percentage of veterans benefited (i.e., as civil service exam candidates), the policy was seen as symbolically significant. Veterans vented their anger on women's organizations that had supported the court case, resorting to bomb threats, cyber violence (use of the Internet to abuse or threaten [in this case] women), and threatening phone calls (Yoon, 2001 interview). The system was overhauled after the elections, but this example suggests that the rule of law is still not fully institutionalized.
10. There were 811 in 1977, over 3,000 by 1996 and 6,892 lawyers and 1923 judges by 2003.

11. *Minbyŏn's* public profile has increased significantly under Noh Moo Hyun: he is a long-term member and has appointed a number of *minbyŏn* colleagues to decisionmaking roles within his administration.
12. See statistics on workforce gender composition at the Ministry of Justice (www.moj.go.kr).
13. After the passage of the 1994 Act on the Punishment of Sexual Crime and Protection of Victims Thereof, the number of reported rapes increased by approximately 40 percent between 1995 and 2000 (4,844 to 6,855) (National Policy Agency, 2001), whereas in the case of the 1998 Special Act for the Punishment of Domestic Violence the number of arrests rose from 4,002 to 14,105 between 1998 and 2000 (ibid.). According to the Supreme Prosecutors' Office, by 2002 there was a 40.8 percent prosecution rate for family violence offenders and in the case of sexual violence a 58.4 percent prosecution rate by 2003 (www.sppo.go.kr).
14. The crude marriage rate peaked at 10.6 (per 1,000 population) in the mid-1980s, but had fallen to 6.3 in 2003 as couples prioritized academic achievement and careers over starting a family. The average age of marriage is now 30.6 years for men and 27.5 years for women, up by more than 2 years since 1995 (Lee H., 2005).

Chapter 6 Policy Change

1. Efforts to secure greater political rights for women (discussed in chapters 7–9), whether through the passage of the Women's Basic Development Act (WBDA) in 1995, the establishment of new WPMs, or political quotas for women in the 2000 Political Party Law, have engendered opposition from institutional—not civil society—actors. Because these reforms challenge institutional structures, they give rise to opposition among political elites who are concerned to protect turf and/or votes.
2. Activists opposed the Dispatch Law because it was designed to enhance labor flexibility by introducing more temporary and part-time positions, which in Korea lack benefits or security and can require full-time work for part-time pay (Chong, 2002 interview).
3. Calls for sexual harassment and indirect discrimination prevention and redress provisions were unsuccessful during the 1995 reform campaign (Cho S., 2002 interview).
4. For example, although the KNCW believed that the decision to replace menstruation leave with extended maternity leave should be determined by company-level collective bargaining, they did not voice this stance publicly (Kim K. H., 1998).
5. MoL Equal Employment Promotion Office director Shin Myung argued: "In 1995 no one knew what was meant by sexual harassment—but there has to be sufficient awareness to know the meaning of the term. This is the role of social movements" (2002 interview).

6. Employers, however, thwarted women's demands for leave in the cases of miscarriage, stillbirths, and regular prenatal checkups (Lee H. S., 2000 interview).

7. Employers estimated that the policy would cost 853.8 billion won (Paik J., 2002: 61), but women's organizations put the cost at 36.6 billion won, and the MoL at 165.7 billion (Yang, 2002: 81).

8. According to a MoL survey of 1,740 workplaces in 2000, only 21 percent implemented the 60-day paid maternity leave (*Korea Herald*, August 26, 2000). However, whereas 3,685 women and 78 men took maternity/paternity leave in 2002, the figures had almost doubled a year later to 6,712 women and 104 men (KWDI, 2004: 391).

9. Women opposed the same-surname/same-clan marriage ban because "it perpetuates the notion that only paternal lineage counts in tracing one's roots" (Kim R., 1994: 154). Although overturned by the Constitutional Court in 1997, the revision passed into law only because of congressional inaction (Yang, 2002).

10. As part of a broader public awareness campaign, MOGE awarded the Korean Broadcasting System (KBS) drama *Yellow Handkerchief*, which dealt with the ramifications of the patriarchal headship system, its annual media award for "fostering a sense of gender equality."

11. Although no female legislators voted against abolishing the family headship system, six congresswomen were absent for this important vote (four from the URI Party and two from the GNP). An additional two women from the GNP were present for the vote, but abstained.

12. The usually reform-oriented Constitutional Court delayed ruling on the constitutionality of the family headship system following the presentation of a case involving a divorced woman who had been prevented from registering her child on her family registry in 2000. It finally overturned the family law (6-3) after a series of hearings with experts in 2003–04.

13. Even if the father relinquished his right to custody, "he remained the sole parental authority" and needed to be referred to on all matters regarding the child's welfare (Lee K., 1995).

14. Married daughters were only eligible to one-quarter of a son's share of the parental inheritance and until 1997 this had also applied to single daughters.

15. Judicial professionals claimed a separate law was unnecessary as rape was already included in the Criminal Code. However, the Code defined rape as a crime against chastity.

16. The KWAU and KNCW joined forces with the National Professors' Association, the Korean Elderly Helpline, the Korea Differently Abled Federation, two national nursing associations, human rights groups, and the PSPD and CCEJ (Lee H. and Jong, 1999).

17. Activists have also organized campaigns against date rape, sexual harassment on campus, and cyber violence (Lee M., 2002 interview).

18. Various surveys conducted by different researchers and using different sample populations and definitions of family violence estimated that between 30 and 48 percent of all Korean women had experienced some form of domestic violence (Byun, 2000).

19. For numbers on arrest rates, see Koran National Police Agency (www.police.go.kr). Note that the sentencing rates, as calculated by the Supreme Prosecutor's Office, have fluctuated widely, ranging from 12.4 percent in 1998 to 4.8 percent in 2000, 40.8 percent in 2002, and 19.1 percent in 2003 (www.sppo.go.kr).

20. When MOGE proposed in 2001 to revise the Special Act on Sexual Violence to include marital rape, there was a strong outcry among men who retorted: "We'll be too scared to sleep with our wives" or "The law will be abused by women." However, following an August 2004 Seoul District ruling whereby a man was sentenced for sexually assaulting his wife, the URI Party submitted a revision bill in March 2005 to have marital rape or sexual assault against a spouse included in the definition of family violence (*Arirang News*, 2005).

21. These revisions included a special provision to outlaw the use of secret cameras in public toilets "to satisfy perpetrators' sexual desires" and harsher sentences for rapists of minors and disabled people.

22. The Korean sexual violence prevention movement has relied heavily on U.S. examples in drafting legislation and related policies (Shin H., 2000 interview).

23. According to MOGE, the total number of women who availed themselves of the 1366 women's hotline increased from 42,706 in 1998 to 156,805 in 2003 (www.moge.go.kr).

Chapter 7   State Transformation

1. Femocrats in the Seoul City and provincial governments have suggested, however, that their potential to bring about change is limited by budget constraints and a lack of gender awareness among conservative, predominantly older, male colleagues (Noh, 2000 interview; Chung, 2001 interview).

2. A research body akin to the KWDI was virtually unprecedented internationally when it was first founded, and even today few countries can boast a comparable organization (Byun, 2000 interview).

3. The KWDI initially had 164 research staff but in 1998 this was reduced to 91 when the government scaled back funding to 70 percent of the KWDI total budget as part of broader civil service restructuring (Park Y., 2000 interview).

4. In terms of funding, the KWDI's annual budget increased from around 4 billion Won in the late 1980s to 7 billion Won by 1995; after dipping in 1998, the budget had increased to near 10 billion Won by 2002 (Jung, 2004).

5. Established in 1983, the WPEC was headed by the prime minister and had 20 staff (later 35 under Kim Young-sam) and 10 civilian experts. It was mandated to oversee Korea's entry into CEDAW, develop the KWDI's research results into a concrete policy agenda, and monitor the implementation of women-related policies. Although annual meetings helped to increase public officials' awareness of gender issues (e.g., Lee K., 2002 interview), with few clear targets and no enforcement power, WPEC's ultimate ineffectiveness was virtually assured (Kwon Y., 2000 interview).

6. Only 235 cases were filed in 2000 (MOGE, 2001), partially because of the requirement that victims use their real names to proceed with a formal investigation. Counseling services are available, however, for women unwilling to give their real identity (Chang, 2001 interview).

7. *Yŏsŏng-bu* translates as "Ministry of Women" rather than "Ministry of Gender Equality," suggesting that although the government seeks to present a progressive gender-sensitive image internationally, the concept of gender equality is still regarded with some mistrust within Korean political society.

8. In June 2004, staff numbers increased to 139 (Kim, 2005 interview). The MOGE's budget expanded from 36 billion won in 2001 to 45 billion won in 2004 (statistics from Ministry of Planning and Budget [www.mpb. go.kr/english]).

9. Although a 2002 WBDA revision provided for the expansion of WFPs into all government agencies, in practice they are active only in ten ministries: the original six as well as the Ministries of Science and Technology; Commerce, Industry, and Energy; Culture and Tourism; and the Office for Government Policy Coordination. Activists and femocrats had hoped that by assigning existing staff specific policy coordination and oversight responsibilities, and thereby minimizing the need for new funding and staff resources, that bureaucratic resistance would be contained. Full-scale implementation, however, was later shelved as it proved too difficult to carry out (Park, 2005 interview).

10. Former minister and ex-KNCW president, Lee Yon-sook, appointed as the last MPA2 minister under Kim Young-sam, is an exception here.

11. Although assigning these portfolios to MOGE heightens the chances that key gender-related policy areas will be approached from a feminist perspective, it is not fully compatible with the women's movement's call for broader gender mainstreaming.

12. Established in December 1997, "1366" was initially managed by the MHSW, but was transferred to the MOGE in January 2001. It provides emergency counseling and puts victims in contact with medical and legal counseling services and shelters.

13. Following the MOGE's establishment, the (S)CCWA was upgraded to the status of a standing committee, which entitled it to additional research staff, funds, etc.

14. Upgrading the (S)CCWA was delayed until March 2002 owing to concerns that participation in a standing committee on women's affairs would prove unpopular. An exception was eventually made to the regulation stipulating that legislators could belong to only one standing committee so that CCWA members could retain membership of a second committee (Kim S., 2002 interview).

15. Because of an emphasis on training generalists not specialists, and the more practical need to check potential corruption, officials are rotated regularly, within and across ministries.

Chapter 8   Women's Political Representation

1. The only high-profile female politician in Korea to enjoy name recognition because of a male relative is President Park's daughter, Park Geun-Hye. After withdrawing from political life following her father's 1979 assassination, Park reemerged to be elected to Congress in 1998 and led the GNP into the 2004 congressional elections.

2. Key examples include Kwon Young-Ja (1996–2000), a celebrated political dissident who had been fired as a journalist with the *Dong-A Daily* in the early 1980s for censorship violations; Lee Mi-Kyoung (1996–present); and Han Myung-Sook (2000–01; 2004–present). The latter two were former directors of the KWAU.

3. The 2004 GEM did not reflect the April 2004 election results, and thus Korea retained a low score (68th out of 78 countries) (UNDP, 2004).

4. These included the Korean Women's Political Research Center (1989), the Korean Institute for Women and Politics (1990), and the KNCW's "Special Committee on Political Issues" (1992) as well as the YWCA and the League of Women Voters.

5. Political representation was not a major focus of the KWAU at this juncture, and no member organization specifically focused on women's formal political involvement.

6. In the 1998 local elections, the National Congress Party (NCP) nominated 33 percent, the ULD just 16.3 percent, and the GNP 36.1 percent (KWDI, 2002b).

7. The "386 generation" refers to women (and men) born in the 1960s, who were democracy activists in the 1980s and in their thirties when the term was first coined.

8. Public support for mandatory quotas was limited, with 49 percent (47 percent women to 40 percent men) arguing that parties should voluntarily implement quotas compared with 39 percent in favor of compulsory provisions (KWDI, 2000: 282).

9. In the 2002 local elections, hopes of breaking the two-digit barrier for women's participation remained unfulfilled, with women securing 9.2 percent

of provincial seats and just 2.2 percent at the city/county council level (Moon M., 2002).

10. Statistics from MOGAHA (www.mogaha.go.kr).

11. More recent data is not available, according to MOGE spokespeople.

12. Because military service is compulsory for all able-bodied men, feminists argued that the 1997 Support for Discharged Soldiers Act was tantamount to gender discrimination. A 1999 Constitutional Court ruling on a case brought by four women and a disabled man endorsed this argument: "The veterans' extra point system is an unfinanced attempt to support veterans that ends up shifting burdens to the socially weak such as women and the handicapped" (Constitutional Court, 1999).

13. See note 10.

14. Statistics from MOGE (www.moge.go.kr).

15. Although activists have pushed parties to establish a 30 percent quota for decisionmaking ranks, progress has been slow (Kim W. et al., 2001a). As MDP officer Kim Young-Ae explains:

> Although we kept the promise to develop women's positions in the National Assembly and at the local level, how about inside our party? Now is the time—let us show the people! But it is not easy . . . they argue we should fight equally and not demand to be privileged with a 30 percent quota . . . But throughout our history women have been strongly repressed—we don't have an equal culture . . . The spaces are very male and they don't want to give that up. (2000 interview)

16. See statistics from the National Election Commission (www.nec.go.kr).

Chapter 9   Conclusions

1. An important exception is the analysis by Na and Cha (2000) of survey data from 1979 and 1998 on generational change and cultural values.

2. Similarly, a 1999 survey by the NSO found that among double-income households, 51 percent thought the division of household affairs was fairly shared, but for couples with only a single income-earner, the figures were much lower: 7.5 percent in the case of male breadwinners and 26.5 percent for female breadwinners (NSO, 2002: 97).

3. Recent anthropological work by Janelli and Yim (2002) on the Korean corporate sector suggests that even the small improvements seen in promoting women to senior positions have been motivated by concerns about corporate image:

> The main owners (of the *chaebol*), sensitive about their public image in light of the problematic legitimacy of their huge enterprises and their personally privileged positions, began to hire women openly for managerial track positions. (132)

4. Feminists have noted, however, that Korea's democratization process has coincided with a society-wide embrace of a culture of consumption, in which women and their bodies have become constructed as symbols of successful consumer capitalism (e.g., Kim E., 1994; Abelmann, 1997; Kendall, 2002). Accordingly, sociocultural pressures to tame and mold one's body according to exacting standards of beauty have contributed to rapidly rising rates of eating disorders as women seek to attain unrealistic body sizes, as well as a burgeoning plastic surgery industry. Interviews with patients suggest that such surgery is often in part motivated by a desire to fit the appearance requirements to which many companies still informally adhere (e.g., Park M., 2002).

5. See statistics on gender violence at MOGE (www.moge.go.kr).

6. Estimates are likely to reflect shifts in willingness to discuss such sensitive issues as much as a changing prevalence of family violence.

7. This attitude is partly attributable to the practice whereby husbands typically hand their wages over to their wives, who then manage the household pursestrings. A 2002 survey for example found that 55.1 percent of homemakers are the major decisionmakers in household spending (*Joongang Daily*, September 16, 2002).

8. One such example was the alliance formed between the Lotte Hotel labor union in the case of sexual harassment legislative reform.

9. In many nascent democracies, cross-sector coalitions have proved unsustainable, with broader alliances hampered by the reemergence of social divisions (whether class, ideological, or ethnic) that were bracketed during the anti-authoritarian struggles. A case in point is the Latin American human rights movement where the largely middle-class activists, who campaigned on behalf of the disappeared and political prisoners during the authoritarian period, have more recently ignored issues of police brutality that primarily affect working-class populations (e.g., Fuentes, 2004).

Glossary

100-Member Committee (to pull out
  the roots of sexual violence in
  social movements)
All Citizens United for
  Protecting the Traditional
  Family System
Alternative Culture
Association of Bereft Families of
  Persons of National
  Independence Merit
Blue House
Buddhist Commission for Human Rights
Catholic National Federation for Justice
Center for Korean Women and
  Politics
Christian Party
Citizens' Coalition for
  Economic Justice

Citizens' Coalition for Fair Elections
Citizens for Abolition of the
  Family Headship System
Citizens' Times
Comfort Women
Congressional Blacklist Campaign
Congressional Committee on
  Women's Affairs
Democratic Labor Party
Fathers Who Think of Their Daughters'
  Welfare
Federation of Korean
  Industries
Federation of Korean Trade Unions
Feminist Artist Group ("Puff of breath")

Sahoe undong nae
  sŏngpongnyŏk ppuri pŏbgi
  100in wiwŏnhoe (100inwei)
Chŏnt'ong kajokjedo suho
  pŏmgungmin
  yŏnhaphoe
Tto hanaŭi munhwa
Tongnip
  yugongja
  yujokhoe
Ch'ŏng wadae
Pulgyo ingwŏn wiwŏnhoe
Chongwi kuhyŏn sajedan
Hankuk yŏsŏng kwa
  chŏngch'i sentŏ
Hankuk kidok-dang
Kyŏng shillyŏn/ kyŏngjae
  chŏngui shilch'ŏn
  shimin yŏnhap
Parŭn sŏn'gŏ shimin moim
Hojuche paeji oehan
  shiminŭi moim
Shimin ilbo
Chŏngshindae
Kukhoe naksŏn undong
Kukhoe yŏsŏng t'ŭkŭi
  wiwŏnhoe
Minju nodong-dang
Ttal sarang abŏji moim

Chŏn'guk kyŏngjaein
  yŏnhaphoe
Hankuk noch'ong
Ipgim

Gender Complaints Unit	Namyŏ ch'abyŏl shingo sentŏ
Grand National Party	Hannara-dang
Green Korea	Noksaek yŏnhap
Hyundai Asan Foundation	Hyundai asan chedan
Judicial Research and Training Institute	Pŏpwŏn kongmuwŏn kyoyukwŏn
Korea Differently Abled Federation	Hankuk changaein tanch'ae ch'ong yŏnmaeng
Korea Legal Aid Center for Family Relations	Hankuk kajŏng pŏpnyul sangdamso
Korea Sexual Violence Relief Center	Hankuk sŏngpongnyŏk sangdamso
Korea Women's Hotline	Hankuk yŏsŏngŭi chŏnhwa yŏnhap
Korea Women's Political Solidarity	Yŏsŏng chŏngch'i seryŏk minju yŏndae
Korean Association for the Elderly	Taehan noinhoe
Korean Christian Action Organization	Kidokkyo yulli shilch'ŏn undong
Korean Christian Council	Hankuk kidokkyohoe
Korean Church Women United	Hankuk kyohoe yŏsŏng yŏnhaphoe
Korean Clans United	Hankuk shijok ch'ong yŏnhaphoe
Korean Confederation of Trade Unions	Chongguk minju nodong chŏnhap chŏng yŏnmaeng (minju nojŏng)
Korean Council for the Women Drafted for Military Sexual Slavery by Japan	Hankuk chongshindae munjae daech'aek hyŏpŭihoe
Korean Council of Citizens' Movements	Shimin yŏp/ Hankuk Shimin undong tanch'ae
Korean Differently Abled Women United	Hankuk yŏsŏng changaein yŏnhap
Korean Elderly Helpline	Hankuk noin chŏnwha
Korean Employers' Federation	Hankuk kyŏngyongja ch'ong hyophoe
Korean Family Law Reform Movement	Kajok pŏpkaejŏng undong
Korean Federation of Housewives' Clubs	Hankuk kajŏngchubu yŏnhap
Korean Federation of the Environmental Movement	Hankuk hwan'gyŏng undong yŏnhap
Korean Institute for Alternative Social Policy	Hankuk taehan sahoe chŏngch'aek kyohwan
Korean National Council of Women	Hankuk yŏsŏng tanch'ae yŏpŭihoe
Korean Peasants' League	Hankuk nongminhoe chŏngyŏnmaeng
Korean Research Institute of Sexual Violence	Hankuk sŏngpongnyŏk yŏn'guso

Korean Research Institute on the
Rights of the Differently Abled
Korean Women Political Culture
Research Center
Korean Women Workers
Association United
Korean Women's Christian
Academy
Korean WomenLink
Korean Women's Association United

Korean Women's Development Institute
Korean Women's Hotline
Korean Women's Political Caucus

Korean Women's Political Research Center

Korean Women's Political Solidarity

Korean Women's Studies Association
Korean Women's Trade
Union
Lawyers for a Democratic
Society
League of Women
Voters
Millennium Democratic Party
Ministry of Gender Equality
Ministry of Political Affairs No. 2
National Congress Party (NCP)
National Election
Commission
National Professors Association
New Democratic Republican Party
New Korea Democratic Party
New Village Movement
NGO Times
Peace and Democracy Party
People's Solidarity for Participatory
Democracy
Presidential Commission on
Women's Affairs
Sarangbang Group for Human Rights
Seoul Women's Trade Union

Changaein kwŏnik munhwa
yŏn'guso
Hankuk yŏsŏng chŏngch'i
munhwa yŏn'guso
Hankuk yŏsŏng nodongja
hyŏpŭihoe
Hankuk yŏsŏng kidokkyo
sahoe yŏnguhoe
Hankuk yŏsŏng minuhoe
Hankuk yŏsŏng tanch'ae
yŏnhap
Hankuk yŏsŏng kaebalwŏn
Hankuk yŏsŏngŭi chŏnhwa
Hankuk yŏsŏng chŏngch'i
yŏnmaeng
Hankuk yŏsŏng chŏngch'i
yŏn'guso
Yŏsŏng chŏngch'i seryŏk
minju yŏndae
Hankuk yŏsŏng hakhoe
Chŏn'guk yŏsŏng nodong
chohap
Minbyŏn/minju sahoirul
ŭihan byonhosa moim
Hankuk yŏsŏng yugwŏnja
yŏnmaeng
Sae ch'ŏn nyŏn minju-dang
Yŏsŏng-bu
Chongmu che-i gwanshil
Kukhoe chŏng-dang
Chungang sŏn'gŏ kwalli
wiwŏnhoe
Chŏnkuk kyosu hyŏpŭihoe
Shin minju konghwa-dang
Sae Hankuk minju-dang
Saemaŭl undong
Shiminŭi shinmun
P'yŏnghwa minju-dang
Ch'amyŏ
yŏndae
Taetongnyŏng yŏsŏng
t'ŭkŭi wiwŏnhoe
ingwŏn undong sarangbang
Seoul yŏsŏng noch'ohap

Sunggyunggwan Confucian Association — Songgyun'gwan yurim tanch'ae
Special Congressional Committee on Reform of Political Legislation — Chŏngch'i pŏp kaejŏngŭl ŭihan t'ŭkbyŏl wiwŏnhoe
Students' Action and Solidarity — Haksaeng yŏndae
Tripartite Commission — Nosajŏng wiwŏnhoe
United Liberal Democrats — Chayu minju yŏnmaeng-dang
URI Party/Our Open Party — Yŏllin uri-dang
Veteran Affirmative Action Policy — Kasanjŏm chedo
Women 21 — Hankuk yŏsŏng tanch'ae yŏnhap
Women Chemists Association — Yŏsŏng yaksahoe
Women for Equality and Peace — Yŏsŏng p'yŏnguhoe
Women Times — *Wŏmŭn T'aimjŭ*
Women's Associations United for Reformation of the Labor Laws — Yŏsŏng nodong pŏp kaejŏng yŏndae
Women's Focal Points — Yŏsŏng chŏngch'aek damdanggwan

Women's News — *Yŏsŏng shinmun*
Women's Policy Evaluation Committee — Yŏsŏng chŏngch'aek p'yonga wiwŏnhoe

Women's Solidarity for the Introduction of a Women's Quota — Malgŭn chŏngch'i yŏsŏng netwŏk
Women's Solidarity for the Presidential Elections — 2002 daesun yŏsŏng yŏndae
Women's Union for Revision of Family Law — Kajok pŏpkaejŏngnyul ŭihan yŏsŏng yŏnhap
Working-Class Power — Nodongja him

Bibliography

Abdollohian, Mark, Kacek Kugler, and Hilton Root. 2000. "Economic Crisis and the Future of Oligarchy." In *Institutional Reform and Democratic Consolidation in Korea*, edited by Larry Diamond and Doh-Chull Shin. Stanford: Hoover Institution Press.

Abelmann, Nancy. 1997. "Women's Class Mobility and Identities in South Korea: A Gendered, Transnational, Narrative Approach." *The Journal of Asian Studies* 56, no. 2: 398–420.

Adelman, Irma. N.d. "Social Development in Korea 1953–1993." Working Paper (are.berkeley.edu/~adelman/KOREA.DOC).

Ahn, Kyong-Whan. 1994. "The Growth of the Bar and Changes in the Lawyer's Role." In *Technology and Law in the Pacific Community*, edited by Philip Lewis. Boulder: Westview Press.

——— 1997. "The Influence of American Constitutionalism on South Korea." *Southern Illinois University Law Journal* 22, no. 71: 71–115.

Alvarez, Sonia. 1990. *Engendering Democracy in Brazil: Women's Movements in Transition Politics*. Princeton: Princeton University Press.

Alvarez, Sonia, Evelina Dagnino, and Arturo Escobar. 1998. *Cultures of Politics, Politics of Cultures: Revisioning Latin American Social Movements*. Boulder: Westview Press.

Amsden, Alice. 1989. *Asia's Next Giant: South Korea and Late Industrialization*. New York: Oxford University Press.

Anderson, Benedict. 1991. *Imagined Communities: Reflections on the Origin and Spread of Nationalism*. London: Verso.

Arirang News. 2005. "Martial Rape to Face Punishment." May 3 (www.arirangtv.com/english/news/news_body.asp?news_no=58695&title=National).

Atienza, Maria. 2000. "Gender and Local Governance in the Philippines." In *Democracy and the Status of Women in East Asia*, edited by Rose Lee and Cal Clark. Boulder: Lynne Rienner Publishers.

Baek, Hyun-Suk. 2003. "How Much Has Been Achieved in Terms of Abolishing the Family Headship System? Who Will Take Control of the Debate?" May 27. *Woman Times*. Seoul: (www.iwomantimes.com).

Bai, Moo-Ki and Cho Woo-Hyun. 1995. *Women's Wages and Employment in Korea*. Seoul: Seoul National University Press.

Barrig, Maruja. 1994. "The Difficult Equilibrium between Bread and Roses: Women's Organizations and Democracy in Peru." In *The Women's Movement in Latin America*, edited by Jane Jaquette. Boulder: Westview Press.

Basu, Amrita. 1995. *The Challenge of Local Feminisms: Women's Movements in Global Perspective*. Boulder: Westview Press.

Besse, Susan. 1996. *Restructuring Patriarchy: The Modernization of Gender Inequality in Brazil, 1914–1940*. Chapel Hill: University of North Carolina.

Blofield, Merike. 1998. "The Politics of Abortion in Chile and Argentina: Public Opinion, Social Actors and Discourse, and Political Agendas." Paper presented at the Latin American Studies Association, Chicago.

Brinton, March. 2001. *Women's Working Lives in East Asia (Studies in Social Inequality)*. San Francisco: Stanford University Press.

Brock, Karen, Andrea Cornwall, and John Gaventa. 2001. "Power, Knowledge and Political Spaces in the Framing of Poverty Policy." Institute of Development Studies Working Paper 143. Sussex: Institute of Development Studies.

Burton, Michael and Jai Ryu. 1997. "South Korea's Elite Settlement and Democratic Consolidation." *Journal of Political and Military Sociology* 25, no. 1: 1–24.

Bystydzienski, Jill. 1995. "Women's Equality Structures in Norway: The Equal Status Council." In *Comparative State Feminism*, edited by Dorothy McBride Stetson and Amy Mazur. London: Sage Publications.

Byun, Whasoon. 2000. "Research on Sex, Gender, Sexuality, and Violence against Women." *Women's Studies Forum* 17. Seoul: KWDI (www2.kwdi.re.kr/board/view.php?db=project&category=&no=130&page=8).

Caldiera, Teresa. 1996. "Crime and Individual Rights: Reframing the Question of Violence in Latin America." In *Restructuring Democracy: Human Rights, Citizenship, and Society in Latin America*, edited by Elizabeth Jelin and Eric Hershberg. Oxford: Westview Press.

———— 1998. "Justice and Individual Rights: Challenges for Women's Movements and Democratization in Brazil." In *Women and Democracy: Latin America and Central and Eastern Europe*, edited by Jane Jaquette and Sharon Wolchik. Baltimore: Johns Hopkins University Press.

Callahan, William. 1998. "Comparing the Discourse of Popular Politics in Korea and China: From Civil Society to Social Movements." *Korea Journal* 39, no. 1: 277–322.

Carroll, Susan. 1994. *Women as Candidates in American Politics*. Bloomington: Indiana University Press.

Cha, Dong-Se, Kwang-Suk Kim, and Dwight Perkins. 1997. *The Korean Economy 1945–1995: Performance and Vision for the 21st Century*. Seoul: Korea Development Institute.

Cha, Insoon. 2004. "A Study on Women's Policy of Local Government in Korea Centering on Budget," Ph.D. thesis, Department of Women's Studies, Ewha Womans University, Seoul.

Chalmers, Douglas, Carlos Vilas, Katherine Hite, Scott Martin, Kerianne Piester, and Monique Segarra. 1997. *The New Politics of Inequality in Latin America: Rethinking Participation and Representation*. New York: Oxford University Press.

Chang, Kyung-Sup. 1995. "Gender and Abortive Capitalist Social Transformation: Semi-Proletarianization of South Korean Women." *International Journal of Comparative Sociology XXXVI*, no. 1–2: 61–82.

——— 1997. "The Neo-Confucian Right and Family Politics in South Korea: The Nuclear Family as an Ideological Construct." *Economy and Society* 26, no. 1: 22–43.

Chang, Pilwha. 1994. "The Gender Division of Labour at Work." In *Gender Division of Labor in Korea*, edited by Cho Hyoung and Chang Pilwha. Seoul: Ewha Womans University Press.

——— 2005 "Talking about Sexuality." In *Women's Experiences and Feminist Practices in South Korea*, edited by Chang Pilwha and Kim Eunshil. Seoul: Ewha Womans University Press.

Chang, Yoon-Son. 2004. "Haste to Abolish the Family Headship System as the 17th Congress Opens." May 6. *Women 21*. Seoul: KWAU (in Korean).

Chang, Yoekyong. 1999. "Women's Strategy in Cyberspace: More Political Imagination." Seoul: Jinbonet (http://lmedia.nodong.net/1999/archive/e21.htm).

Chant, Sylvia and Nikki Craske. 2003. *Gender in Latin America*. New Jersey: Rutgers University Press.

Chin, Mikyung. 2000. "Self-Governance, Political Participation, and the Feminist Movement in South Korea." In *Democracy and the Status of Women in East Asia*, edited by Rose Lee and Cal Clark. Boulder: Lynne Rienner Publishers.

Ching, Miriam and Louie Yoon. 1995. "Minjung Feminism: Korean Women's Movement for Gender and Class Liberation." *Women's Studies International Forum* 18, no. 4: 417–30.

Cho, Hae-Joang. 1994. "The 'Woman Question' in the Minjok-Minju Movement: A Discourse Analysis of a New Women's Movement in 1980's Korea." In *Gender Division of Labor in Korea*, edited by Cho Hyung and Chang Pilwha. Seoul: Korea, Ewha Womans University Press.

——— 2002. "Living with Conflicting Subjectivities: Mother, Motherly Wife, and Sexy Woman in the Transition from Colonial-Modern to Postmodern Korea." In *Under Construction: The Gendering of Modernity, Class, and Consumption in the Republic of Korea*, edited by Laurel Kendall. Honolulu: University of Hawaii Press.

Cho, Hee-Yeon. 2000. "Democratic Transition and Changes in Korean NGOs." *Korean Journal* 40, no. 2: 275–304.

Cho, Ju-Hyun. 2005. "The Politics of Gender Identity: The Women's Movement in Korea in the 1980s and 1990s." In *Women's Experiences and Feminist Practices in South Korea*, edited by Chang Pilwha and Kim Eunshil. Seoul: Ewha Womans University Press.

Cho, Lee Yeo-wol. 2002. "Disclosing Sexual Violence Perpetratros Cannot Be Considered Defamation." *WomenNews*. November 6.

Cho, Mi-Kyung. 1998. "The Relationship between Social Change and Family Law in Korea." In *The Changing Family: Family Forms and Family Law*, edited by John Eekelaar and Thandababtu Nhlapo. Oxford: Hart Publishing.

Cho, Oakla. 1998. "The Problem of Identity among Peasant Women in Korea. *Korea Journal* 38: 66–81.

Cho, Soon-Kyoung. 1994. "The Limits and Possibilities of the Women's Movement in Korea." In *Gender Division of Labor in Korea*, edited by Cho Hyung and Chang Pilwha. Seoul: Korea Womans University Press.

Cho, Uhn. 1996. "Female Labor in Korea: Economically Active but Not Empowered." *Asian Women* 2: 55–75.

Choi, Sook-Kyung. 1985. "Formation of Women's Movements in Korea: From the Enlightenment Period to 1910." *Korea Journal* 25, no. 1: 4–15.

Choo, Hakchung. 1985. "Estimation of Size Distribution of Income and Its Sources of Change in Korea, 1982." Seoul: KDI Working Paper #8515.

Choy, Linda. 2001. "Breaking Through: A Right of Passage for Feminist Artists in Korea" (www.artwomen.org/Jongmyo/index.htm).

Christensen, Ray. 2000. "The Impact of Electoral Rules in Japan." In *Democracy and the Status of Women in East Asia*, edited by Rose Lee and Cal Clark. Boulder: Lynne Rienner Publishers.

Chuchryk, Patricia. 1994. "From Dictatorship to Democracy: The Women's Movement in Chile." In *The Women's Movement in Latin America: Participation and Democracy*, edited by Jane Jaquette. Oxford: Westview Press.

Chun, Kyung Ock. 1996. "Women's Political Empowerment in Korea: Legitimacy and Prospects." *Asian Women* 2: 17–53.

Clark, Cal and Rose Lee. 2000. "Democracy and 'Softening' Society." In *Democracy and the Status of Women in East Asia*, edited by Rose Lee and Cal Clark. Boulder: Lynne Rienner Publishers.

Clark, Donald. 1997. "History and Religion in Modern Korea: The Case of Protestant Christianity." In *Religion and Society in Contemporary Korea*, edited by Lewis Lancaster and Richard Payne. University of California, Berkley: Institute of East Asian Studies.

Collier, David. 1979. "The Bureaucratic-Authoritarian Model: Synthesis and Priorities for Future Research." In *The New Authoritarianism in Latin America*, edited by David Collier. Princeton, New Jersey: Princeton.

Collier, Ruth Berins and David Collier. 1991. *Shaping the Political Arena: Critical Junctures, the Labor Movement, and Regime Dynamics in Latin America*. New Jersey: Princeton.

Constitutional Court. 1999. "Opinion on Constitionl Complaint against Article 8 (1) Of the Support for Discharged Soliders Act (11–2 KCCR 770, 98Hun-Ma363, December 23, 1999, Full Bench) 32." Korea: Constitutional Court.

Corcoran-Nantes, Yvonne. 1993. "Female Consciousness or Feminist Consciousness? Women's Consciousness Rising in Community-Based

Struggles in Brazil." In *"ViVa": Women and Popular Protest in Latin America*, edited by Sarah Radcliffe and Sallie Westwood. London: Routledge.

Cotton, James. 1995. *Politics and Policy in the New Korean State: From Roh Tae Woo to Kim Young Sam*. New York: St. Martin's Press.

Craske, Nikki. 1998. "Remasculinisation and the Neoliberal State in Latin America." In *Gender Politics and the State*, edited by Vicki Randall and Georgina Waylen. New York: Routledge.

——— 1999. *Women and Politics in Latin America*. New Brunswick: Rutgers University.

Craske, Nikki and Maxine Molyneux. 2002. *Gender and the Politics of Rights and Democracy in Latin America*. New York: Palgrave.

Croissant, Aurel. 2002a. "Electoral Politics in South Korea." In *Electoral Politics in Southeast and East Asia*, edited by Aurel Croissant, Gab Bruns, and Marie John. Singapore: Friedrich-Ebert-Stiftung.

——— 2002b. "Electoral Systems in Asia as Elements of Consensus and Majoritarian Democracy: Comparing Seven Cases." In *Redefining Korean Politics: Lost Paradigm and New Vision*, edited by Young-Rae Kim, Hochul Lee, and In-Sah Mah. Seoul: Korea Political Science Association.

Cumings, Bruce. 1997. *Korea's Place in the Sun: A Modern History*. New York: Norton and Company.

Curtis, Gerald. 1998. "A 'Recipe' for Democratic Development." In *Democracy in East Asia*, edited by Larry Diamond and Marc Plattner. Baltimore: Johns Hopkins University Press.

Dahlerup, Drude. 1998. "Using Quotas to Increase Women's Political Representation." In *Women in Parliament: Beyond the Numbers*, edited by Azza Karam. Stockholm: International IDEA.

Darcy, R., Susan Welch, and Janet Clark. 1994. *Women, Elections and Representation*. Lincoln: University of Nebraska Press.

Deuchler, Martina. 1992. *The Confucian Transformation of Korea: A Study of Society and Ideology*. Cambridge: Council of East Asian Studies, Harvard University.

Deutsch, Sandra McGee. 1991. "The Catholic Church, Work and Womanhood in Argentina, 1890–1930." *Gender & History* 3: 304–25.

Diamond, Larry. 1999. *Developing Democracy: Toward Consolidation*. Baltimore: Johns Hopkins University Press.

Diamond, Larry and Marc Plattner. 1998. *Democracy in East Asia*. Baltimore: Johns Hopkins University Press.

Diamond, Larry and Doh-Chull Shin. 2000. *Institutional Reform and Democratic Consolidation in Korea*. Stanford: Hoover Institution Press.

Doh, Soowon. 2001. "How Do Political Opportunities Matter for Social Movements?: Political Opportunity, Misframing, Pseudosuccess, and Pseudofailure." *The Sociological Quarterly* 42: 437–66.

Dong, Kim Sung-hye. 2003. "Seoul District Court Supports Women Artists' Freedom of Expression." *WomenNews*. June 23. Seoul.

Dong, Won-Mo. 1993. "The Democratization of South Korea: What Role Does the Middle Class Play?" In *Korea Under Roh Tae Woo: Democratization,*

Northern Policy, and Inter-Korean Relations, edited by James Cotton. Canberra: Australia National University.

Dore, Elizabeth and Maxine Molyneux (eds.). 2000. *Hidden Histories of Gender and the State in Latin America*. Durham: Duke University Press.

Drakulic, Slavenka. 1993. "Women and the New Democracy in the Former Yugoslavia." In *Gender Politics and Post-Communism (Reflections from Eastern Europe and the Former Soviet Union)*, edited by Nanette Funk and Magda Mueller. New York: Routledge.

Duncan, John. 1997. "Confucian Social Values in Contemporary South Korea." In *Religion and Society in Contemporary Korea*, edited by Walter Slote, George De Vos, and Robert Eno. New York: State University of New York Press.

Eisenger, Peter. 1973. "The Conditions of Protest Behavior in American Cities." *American Political Science Review* 67: 11–28.

Eisenstein, Hester. 1995. *Inside Agitators: Australian Femocrats and the State*. Philadephila: Temple University Press.

Elson, Diane. 1997. "Gender-Neutral, Gender-Blind, or Gender-Sensitive Budgets?: Changing the Conceptual Framework to Include Women's Empowerment and the Economy of Care." Paper presented at Preparatory Country Mission to Integrate Gender into National Budgetary Policies and Procedures. London: Commonwealth Secretariat.

EPIC (Election Process Information Collection). 2005. Seoul (epicproject.org/ace/compepic/en/country$KR+ES).

Escandon, Carmen Ramos. 1994. "Women's Movements, Feminism, and Mexican Politics." In *The Women's Movement in Latin America: Participation and Democracy*, edited by Jane Jaquette. Boulder: Westview Press.

Evans, Peter. 1995. *Embedded Autonomy: States and Industrial Transformation*. Princeton: Princeton University Press.

Farris, Catherine. 2000. "Contradictory Implications of Socialism and Capitalism under East Asian Modernity; in China and Taiwan." In *Democracy and the Status of Women in East Asia*, edited by Rose Lee and Cal Clark. Boulder: Lynne Rienner Publishers.

Feijoo, Maria Del Carmen. 1998. "Democratic Participation and Women in Argentina." In *Women and Democracy: Latin America and Central and Eastern Europe*, edited by Jane Jaquette and Sharon Wolchik. Baltimore: Johns Hopkins University Press.

Fisher, Jo. 1993. *Out of the Shadows: Women, Resistance and Politics in South America*. London: Latin American Bureau.

Franco, Jean. 1998. "Defrocking the Vatican: Feminism's Secular Project." In *Cultures of Politics, Politics of Cultures: Re-Visioning Latin American Social Movements*, edited by Sonia Alvarez and Arturo Escobar. Boulder: Westview Press.

Fraser, Nancy. 1993. "Rethinking the Public Sphere: A Contribution to the Critique of Actually Existing Democracy." In *The Phantom Public Sphere*, edited by Bruce Robbins. Minneapolis: University of Minnesota Press.

Friedman, Elisabeth. 2000. *Unfinished Transitions: Women and the Gendered Development of Democracy in Venezuela, 1936–1996*. Pennsylvania: Pennsylvania State University Press.

Frohmann, Alicia and Teresa Valdes. 1995. "Democracy in the Country and in the Home: The Women's Movement in Chile." In *The Challenge of Local Feminisms: Women's Movements in Global Perspective*, edited by Amrita Basu. Boulder: Westview Press.

Fuentes, Claudio. 2004. *Contesting the Iron Fist: Advocacy Networks and Political Violence in Democratic Argentina and Chile*. New York: Routledge.

Funk, Nanette and Magda Mueller (eds.). 1993. *Gender Politics and Post-Communism (Reflections from Eastern Europe and the Former Soviet Union)*. New York: Routledge.

Gal, Susan and Gail Kligman. 2000. *The Politics of Gender after Socialism: A Comparative-Historical Essay*. Princeton: Princeton University Press.

Garreton, Manuel Antonio. 1996. "Human Rights in Democratization Processes." In *Constructing Democracy—Human Rights, Citizenship, and Society in Latin America*, edited by Elizabeth Jelin and Eric Hershberg. Boulder: Westview Press.

Gereffi, Gary and Donald Wyman. 1990. *Manufacturing Miracles: Paths of Industrialization in Latin America and East Asia*. Princeton: Princeton University Press.

Gideon, Jasmine. 2002. "Economic and Social Rights: Exploring Gender Differences in a Central American Context." In *Gender and the Politics of Rights and Democracy in Latin America*, edited by Nikki Craske and Maxine Molyneux. New York: Palgrave.

Gills, Barry and Dong-Sook Shin Gills. 2000. "Globalization and Strategic Choice in South Korea: Economic Reform and Labor." In *Korea's Globalization*, edited by Samuel Kim. Cambridge: Cambridge University Press.

Goven, Joanna. 1993. "Gender Politics in Hungary: Autonomy and Antifeminism." In *Gender Politics and Post-Communism (Reflections from Eastern Europe and the Former Soviet Union)*, edited by Nanette Funk and Magda Mueller. New York: Routledge.

Grootaert, Christiaan and Thierry van Bastelaer. 2002. *The Role of Social Capital in Development: An Empirical Assessment*. Cambridge: Cambridge University Press.

Guy, Donna. 1991. *Sex and Danger in Buenos Aires: Prostitution, Family and Nation in Argentina*. Lincoln: University of Nebraska Press.

Ha, Yong-Chool. 1995. "Neo-Familism: Social Consequences of Industrialization in South Korea." In *Colonialism, Neo-Familism and Rationality: Persectives on Korean Issues*, edited by Ha Yong-Chool, Kim Yung-Myung, Kim Chae-Han, and Bruce Bueno de Mesquita. Seoul: Sowha Publishing Co.

Haas, Anna Liesl. 2000. "Legislating Equality: Institutional Politics and the Expansion of Women's Rights in Chile." Ph.D. dissertation, Department of Political Science, University of North Carolina at Chapel Hill.

Hahm, Chaibong. 1997. "The Confucian Political Discourse and the Politics of Reform in Korea." *Korea Journal* 37, no. 4: 65–77.

Hahm, Sung-Deuk and Christopher Plein. 1997. *After Development: The Transformation of the Korean Presidency and Bureaucracy*. Washington: Georgetown University Press.

Hahn, Chungja. 2001a. "A Study of Local Government Heads' Sensitivity to Women's Problems." *Women's Studies Forum* 17. Seoul: KWDI (www2.kwdi. re.kr/board/view.php?db=project&category=&no=129&page=8).

———— 2001b. "A Study of the Situation of Sexual Harassment in Business Following the Implementation of Legal Regulations and Its Improvements." *Women's Studies Forum* 18. Seoul: KWDI (http://www.kwdi.re.kr/data/02forum-10.pdf).

Han, Chongja and Kim In-Soon. 2001. "Research on the Implementation of Sexual Harassment Legal Regulations in the Workplace and Directions for Future Improvements." Seoul: KWDI.

Han, Sang-Jin. 1997. "The Public Sphere and Democracy in Korea: A Debate on Civil Society." *Korea Journal* 37, no. 4: 78–97.

Han, Heon-woo. 2001. "Survey on 555 people in Seoul: Although They Have Been Child, 68% of Them May Divorce, 70% of Women Can Make Sacrifices." *Chosun Ilbo*. August 21 (in Korean).

Hartman, Heidi. 1981. "The Unhappy Marriage of Marxism and Feminism: Towards a More Progressive Union." In *Women and Revolution: Discussion of the Unhappy Marriage of Marxism and Feminism*, edited by Lydia Sargent. Montreal: Black Rose Books.

Hayes, Sean. 2003. "Divorce at Home and Abroad No Simple Matter." *Korea Herald*. July 13.

Helgesen, Geir. 1997. *Democracy and Authority in Korea: The Cultural Dimension in Korean Politics*. London: Palgrave Macmillan.

Hochstetler, Kathryn. 1997. "The Evolution of the Brazilian Environmental Movement and Its Political Roles." In *The New Politics of Inequality in Latin America: Rethinking Participation and Representation*, edited by Douglas Chalmers, Carlos Vilas, Katherine Hite, Scott Martin, Kerianne Piester, and Monique Segarra. New York: Oxford University Press.

Holston, James and Teresa Caldeira. 1998. "Democracy, Law and Violence: Disjunctions of Brazilian Citizenship." In *Fault Lines of Democracy in Post-Transition Latin America*, edited by Felipe Aguero and Jeffrey Stark. Miami: North-South Center Press.

Honculada, Jurgette and Rosalinda Pineda Ofreneo. 2003. "The National Commission on the Role of Filipino Women, the Women's Movement and Gender Mainstreaming in the Philippines." In *Mainstreaming Gender, Democratizing the State? Institutional Mechanisms for the Advancement of Women*, edited by Shirin Rai. Manchester: Manchester University Press.

Htun, Mala. 2003. *Sex and the State: Abortion, Divorce, and the Family under Latin American Dictatorships and Democracies*. Cambridge: Cambridge University Press.

Htun, Mala and Mark Jones. 2002. "Engendering the Right to Participate in Decision-Making: Electoral Quotas and Women's Leadership in Latin

America." In *Gender and the Politics of Rights and Democracy in Latin America*, edited by Nikki Craske and Maxine Molyneux. New York: Palgrave.

Huang, Changling. 2003. "Democracy and the Politics of Difference: Gender Quota in Taiwan." Paper prepared for delivery at the 2002 Annual Meeting of the American Political Science Association.

IPU (Inter-Parliamentary Union). 2005. "Women in Parliament" (www.ipu.org/wmn-e/world.htm).

Janelli, Robert and Dawn-hee Yim. 2002. "Gender Construction in the Offices of a South Korean Conglomerate." In *Under Construction: The Gendering of Modernity, Class, and Consumption in the Republic of Korea*, edited by Laurel Kendall. Honolulu: University of Hawaii Press.

Jaquette, Jane. 1994. *The Women's Movement in Latin America: Participation and Democracy*. Boulder: Westview Press.

——— 1995. "Rewriting the Scripts: Gender in the Comparative Study of Latin American Politics." In *Latin America in Comparative Perspective: New Approaches to Methods and Analysis*, edited by Peter Smith. Boulder: Westview Press.

Jaquette, Jane and Sharon Wolchik (eds.). 1998. *Women and Democracy: Latin America and Central and Eastern Europe*. Baltimore: Johns Hopkins University Press.

Jelin, Elizabeth and Eric Hershberg, 1996. *Constructing Democracy: Human Rights, Citizenship and Society in Latin America*. Boulder: Westview Press.

Jenkins, Craig and Bert Klandermans. 1995. *The Politics of Social Protest: Comparative Perspectives on States and Social Movements*. Minneapolis: University of Minnesota Press.

Jeon, Jin-bae. 2002. "Divorcing Parents Want to Shed Kids with Spouse." *JoongAng Daily*. October 21.

Ji, Uhn-Hee. 2002. "Analyzing the Women's Movement from Within: With a Focus on the Activities of the Korean Women's Association United." Seoul: KWAU.

Johnson, Niki. 2002. "In Pursuit of the Right to Be Free from Violence: The Women's Movement and State Accountability in Uruguay." In *Gender and the Politics of Rights and Democracy in Latin America*, edited by Nikki Craske and Maxine Molyneux. New York: Palgrave.

Jones, Nicola. 2003. "Mainstreaming Gender: South Korean Women's Civic Alliances and Institutional Strategies, 1987–2002." Ph.D. dissertation, Department of Political Science, University of North Carolina at Chapel Hill.

JoongAng Daily. 2002. "Homemakers Relish Power of Controlling Family Purse." September 16.

JoongAng Daily. 2002. "Barriers and Guilt Still Remain for Professional Women in Korea." October 21.

JoongAng Daily. 2002. "Times Change, but Not Men's Attitudes about Women's Worth." October 28.

Jung, Soon-Young. 2004. "The Role of National Mechanisms in Promoting Gender Equality and the Empowerment of Women: Achievements, Gaps and Challenges." Paper presented at United Nations Division for the Advancement of Women Conference. Rome (http://www.un.org/womenwatch/daw/egm/nationalm2004/resource-papers/RP.8_Jung.pdf).

Kang, David. 2001. "The Institutional Foundation of Korean Politics." In *Understanding Korean Politics*, edited by Soong-Hoom Kil and Chung-in Moon. New York: State University of New York Press.

Kang, Eliot. 2003. "The Developmental State and Democratic Consolidation in South Korea." In *Korea's Democratization*, edited by Samuel Kim. Cambridge: Cambridge University Press.

Karl, Terry. 1990. "Dilemmas of Democratization in Latin America." *Comparative Politics* 23: 1–22.

KCTU (Korean Confederation of Trade Unions). 2000. "Hotel Lotte Labour Union Strike White Paper in 2000." Seoul: KCTU Service Industry Federation.

Kendall, Laurel. 1996. *Getting Married in Korea: Of Gender, Morality, and Modernity*. Berkeley: University of California Press.

——— 2002. *Under Construction: The Gendering of Modernity, Class, and Consumption in the Republic of Korea*. Honolulu: University of Hawaii Press.

KIHASA (Korean Institute of Health and Social Affairs). 1992. "Impact of Fertility Decline on Population Policies and Programme Strategies." Seoul: KIHASA.

Kil, Soong-Hoom and Chung-in Moon. 2001. *Understanding Korean Politics*. New York: State University of New York Press.

Kim, Byung-Kook. 1998. "Korea's Crisis of Success." In *Democracy in East Asia*, edited by Larry Diamond and Marc Plattner. Baltimore: Johns Hopkins University Press.

Kim, Byung-suh. 1994. "Value Orientations and Sex-Gender Role Attitudes: On the Comparability of Attitudes of Koreans and Americans." In *Gender Division of Labor in Korea*, edited by Cho Hyoung and Chang Pilwha. Seoul: Ewha Womans University Press.

Kim, Chan-Jin. 2000. "Korean Attitudes towards Law." *Pacific Rim Law and Policy Journal* 10, no. 1.

Kim, Cho-Soo. 1983. "A Study on Amendment of the Family Law for Rational Implementation of Family Planning Program in Korea (1973)." In *Introduction to the Law and Legal System of Korea*, edited by S. H. Song. Seoul: Kyung Mun Sa Publishing Co.

Kim, Elim. 1995. "The Current Laws on Women in Korea." *Women's Studies Forum* 12: 33–47. Seoul: KWDI.

Kim, Elim, Deukkyoung Yoon, and Hyunmee Park. 2000. "A Study on the Laws Concerning Sexual and Domestic Violence. *Women's Studies Forum* 17. Seoul: KWDI (http://www2.kwdi.re.kr/board/view.php?db=project&category=&no=132&page=7).

Kim, Eun-Mee. 2000. "Reforming the Chaebols." In *Institutional Reform and Democratic Consolidation in Korea*, edited by Larry Diamond and Shin-Doh Chull. Stanford: Hoover Institution Press.

Kim, Eun-Shil. 1994. "The Discourse of Nationalism and Women: Critical Readings on Culture, Power and Subject." *Journal of Korean Women's Studies* 10.

———— 2005. "Women and Discourses of Nationalism: Critical Readings of Culture, Power and Subject." In *Women's Experiences and Feminist Practices in South Korea*, edited by Chang Pilwha and Kim Eun-Shil. Seoul: Ewha Womans Press.

Kim, Hyun-Mee. 1996. "The Politics of Korean Working Class Women." *Asia Journal* 3, no. 1: 63–81.

———— 1999. "Feminist Reflections on Women's Labour Rights in Contemporary Korea." Symposium (June 11, 1999): Feminist Analyses of Modernity in East Asia: China, Japan and Korea Asian Center for Women's Studies, Ewha Womans University, Seoul.

Kim, Kwang-Ok. 1996. "The Reproduction of Confucian Culture in Contemporary Korea: An Anthropological Study." In *Confucian Traditions in East Asian Modernity: Moral Education and Economic Culture in Japan and the Four Mini-Dragons*, edited by Tu Weiming. Cambridge: Harvard University Press.

Kim, Kyung-Ai. 1996. "Nationalism: An Advocate of, or a Barrier to, Feminism in South Korea." *Women's Studies International Forum* 19, no. 1/2: 66–74.

Kim, Kyung-Hee. 1998. "Gender Politics in South Korea: The Contemporary Women's Movement and Gender Policies, 1980–1996." Ph.D. dissertation in Department of Sociology. Madison: University of Wisconsin.

Kim, Kyoung-Hee. 2002. "A Frame Analysis of Women's Policies of Korean Government and Women's Movements in the 1980s and 1990s." *Korea Journal* 42, no. 2: 5–36.

Kim, Pan-Suk. 2002. "The Development of Korean NGOs and Governmental Assistance to NGOs." *Korea Journal* 42, no. 2: 279–303.

Kim, Rose. 1994. "The Legacy of Institutionalized Gender Inequality in South Korea: The Family Law." *Boston College: Third World Law Journal* 14: 145.

Kim, Rose. 2000. "Democratic Consolidation and Gender Politics in South Korea." In *Democracy and the Status of Women in East Asia*, edited by Rose Lee and Cal Clark. Boulder: Lynne Rienner Publishers.

Kim, Samuel. 2000. "Korea and Globalization (*Segyehwa*): A Framework for Analysis." In *Korea's Democratization*, edited by Samuel Kim. Cambridge: Cambridge University Press.

———— 2003. "Korea's Democratization in the Global-Local Nexus." In *Korea's Democratization*, edited by Samuel Kim. Cambridge: Cambridge University Press.

Kim, Seung-Kyung. 1997. *Class Struggle or Family Struggle? The Lives of Women Factory Workers in South Korea*. Cambridge. Cambridge University Press.

Kim, Suk-Ja. 2003. "Towards a New Childcare Policy." *Women's Policy Forum* 4. Seoul: KWDI (www2.kwdi.re.kr/).

Kim, Sun-Hyuk. 1997. "State and Civil Society in South Korea's Democratic Consolidation: Is the Battle Really Over." *Asian Survey* 37: 1135–44.

Kim, Sun-Hyuk. 2000. *The Politics of Democratization: The Role of Civil Society.* Pittsburgh: University of Pittsburgh Press.

———— 2003. "Civil Society in Democratizing Korea." In *Korea's Democratization*, edited by Samuel Kim. Cambridge: Cambridge University Press.

Kim, Sun-uk. 1995. "Meaning of the Quota System as a Policy for Women and Its Introduction Methods." *Women's Studies Forum* 11. Seoul: KWDI (www2. kwdi.re.kr/board/view.php?db=project&category=&no=39&page=14).

———— 2005. "An Analysis of Legislative Policy Related to the Implementation of the Convention on the Elimination of All Forms of Discrimination against Women (CEDAW) in Korea." In *Women's Experiences and Feminist Practices in South Korea*, edited by Chang Pilwha and Kim Eun-Shil. Seoul: Ewha Womans Press.

Kim, Tae-Hong. 2001. "Integrating Unpaid Work into National Policy in the Republic of Korea." Paper presented at UNESCAP Workshop on Integrating Paid and Unpaid Work in National Systems, Bangkok.

Kim, Wonhong and Eunkyoung Kim. 1998. "Recommendations to Reform the Electoral Structure and Guarantee Women's Representation." *Women's Studies Forum.* Vol. 15. Seoul: KWDI (www2.kwdi.re.kr/board/view.php?db=project&category=&no=57&page=10).

Kim, Wonhong, Hyeyoung Kim, and Eunkyung Kim. 2001a. *Korean Women's Political Participation after Independence and Future Tasks.* Seoul: KWDI Research Report.

Kim, Wonhong, Haeyoung Kim, and Eunkyung Kim. 2001b. "Measures to Increase the Number of Females in the Decision-Making Positions in Political Parties." *Women's Studies Forum* 17. Seoul: KWDI (http://www2.kwdi.re.kr/board/view.php?db=project&category=&no=57&page=10).

Kim, Wonhong, Haeyoung Kim, and Minjung Kim. 2002. "A Study of the Policy-Oriented Voting Behavior of Female Voters." *Women's Studies Forum* 19. Seoul: KWDI (http://www2.kwdi.re.kr/board/view.php?db=project&category=&no=157&page=5).

Kim, YangHee, Kim HongSook, and Kim KyungHee. 2000. "Research on a Citizen Awareness Survey about Women's Policy in the 21st Century." *Women's Studies Forum* 17. Seoul: KWDI (www2.kwdi.re.kr/).

Kim, YangHee, Kim KyungHee, Kim HongSook, and Lee SuYon. 2001. "Survey of Experts and the General Public on 21st Century Gender Mainstreaming." *Women's Studies Forum* 18. Seoul. KWDI (http://www2.kwdi.re.kr/board/view.php?db=project&category=5&no=144).

Kim, Yong-Joon. 1999. "Constitutional Adjudication System: Experience of Korea." *Harvard Asia Quarterly* (www.fas.harvard.edu/~asiactr/haq/200001/0001a002.htm).

Kim, Yu-Soon and Dianne Harrison. 1999. "Housework, Gender Role Attitudes, Perceived Fairness, and Marital Quality of Korean Working Wives." *Arete* 23: 21–32.

Ko, Dae-hoon. 2002. "Women Targeted for High Level State Jobs." *JoongAng Daily*. October 28.

Koh, Byong-Ik. 1996. "Confucianism in Contemporary Korea." In *Confucian Traditions in East Asian Modernity: Moral Education and Economic Culture in Japan and the Four Mini-Dragons*, edited by Tu Weiming. Cambridge: Harvard University Press.

Koo, Hagen. 2001. *Korean Workers: The Culture and Politics of Class Formation*. Ithaca: Cornell University Press.

Korea Herald. 2000. "Korea Suffers Loss of Female Workers due to Poor Childcare." August 26.

Korean Civil Service Commission. 2002. "Women Targeted for High-Level State Jobs." Seoul: Korean Civil Service Commission.

Korean National Assembly. 2005. *Official Report* no. 252/8: 82–83. Seoul: Korean National Assembly.

Kwak, Jin-Young. 2002. "Open System or Cartelized System? Redefining the Korean Party System after Democratization." In *Redefining Korean Politics: Lost Paradigm and New Vision*, edited by Young-Rae Kim, Hochul Lee, and In-Sub Mah. Seoul: Korean Political Science Association.

KWAU. 1998. *Korea Shadow Report for the Third and Fourth CEDAW Report of the Korean Government*. June. Seoul: Korean Women's Association United.

———— 2004. "KWAU Forum on the Congressional Election Action Controversy." *Women 21 News Magazine* (www.women21.or.kr).

KWDI. 2000. *Korean Women's Statistical Yearbook*. Seoul: KWDI (in Korean).

———— 2002. "6.13 Local Election: Status of Successful Female Candidates." Seoul: KWDI.

———— 2004. *Women's Statistical Year Book*. Seoul: KWDI.

KWDI and MOGE. 2005. "8.7% of Male Servants Attend Gender Equality Training." February 17 News (www.kwdi.re.kr).

Kwon, Huck-Ju. 1999. *The Welfare State in Korea: The Politics of Legitimation*. Oxford: St. Anthony's College.

Kwon, Ohboon. 2000. "Military Gender Politics Seen through the Process of Signifying Military Experience: Focusing on Cases of Co-Ed Universities." M.A. dissertation. Seoul: Ewha Womans University.

Kwon, Yong-Ja. 1995. "A Study of Korean Women's Policy: Equality, Participation, Welfare." Ph.D. dissertation, Sungshin Women's University.

KWWAU (Korea Women's Studies Institute and the Korean Federation of Trade Unions). 1998. "Organizational Strategies of Irregular Women Workers." Seoul: KWWAU.

Lee, Chul-Woo. 1998. "Talking about Korean Legal Culture: A Critical Review of the Discursive Production of Legal Culture in Korea." *Korea Journal* 38, no. 3: 45–75.

Lee, Hye-Kyung, 1994. "Gender Division of Labor and the Authoritarian Developmental State." In *Gender Division of Labor (in) Korea*, edited by Cho Hyoung and Chang Pilwha. Seoul: Ewha Womans University Press.

Lee, Hyo-sik. 2005. "Divorce Decrease for 1st Time in 16 Years." *Korea Times*. March 30.

Lee, Hyunsook and Choon-Sook Jong. 1999. "History of the Domestic Violence Prevention Movement." In *History of the Korean Women's Human Rights Movement*, edited by Korea Women's Studies Association. Seoul: Hanwool Academy (in Korean).

Lee, Jung-Bock. 2001. "The Political Process in Korea." In *Understanding Korean Politics: An Introduction*, edited by Soong-Hoom Kil and Chung-in Moon. Albany: State University of New York Press.

Lee, Kay 1995. "Confucian Ethics, Judges and Women: Divorce under the Revised Korean Family Law." *Pacific Rim Law and Policy Journal* 4: 479–512.

Lee, Kyung-soon and Ellen Bishop. 1998. *The May 18 Kwangju Democratic Uprising*. Kwangju: The May 18 History Compilation Committee of Kwangju City.

Lee, Manwoo. 1990. *The Odyssey of Korean Democracy: Korean Politics, 1987–1990*. Westport: Praeger Publishers.

Lee, Rose. 2000. "Democratic Consolidation and Gender Politics in South Korea." In *Democracy and the Status of Women in East Asia*, edited by Rose Lee and Cal Clark. Boulder: Lynne Rienner Publishers.

Lee, Rose and Cal Clark. 2000. *Democracy and the Status of Women in East Asia*. Boulder: Lynne Rienner Publishers.

Lee, So-Hee. 2002. "The Concept of Female Sexuality in Korean Political Culture" In *Getting Married in Korea: Of Gender, Morality, and Modernity*, edited by Laurel Kendall. Berkeley: University of California Press.

Lee, Soo-jeong. 2000. "NGOs in Korea—KWAU Tries to Expand Women's Role in Politics." *Korea Times*. April 16.

Lee, Young-Jo. 2000. "The Rise and Fall of Kim Young Sam's Embedded Reformism." In *Institutional Reform and Democratic Consolidation in Korea*, edited by Larry Diamond and Shin Doh-Chull. Stanford: Hoover Institution Press.

Leipziger, Danny, David Dollar, A. F. Shorrocks, and S. Y. Song. 1992. *The Distribution of Income and Wealth in Korea*. EDI Development Studies, World Bank, Washington, D.C.

Lie, John. 1995. "The Transformation of Sexual Work in 20th Century Korea." *Gender and Society* 9: 310–27.

Lienesch, Michael. 1993. *Piety and Politics in the New Christian Right: Redeeming America*. Chapel Hill: University of North Carolina Press.

Lijphart, Arend. 1984. *Democracies: Patterns of Majoritarian and Consensus Government in Twenty-One Democracies*. New Haven: Yale University Press.

Ling, Bettina and Charlotte Bunch. 1999. *Aung San Suu Kyi: Standing Up for Democracy in Burma*. New York: Feminist Press.

Ling, L. H. M. 2000. "The Limits of Democratization for Women in East Asia." In *Democracy and the Status of Women in East Asia*, edited by Rose Lee and Cal Clark. Boulder: Lynne Rienner Publishers.

Linz, Juan and Alfred Stepan. 1996. *Problems of Democratic Transition and Consolidation: Southern Europe, South America, and Post-Communist Europe.* Baltimore: Johns Hopkins University Press.

Lowy, Michael. 1996. *The War of Gods: Religion and Politics in Latin America.* London: Verso.

Lukes, Steven. 1974. *Power: A Radical View.* Hampshire: Macmillan.

Lycklama a Nijeholt, Geertje, Virginia Vargas, and Saskie Wieringa. 1998. *Women's Movements and Public Policy in Europe, Latin America, and the Caribbean.* New York: Garland.

Macaulay, Fiona. 2000. "Getting Gender on the Policy Agenda: A Study of a Brazilian Feminist Lobby Group." In *Hidden Histories of Gender and the State in Latin America*, edited by Elizabeth Dore and Maxine Molyneux. Durham: Duke University Press.

———— 2002. "Taking the Law into Their Own Hands: Women, Legal Reform and Legal Literacy in Brazil." In *Gender and the Politics of Rights and Democracy in Latin America*, edited by Nikki Craske and Maxine Molyneux. London: Palgrave.

Mah, In-Sub. 2002. "Weak Labor and the Poverty of Social Welfare in South Korea." In *Redefining Korean Politics: Lost Paradigm and New Vision*, edited by Young-Rae Kim, Hochul Lee, and In-Sah Mah. Seoul: Korea Political Science Association.

Mainwaring, Scott and Timothy Scully. 1995. *Building Democratic Institutions: Party Systems in Latin America.* Stanford: Stanford University Press.

Mainwaring, Scott and Eduoardo Viola. 1984. "New Social Movements, Political Culture, and Democracy: Brazil and Argentina." *Telos* 61: 17–52.

Manarin, Glenn. 2000. "South Korea's Campaign School." *UNESCO Courier* (www.unesco.org/courier/2000_06/uk/doss25.htm).

Matland, Richard. 2003. *Women's Access to Political Power in Post-Communist Europe.* Oxford: Oxford University Press.

Matsui, Yayori. 1999. *Women in the New Asia: From Pain to Power.* London: Zed Books.

McCarthy, John and Mayer Zald. 1977. "Resource Mobilization and Social Movements: A Partial Theory." *American Journal of Sociology* 82, no. 6: 1212–41.

Melucci, Alberto. 1980. "The New Social Movements: A Theoretical Approach." *Social Science Information* 19: 199–226.

Meyer, Mary and Elisabeth Prugl. 1999. *Gender Politics in Global Governance.* New York: Rowman and Littlefield Publishers.

Min, Dong-ki and Min Song-jae. 2004. "Nation Deeply Polarized Amid Widespread Display." *JoongAng Daily.* March 12.

Min, Kyung-Ja. 1999. "Sexual Violence Women's Movement History." In *History of the Korean Women's Human Rights Movement*, edited by Korea Women's Studies Association. Seoul: Hanwool Academy (in Korean).

Minbyun (Lawyers for a Democratic Society). 2004. "About Minbyun" (minbyun.jinbo.net/english/).

Mo, Jongryn and Chung-In Moon. 1999. *Democracy and the Korean Economy.* Stanford: Hoover Institution Press.

MOGE. 2001. "Women's White Paper." Seoul: Ministry of Gender Equality (in Korean).

——— 2002a. "2002 Evaluation and Plan of Major Operations." Seoul: Ministry of Gender Equality.

——— 2002b. "Gender-Related Policies in Korea." Seoul: Ministry of Gender Equality.

——— 2003. "2003 Budget for Improving Rights Projects." Seoul: Ministry of Gender Equality.

MoL. 2004. "Analysis on the Current State of Childbirth Leaves and Child-Care Temporary Retirements Taken in the First Half of 2004." Seoul: Ministry of Labor.

Molyneux, Maxine. 1985. "Mobilization without Emancipation? Women's Interests, the State and Revolution in Nicaragua." *Feminist Studies* 2, no. 2: 227–54.

Montecinos, Veronica. 1999. "Neo-Liberal Economic Reforms and Women in Chile." In *Women in the Age of Economic Transformation: Gender Impact of Reform in Post-Socialist and Developing Countries.* London: Routledge.

Moon, Catherine. 1997. *Sex among Allies.* New York: Colombia University Press.

Moon, Chung-In and Jongryn Mo. 1999. "Korea after the Crash." *Journal of Democracy* 10, no. 3: 150–64.

Moon, Chung-In and Sang-Hoom Lim. 2001. "The Politics of Economic Rise and Decline in South Korea." In *Understanding Korean Politics*, edited by Soong-Hoom Kil and Chung-In Moon. Albany: State University of New York Press.

Moon, Chung-In and Sang-Young Rhyu. 2002. "The State, Structural Rigidity and the End of Asian Capitalism." In *Politics and Markets in the Wake of the Asian Crisis*, edited by Richard Roinson, Mark Beeson, Kanishka Jayasuriya, and Hyuk-Rae Kim. London: Routledge.

Moon, Kyung-ran. 2005. "Female Officials Rise to Higher Ranks and Stir Controversy." *JoongAng Daily*. March 8.

Moon, Min-kyung Shin. 2002. "Once again Falling Short of 10%—Successful Women Candidates in the June 13 Local Elections." *WomenNews*. June 27.

Moon, Seung-sook. 1994. "Economic Development and Gender Politics in South Korea (1963–1992)." Ph.D. dissertation, Department of Sociology, Brandies University, Massachusetts.

——— 1998. "Begetting the Nation: The Androcentric Discourse of National History and Tradition in South Korea." In *Dangerous Women: Gender and Nationalism*, edited by Elaine Kim and Chungmoo Choi. New York: Routledge.

——— 2002. "Carving Out Space: Civil Society and the Women's Movement in South Korea." *Journal of Asian Studies* 61, no. 2: 473–500.

——— 2003. "Redrafting Democratization through Women's Representation and Participation in the Republic of Korea." In *Korea's Democratization*, edited by Samuel Kim. Cambridge: Cambridge University Press.

Moser, Caroline. 1993. "Adjustment from Below: Low-Income Women, Time and the Triple Role in Guayaquil, Ecuador." In *"ViVa" Women and Popular Protest in Latin America*, edited by Sarah Radcliffe and Sallie Westwood. New York: Routledge.

Myung, Jin-sook, Nicola Jones, and Yoon Jung-sook. 2002. "Towards a Less Intrusive Childbirth and Reproductive Health Culture: An Action Research Project Aimed at Reducing the Prevalence of Caesarian Sections in South Korea 2000–2001." Paper prepared for the 6th APSAM Conference, Kunming, China.

Na, Eun-Yeong and Cha Jae-Ho. 2000. "Changes in Values and the Generation Gap between the 1970s and the 1990s in Korea." *Korea Journal*: 285–324.

Nam, Jeong-Lim. 1994. "Women's Role in Export Dependence and State Control of Labor Unions in South Korea." *Women's Studies Int. Forum* 17, no. 1: 57–67.

——— 1995. "Reforming Economic Allocations in the Family: The Women's Movement and the Role of the State in South Korea." *Women's Studies International Forum* 18, no. 2: 113–23.

Nam, Yoon In-Soon, 2004. "What 39 Women Legislators Must Do First." *Korean Women's Association United News Magazine*. April 23. Seoul.

Nash, June and Helen Safa (eds.). 1986. *Women and Change in Latin America: New Directions in the Study of Sex and Class*. Westport: Bergin and Garvey Publishers.

NHRCK (National Human Rights Commission of Korea). 2003. "Hoju System Is Unconstitutional and a Violation of Human Rights." The Asia Pacific Forum of National Human Rights Institutions (www.asiapacificforum.net/member/docs/korea_news.htm#hoju).

National Police Agency. 2001. *White Paper on Police*. Seoul: National Police Agency.

Nowakowska, Urszula 2001. "Women's Reproductive Rights." In *Polish Women in the 90s*, edited by The Women's Rights Center, Warsaw (free.ngo.pl/temida/contents.htm).

NSO. 2002. *Social Indicators in Korea*. Seoul: National Statistics Office.

O'Connor, Julia, Ann Shola Orloff, and Sheila Shaver. 1999. *States, Markets, Families: Gender, Liberalism, and Social Policy in Australia, Canada, Great Britain and the United States*. Cambridge: Cambridge University Press.

O'Donnell, Guillermo. 1994. "Delegative Democracy." *Journal of Democracy* 5: 55–69.

O'Donnell, Guillermo and Philippe Schmitter. 1989. *Transitions from Authoritarian Rule: Tentative Conclusions about Uncertain Democracies*. Baltimore: Johns Hopkins University Press.

Oh, Hye-ran. 1997. "Activities of Women's Organizations in Korea: Focusing on the Activities of the Korean National Council of Women since the 1980s." *Asian Women* 5: 145–55.

Oxhorn, Philip. 1995. *Organizing Civil Society: The Popular Sectors and the Struggle for Democracy in Chile*. University Park: Pennsylvania State University Park.

Paik, Jina. 2002. "Formulation of and Discourse on Women." *Korea Journal* 2, no. 2: 37–67.

Pak, Unjong. 2002. "Reinforcement of Legal Protection for Working Women: Focusing on Discrimination and Sexual Harassment." *Korea Journal* 42, no. 2: 160–80.

Palley, Marian Lief. 1994. "Feminism in a Confucian Society: The Women's Movement in Korea." In *Women of Japan and Korea*, edited by Joyce Gelb and Marian Lief Palley. Philadelphia: Temple University Press.

Park, Chan-Wook. 2000. "Legislative-Executive Relations and Legislative Reform." In *Institutional Reform and Democratic Consolidation in Korea*, edited by Larry Diamond and Doh-Chull Shin. Stanford: Hoover Institution Press.

——— 2002. "The Rules of the Electoral Game for the National Assembly in Democratic Korea: A Comparative Perspective." In *Redefining Korean Politics: Lost Paradigm and New Vision*, edited by Young-Rae Kim, Hochul Lee, and In-Sah Mah. Seoul: Korea Political Science Association.

Park, Chung-Hee. 1968. *Our Nation's Path: Ideology of Social Reconstruction*. Seoul: Hollym Corporation Publishers.

Park, Kyung-Ae. 1993. "Women and Development: The Case of South Korea." *Comparative Politics* 25, no. 2: 127–45.

——— 1999. "Political Representation and South Korean Women." *The Journal of Asian Studies* 58, no. 2: 432–48.

Park, Moo-jong. 2002. "Looks Do Matter." *Korea Times*. November 21.

Park, Soo-Mee. 2002. "Birds and Bees and Backpacks." *JoongAng Daily*. April 21.

——— 2003. "After 30 Years of Abortion, Protesters Urge Changes." *JoongAng Daily*. February 10.

Park, Yeongran and Jungim Hwang. 2000. "Policy Recommendations to Improve the Linkage of Services for the Victims of Violence against Women." *Women's Studies Forum* 17. Seoul: KWDI (http://www2.kwdi.re.kr/board/view.php?db=project&category=&no=131&page=8).

Payne, Mark, Daniel Zovatto, Fernando Carrillo Florez, and Andres Allamand Zavala. 2002. *Democracies in Development: Politics and Reform in Latin America*. Washington D.C: Inter-American Development Bank.

PCWA. 1999. "National Report on the Implementation of the Beijing Platform for Action." Seoul: Presidential Commission on Women's Affairs.

——— 2000a. "The First Basic Plan on Women's Policy." Seoul: Presidential Commission on Women's Affairs.

——— 2000b. "A Collection of Gender-Related Legal Acts of the Republic of Korea." Seoul: Presidential Commission on Women's Affairs.

Perelli, Carina. 1994. "The Uses of Conservatism: Women's Democratic Politics in Uruguay." In *The Women's Movement in Latin America: Participation and Democracy*, edited by Jane Jaquette. Boulder: Westview Press.

Petras, James, Fernando Ignacio Leiva, and Henry Veltmeyer. 1994. *Democracy and Poverty in Chile: The Limits to Electoral Politics*. Boulder: Westview Press.

Prillman, William. 2000. *The Judiciary and Democratic Decay in Latin America: Declining Confidence in the Rule of Law*. Westport: Praeger Publishers.

Pringle, Rosemary and Sophie Watson. 1992. " 'Women's Interests' and the Post-Structuralist State." In *Destabilizing Theory: Contemporary Feminist Debates*, edited by Michelle Barrett and Anne Phillips. Oxford: Polity Press.

Putnam, Robert. 1993. *Making Democracy Work: Civic Traditions in Modern Italy*. Princeton: Princeton University Press.

Radcliffe, Sarah and Sallie Westwood (ed.). 1993. *"ViVa" Women and Popular Protest in Latin America*. New York: Routledge.

Rai, Shirin (ed.). 2003. *Mainstreaming Gender, Democratizing the State? Institutional Mechanisms for the Advancement of Women*. Manchester: Manchester University Press.

Ramilo, Chat. 2002. "National ICT Policies and Gender Equality/Regional Perspective: Asia." In proceedings from the United Nations Division for the Advancement of Women Expert Group Meeting on "Information and Communication Technologies and Their Impact on and Use as an Instrument for the Advancement and Empowerment of Women," Seoul.

Randall, Vicky and Georgina Waylen (ed.). 1998. *Gender Politics and the State*. London: Routledge.

Rosemblatt, Karin. 1997. "She's not a Libertine, He Doesn't Drink: Popular Morality and the State in Twentieth-Century Chile." Paper presented at the Latin American Studies Association Conference, Continental Plaza Hotel, Guadalajara, Mexico.

Sawer, Marian. 1996. *Femocrats and Ecocrats: Women's Policy Machinery in Australia, Canada and New Zealand*. Geneva: UNRISA.

——— 1998. "Femocrats and Ecocrats: Women's Policy Machinery in Australia, Canada and New Zealand." In *Missionaries and Mandarins: Feminist Engagement with Development Institutions*, edited by Carol Miller and Shahra Razavi. Intermediate Technology Publications.

——— 2003. "The Life and Times of Women's Policy Machinery in Australia." In *Mainstreaming Gender, Democratizing the State? Institutional Mechanisms for the Advancement of Women*, edited by Shirin Rai. Manchester: Manchester University Press.

SCCWA (Special Congressional Committee on Women's Affairs). 1998. *Legislative Process and Future Directions of Women-related Laws*. Seoul: SCCWA (in Korean).

——— 2000. *Women-Related Current Issues and Policy*. Seoul: SCCWA (in Korean).

Schild, Veronica. 1998. "New Subjects of Rights? Women's Movements and the Construction of Citizenship in the 'New Democracies.' " In *Cultures of Politics Politics of Cultures: Re-visioning Latin American Social Movements*, edited by Sonia Alvarez, Evelina Dagnino, and Arturo Escobar. Boulder: Westview Press.

Scott, Joan Wallach. 1988. *Gender and the Politics of History*. New York: Columbia University Press.

Seo, Dong-shin. 2005. "Male-Dominated Family Registry System to Change in 2008." *Korea Times*. March 1.

Seo, Min-Ja. 2000. "No Equal Employment Opportunities?" *Korea WomenLink Newsletter* no. 1 (womenlink.or.kr/english/news/news01_04.html).

Seong, Kyoung-Ryung. 2000. "Delayed Decentralization and Incomplete Democratic Consolidation." In *Institutional Reform and Democratic Consolidation in Korea*, edited by Larry Diamond and Doh-Chull Shin. Stanford: Hoover Institution Press.

Seoul Shinmun. 2004a. "Women Don't Want to Marry." June 20.

———— 2004b. "Attitudes about Abortion." November 10 (in Korean).

———— 2004c. "Young Women's Attitudes about Sex before Marriage." December 8 (in Korean).

Seoul Yeonghap News. 2004. "Sexual Harassment: 38% of Women Have Been Sexually Harassed." July 2 (in Korean).

Shafir, Gershon (ed.). 1998. *The Citizenship Debates*. Minneapolis: University of Minnesota Press.

Shim, Young-Hee. 1998. "Sexual Violence and Sexual Harassment in a Risk Society." *Korea Journal* 38, no. 1: 102–30.

———— 2002. "Sexuality Policy in Korea in the 1990s: Changes and Factors." *Korea Journal* 42, no. 2: 136–59.

Shin, Doh-Chull. 1999. *Mass Politics and Culture in Democratizing Korea*. Cambridge: Cambridge University Press.

———— 2003. "Mass Politics, Public Opinion, and Democracy in Korea." In *Korea's Democratization*, edited by Samuel Kim. Cambridge: Cambridge University Press.

Shin, Doh-Chull and Huoyan Shyu. 1997. "Public Opinion in New Democracies: Political Ambivalence in South Korea and Taiwan." *Journal of Democracy* 8, no. 3: 112–13.

Shin, Eui-Hang. 2003. "The Role of NGOs in Political Elections in South Korea: The Case of the Citizens' Alliance for the 2000 General Election." *Asian Survey* 43, no. 4: 697–715.

Shin, Kwang-Yeong. 2004. "The Contentious Politics, Social Movement and the Divided Civil Society in Korea." Paper presented at International Conference on Political Challenges and Democratic Institutions, Taipei.

Siemienska, Renata. 1998. "Consequences of Economic Changes for Women in Poland." In *Women and Democracy: Latin America and Central and Eastern Europe*, edited by Jane Jacquette and Sharon Wolchik. Baltimore: Johns Hopkins University Press.

Siklova, Jirina. 1993. "Are Women in Central and Eastern Europe Conservative?" In *Gender Politics and Post-Communism (Reflections from Eastern Europe and the Former Soviet Union*, edited by Nanette Funk and Magda Mueller. New York: Routledge.

SIPRI. 2002. "SIPRI Military Expenditure Database." Stockholm: Stockholm International Peace Research Institute (www.sipri.org/contents/milap/milex/mex_database1.html).

Smelser, Neil. 1962. *Theory of Collective Behaviour*. London: RKP.

Smith, Christian. 1991. *The Emergence of Liberation Theology: Radical Religion and Social Movement Theory*. Chicago: University of Chicago Press.

Sobritchea, Carolyn (ed.). 2005. *Gender Culture and Society: Selected Readings in Women's Studies in the Philippines*. Seoul: Ewha Womans University Press.

Soh, Chung-Hee Sarah. 1993. "Sexual Equality, Male Superiority, and Korean Women in Politics: Changing Gender Relations in a 'Patriarchal Democracy.' " *Sex Roles: A Journal of Research* 28: 73–90.

——— 1994. *Women in Korean Politics*. Boulder: Westview Press.

Soh, Ji-Young. 2000. "Female Candidates Make Strides." *Korea Times*. April 14.

Sohn, Bong-Scuk. 1994. "Agenda for Social Reform: Women's Political Participation in South Korea." In *Women of Japan and Korea*, edited by Joyce Gelb and Marian Lief Palley. Philadelphia: Temple University Press.

——— 1998. "Gender, State, and Power in South Korea." 1998 AAS Annual Meeting March 26–29, Washington, DC.

Sohn, Seong-Young. 1999. "The Women's Movements in Korea: Transition and Prospects." *Asian Women* 9: 27–44.

Stacey, Judith. 1999. "Virtual Social Science and the Politics of Family Values in the United States." In *Changing Family Values*, edited by Gill Jagger and Caroline Wright. London: Routledge.

Staudt, Kathleen. 1997. "Gender Politics in Bureaucracy: Theoretical Issues in Comparative Perspective." In *Women, International Development, and Politics*, edited by Kathleen Staudt. Philadelphia: Temple University Press.

——— 2003. "Gender Mainstreaming: Conceptual Links to Institutional Machineries." In *Mainstreaming Gender, Democratizing the State? Institutional Mechanisms for the Advancement of Women*, edited by Shirin Rai. Manchester: Manchester University Press.

Steinberg, David. 1997. "Civil Society and Human Rights in Korea: On Contemporary and Classical Orthodoxy and Ideology." *Korea Journal* 37, no. 3: 145–65.

Steinmo, Sven, Kathleen Thelen, and Frank Longstreth. 1992. *Structuring Politics: Historical Institutionalism in Comparative Analysis*. New York: Cambridge University Press.

Sternbach, Nancy Saporta, Marysa Navarro-Aranguren, Patricia Chuchryk, and Sonia E. Alvarez. 1992. *Feminisms in Latin America: From Bogotá to San Bernardo. Signs* 17, no. 2: 393–433.

Stetson, Dorothy McBride and Amy G. Mazur. 1995. *Comparative State Feminism*. London: Sage Publications.

Stevenson. 2000. "Gender Politics and Policy Process in Mexico, 1968–2000: Symbolic Gains for Women in an Emerging Democracy." Ph.D. dissertation, Political Science, University of Pittsburgh.

Stoner, Lynn. 1991. "On Men Reforming the Rights of Men: The Abrogation of the Cuban Adultery Law, 1930." *Cuban Studies* 21: 83–99.

Tarrow, Sidney. 1994. *Power in Movement: Social Movements, Collective Action and Politics*. New York: Cambridge University Press.

Thelen, Kathleen and Sven Steinmo. 1992. "Historical Institutionalism in Comparative Politics." In *Structuring Politics: Historical Institutionalism in Comparative Analysis*, edited by Sven Steinmo, Kathleen Thelen, and Frank Longstreth. New York: Cambridge University Press.

True, Jacqui and Michael Mintrom. 2001. "Transnational Networks and Policy Diffusion: The Case of Gender Mainstreaming." *International Studies Quarterly* 45: 27–57.

Tsuya, Noriko, Larry Bumpass, and Minja Kim Choe. 2000. "Gender, Employment and Housework in Japan, South Korea, and the United States." *Review of Population and Social Policy* no. 9: 195–200.

UIA. 2000. *Yearbook of International Organizations*. Vol. 2. Union of International Associations (ed.). Muenchen: K. G. Saur.

UNDP. 2004. *Human Development Report 2004: Cultural Liberty in Today's Diverse World*. New York: United Nations Development Programme.

Upham, Frank. 1987. *Law and Social Change in Postwar Japan*. Cambridge: Harvard University Press.

US-DoD. 2000. "2000 Report to Congress Military Situation on the Korean Peninsula." United States Department of Defense (www.defenselink.mil/ news/Sep2000/korea09122000.html).

Valenzuela, Maria Elena. 1998. "Women and the Democratization Process in Chile." In *Women and Democracy: Latin America and Central and Eastern Europe*, edited by Jane Jaquette and Sharon Wolchik. Baltimore: Johns Hopkins University Press.

Vargas, Virginia. 2002. "The Struggle by Latin American Feminisms for Rights and Autonomy." In *Gender and the Politics of Rights and Democracy in Latin America*, edited by Nikki Craske and Maxine Molyneux. New York: Palgrave.

Wade, Larry and Jin Wan-Seo. 1996. "Women, Education and Political Volitions in the South Korean Mass Public." *Comparative Political Studies* 29, no. 1: 27–51.

Waylen, Georgina. 1994. "Women and Democratization: Conceptualizing Gender Relations in Transition Politic." *World Politics* 46, no. 3: 327–55.

———— 1996a. *Gender in Third World Politics*. Boulder: Lynne Rienner Publishers.

———— 1996b. "Democratization, Feminism and the State in Chile: The Establishment of SERNAM." In *Women and the State: International Perspectives*, edited by Shirin Rai and Geraldine Lievesley. London: Taylor and Francis.

West, James and Dae-Kyu Yoon. 1992. "The Constitutional Court of the Republic of Korea: Transforming the Jurisprudence of the Vortex?" *The American Journal of Comparative Law* 40, no. 1: 73–199.

Willmott, Ceri. 2002. "Constructing Citizenship in the *Poblaciones* of Santiago, Chile: The Role of Reproductive and Sexual Rights." In *Gender and the Politics of Rights and Democracy in Latin America*, edited by Nikki Craske and Maxine Molyneux. New York: Palgrave.

WomenLink 2001. "Survey on Gender Discrimination in Recruitment Processes" (www.womenlink.or.kr).

WSPE. 2002. "A Comparison and Evaluation of the Women's Platforms of the Candidates for the 16th Presidential Elections, 2002." Seoul: Women's Solidarity for the Presidential Elections.

Yang, Hyunah. 1998. "Envisioning Feminist Jurisprudence in Korean Family Law at the Crossroads of Tradition/Modernity." Ph.D. dissertation, New School for Social Research, New York.

——— 2002. "Unfinished Tasks for Korean Family Policy in the 1990s: Maternity Protection Policy and Abolition of the Family-Head System." *Korea Journal* 42, no. 2: 68–99.

Yee, Jaeyeol. 2000. "The Social Networks of Koreans." *Korea Journal* 40, no. 1: 325–52.

Yi, Eunhee-Kim. 1998. " 'Home Is a Place to Rest': Constructing the Meaning of Work, Family and Gender in the Korean Middle Class." *Korea Journal* 38: 168–213.

Yoon, Dae-Kyu. 1990. *Law and Political Authority in South Korea*. Boulder: Westview Press.

Yoon, Jung-Sook. 2002a. "An Analysis of Korean Local Governments' Budget and Policies." Seoul: WomenLink.

——— 2002b. "Korea: Raising Questions about Women-Related Policies." In *Gender Budgets Make More Cents: Country Studies and Good Practice*, edited by Debbie Budlender and Guy Hewitt. London: Commonwealth Secretariat.

Yoon, Yee-Heum. 1997. "The Contemporary Religious Situation in Korea." In *Religion and Society in Contemporary Korea*, edited by Lewis Lancaster and Richard Payne. Berkeley: University of California Press.

Youm, Kyu-Ho. 1994. "Press Freedom and Judicial Review in South Korea." *Stanford Journal of International Law* 30: 1–40.

Index